Mary Queen of Scots

ANTONIA FRASER

Volume Two

PHOENIX

This edition produced for The Book People Ltd,
Hall Wood Avenue, Haydock, St Helens WA11 9UL

First published in Great Britain in 1969
by Weidenfeld & Nicolson Ltd
First published in paperback in 1970

Paperback edition published in 2002
by Phoenix,
an imprint of Orion Books Ltd,
Orion House, 5 Upper St Martin's Lane,
London WC2H 9EA

A CIP catalogue record for this book is available from the British Library.

ISBN 978 1 4072 1616 4

Printed and bound in Great Britain by
Clays Ltd, St Ives plc

The Orion Publishing Group's policy is to use papers that are natural, renewable
and recyclable products and made from wood grown in sustainable forests. The
loggingand manufacturing processed are expected to conform to the environmental
regulations of the country of origin.

www.orionbooks.co.uk

Contents

PART THREE

The Captivity

CHAPTER NINETEEN
In Foreign Bands

And I'm the sovereign of Scotland
  And mony a traitor there
Yet here I lay in foreign bands
  And never-ending care
                    Robert Burns, Queen Mary's Lament

On Lochleven Mary had been compared by Maitland to a captive lion; the feelings of the Regent Moray on hearing that his sister had escaped from her prison may be compared to those of Prince John, regent of England, when he learnt that his brother King Richard was on his way home, and 'the lion was unloosed'. The Regent Moray was sore amazed, said the Diurnal of Occurrents,[1] more especially because he happened to be at Glasgow when he learnt the evil news, and by now Mary herself had reached nearby Hamilton from Niddry. The regent's first instinct was to desert the unhealthy area of western Scotland – where such loyal Marian lords as Herries and Maxwell held sway in the south, and Argyll, now also a Marian, in the north, to say nothing of the menacing prospect of the key fortress of Dumbarton, still firmly held for the queen, to the west beyond Glasgow. But prudence prevailed: the regent decided to stand firm, rather than let the whole west unite for the queen; as it turned out, he was amply repaid for the steadfast nature of his decision.

Supporters were flocking to the queen, as a result of the series of proclamations in which she once more sought her subjects' allegiance. On 8th May nine earls, nine bishops, eighteen lairds and over 100 lesser supporters declared for her in a joint proclamation. Despite this impressive show of loyalty and strength, Mary was not without her problems. The Hamiltons seized this ripe opportunity of emphasizing their own claims to the succession if both Mary and James disappeared – and their right to act as governors if only Mary did. Another particularly virulent Marian proclamation, thought to be the work of Archbishop Hamilton, referred to Moray as 'an bastard gotten in shameful adultery' and Châtelherault as the 'Queen's dearest father adoptive ... head of the good house of Hamilton'. Although it is unlikely that this proclamation was ever published,[2] its tone certainly makes it clear why Mary feared to remain overlong at Hamilton. Having escaped her Lochleven bonds, she did not wish to become the puppet of another Scottish house. She therefore determined to march towards Dumbarton and here on neutral ground try to draw her subjects back to her. Mary was certainly not particularly anxious to fight Moray before she reached Dumbarton, seeing no advantage in confronting him at the head of a Hamilton force when she might in the future be able to face him backed up by a more truly national army. In her desire to be restored to her throne at all costs, Mary was even prepared to treat with Moray; but the regent refused to enter into negotiations.

The Marian party had by now reached impressive proportions – twice as many as that of the regent, said the queen.[3] Estimates vary from 6000 royalists to Moray's 4000 to 5000 and 3000 respectively; but all agreed that Mary's party had considerable numerical superiority. This preponderance had the fatal effect of encouraging the queen's army to skirt Glasgow narrowly on their route to Dumbarton, in the hopes of drawing the regent into a fight and thus annihilating him. The Hamiltons had, after all, suffered much at Moray's hands; his occupation of the regency was a flagrant insult to their ancient position in Scotland: they now saw an excellent opportunity of obliterating their enemy under what seemed to be ideally weighted conditions. As the Marians reached the small village of Langside, the vanguard under Lord Claud Hamilton stormed forward. Moray was established beyond Langside on the Burgh Muir. He appeared to accept their challenge, despite the Marian numerical superiority. But Moray was fortunate in having two experienced and skilful soldiers beside him – Kirkcaldy of Grange and Morton. Morton remained at Moray's side, in charge of the main battle, while Kirkcaldy rode forward with his hagbutters to harry the royal troops as they entered the narrow main street of Langside.

Under the regent's attack, the border horsemen under Lord Herries did valiantly, and Hamilton's men fought their way gallantly forward. But by an evil chance, the main command of the royal army had been given to Argyll, now made 'Lieutenant of the Kingdom'[4] on the grounds that he had supplied by far the largest amount of men. And now the main body of the royal troops under Argyll's personal command entirely failed to follow up their van. It was said afterwards, to explain his defection, that Argyll had actually fainted, or else had had an exceptionally ill-timed epileptic fit; his enemies pointed out that as he was Moray's brother-in-law and erstwhile comrade, his failure of generalship might have the less medical and more sinister explanation of pre-arranged treachery. Whatever its origin, the temporary suspension of Argyll's faculties proved fatal to the cause of Mary Queen of Scots at Langside. As Kirkcaldy's pikemen fell upon the Hamiltons, they found themselves totally unsupported by Argyll's men who, leaderless and unable or unwilling to withstand a full charge, broke away from it, and fled back towards their native Highlands. The crossfire of the hagbutters, the depredations of the pikemen, and the failure of Argyll combined to bring about a colossal defeat for the queen in which few members of Moray's side were killed even by Herries's gallant charge (although Lords Home and Ochiltree were injured). Over 100 of the queen's party were slain, mainly Hamiltons, and over 300 were taken prisoner, including the faithful Lord Seton, Sir James Hamilton and many other members of his clan.

The queen watched this gloomy contest from a nearby hill. For once might had been allied with right; but sadly, the combination had worked out to the advantage of neither. Mary's servant John Beaton told Catherine de Médicis later that Mary had mounted on her own horse, and like another Zenobia ridden into the battle, to encourage her troops to advance; she would have led them to the charge in person, but she found them all quarrelling among themselves, insensible to her eloquence and more inclined to exchange blows with each other than to attack the rebel host.⁵ Once the battle was clearly decided in favour of Moray, the queen had more pressing problems to deal with than the feuds of her own supporters. She had now to ride, not like Zenobia into battle, but like any fugitive away from the scene of her defeat, and away from the searing sweep of Moray's men. Dumbarton was the obvious target for her – Dumbarton, from which French help could be introduced into the country, or from which France itself could be reached, if the situation became so desperate that the queen had to flee. But Dumbarton was cut off by hostile Lennox country and Moray's forces; guided by Lord Herries, the queen decided to flee south instead, into the south-western territories of Scotland which were still extremely Catholic in feeling as well as loyal to Mary, under the feudal sway of two Catholic magnates, Herries and Maxwell.

The journey itself was rough and wild; the conditions of travel were primitive in the extreme. Afterwards the queen seemed to remember so little about this nightmare flight in her account of it to Nau, that his narrative, so free and detailed during the period of her captivity at Lochleven, degenerates into a mere list of headings. Once she was in captivity, perhaps Mary preferred to throw a veil in her own mind over these last Scottish sufferings, which had been a prelude to the long years of English imprisonment. Immediately after the flight, in June 1568, she gave a description of it to her uncle in France: 'I have endured injuries, calumnies, imprisonment,' she wrote, 'famine, cold, heat, flight not knowing whither, 92 miles across the country without stopping or alighting, and then I have had to sleep upon the ground and drink sour milk, and eat oatmeal without bread, and have been three nights like the owls. ...'⁶ Queen Mary fled first to Dumfries, a journey of about sixty miles; by tradition Lord Herries led her down through the unfrequented passes of the Glenkens and along the west bank of the River Ken. They paused to rest at the head of the valley of the Tarff, at a point now named Queen's hill. The Dee was crossed just beyond the village of Tongland, where her escort destroyed the ancient wooden bridge to avoid pursuit; close by, at Culdoach, Mary received the reviving bowl of sour milk which she mentioned to her uncle.* Having rested at Herries's own castle of Corrah on the way, the queen finally reached the Maxwell castle of Terregles.

It was here at Terregles that the critical decision was taken to flee further on into England. The decision was made by the queen alone. She herself described dolefully to Archbishop Beaton in Paris how her supporters had cautioned her piteously not to trust Queen Elizabeth, since the English in the past had savagely imprisoned a Scottish sovereign, in the shape of James I, and even her own father had not trusted himself to meet Henry VIII at York. The general view was that she should either stay in Scotland – where Herries guaranteed that she could hold out for at least another forty days – or go to France and hope to rally some support there. In retrospect, either course would seem to have been more sensible than seeking an English refuge. We cannot tell what considerations weighed with Mary Stuart to choose it nevertheless, what dreams of friendship and alliance with Elizabeth still possessed her; yet the siren song of Elizabeth's friendship, the mirage of the English succession, were still strong enough in this moment of decision to blot out the stable image of the proven friendship of France, where Mary had actually lived for thirteen years, and which could still be so easily sought from a western port of Scotland, the sea-route past Wales and Cornwall which Mary had taken years before as a child. In France Mary had the inalienable estates and incomes of a queen dowager of the country; as a Catholic queen fleeing from a Protestant country, she had every reason to expect the

---

* Tradition has it that the old woman received the freehold of her croft – for which she had previously paid rent – for this Samaritan deed. This was probably through the good offices of Lord Herries, who was the principal local landowner, and in a position to make such a gesture.

support of her brother-in-law, Charles IX, and Queen Catherine, to say nothing of her Guise relations, of whom the latest scion Henry, duke of Guise, was just rising into a manhood which promised to be as glorious as that of his father Duke Francis. Even if Elizabeth had shown stronger support for Mary against her rebels in the short interval since Carberry Hill than the French king, the patent fact that Mary was a Catholic whereas her insurgents were mainly Protestants meant that the French would always have a vested interest to help the Scottish queen as their co-religionist.

In place of friendly France, Mary Stuart chose to fling herself upon the mercy of unknown England, a land where she had no party, no money, no estates, no relatives except her former mother-in-law, Lady Lennox, who hated her, and Queen Elizabeth herself, whom she had never met personally, and whose permission she had not even obtained to enter the country. As decisions go, it was a brave one, a romantic one even, but under the circumstances it was certainly not a wise one. No human character is static. Different circumstances develop different aspects of the same personality. Perhaps ten months in prison had served to bring out in Mary's nature that streak either of the romantic or of the gambler, which leads the subject fatally on ever to prefer hope and high adventure to the known quantity, and which Mary Stuart passed on so dramatically to many of her later Stuart descendants. From now on, like all captives, Mary Stuart was to live of necessity far more in the world of dreams than in that of reality. Her confinement in Lochleven seemed to have already begun the process of attrition in her powers of judgement. The queen herself summed up the subject of her fatal decision in a sentence at the end of a letter to Beaton towards the end of her life as sad as any she ever wrote: 'But I commanded my best friends to permit me to have my own way....'[7]

The decision once taken, Herries wrote to Lowther, the deputy governor of Carlisle, asking permission for the Scottish queen to take refuge in England. But Mary did not even wait for the return of the messenger. She was now in borrowed linen, and in clothes and a hood lent by the laird of Lochinvar. The hood was especially necessary because her head was shorn of its beautiful red-gold wealth of hair as a precaution against recognition: one of Nau's most poignant headings reads: 'How she caused her head to be shaved.'[8] In this disguise she made her way west from Terregles to the abbey of Dundrennan, lying among trees in a secluded valley at the end of winding roads from Kirkcudbright and Castle Douglas, which finally led down to the coast. Dundrennan, a twelfth-century Cistercian foundation, was one of the most beautiful abbeys in Scotland, but the queen had little time to admire its beauties or even to listen to the soft roar of the sea a mile away. Her mind was on the future and on England. She sent yet another letter to Elizabeth from Dundrennan – 'After God, she has now no hope save in Elizabeth. ...'[9] But having so firmly fixed her earthly hopes on the English queen, Mary seemed to find no point in waiting for an answer to her letter.

On the afternoon of Sunday 16th May she went down to the little port at the mouth of the Abbey Burn from which the monks of Dundrennan used to trade with the continent. From this undistinguished sea shore, she could actually see the coast of England across the Solway Firth. Perhaps the sight encouraged her, for at three o'clock in the afternoon the queen of Scotland embarked in a small fishing boat, with only a tiny party of loyal followers – Lord Herries, Maxwell and Fleming, Lord Claud Hamilton and about sixteen other attendants. In this humble fashion, Mary Stuart, who had been born in such magnificence in the palace of Linlithgow, a princess of Scotland, left her native country in a common fishing boat, never to return.

According to one tradition, during the four-hour journey the queen had a sudden premonition of the fate which awaited her in England, and ordered the boatmen to take her after all to France; but the winds and tide were against her, and the boat went remorselessly on towards England.[10] Nau mentions no such vacillation: when Queen Mary arrived at the small Cumberland port of Workington at seven in the evening, she seemed as elated as ever by the heady wine of optimism. Queen Mary stumbled as she first set foot on English soil: this omen, which might have been interpreted in a sinister light, was on the contrary taken by her followers as a sign that their queen was coming to take possession of the country. At Workington, the queen rested and was given supper, while Lord Herries sent a message to Sir Henry Curwen of Workington Hall, whom he knew of old, to say that he had with him a young heiress whom he had carried off from Scotland with the hope of marrying her to Sir Henry's son. The answer to this inviting proposition came back that Sir Henry was in London but that his house and servants were at Lord Herries's disposal. Already Mary's surprising and sudden arrival at the small port, combined with her marked height and dramatically beautiful appearance, were leading the inhabitants to guess only too easily that they had the famous Scottish queen in their midst. One of the Curwen servants, who was French, did not even have to guess: he recognized Queen Mary immediately and told Lord Fleming that he had seen her majesty before 'in better days'.

The next morning the deputy governor, Lowther, already warned by Herries's letter, arrived with a force of 400 horsemen. In the absence of the governor, Lord Scrope, who was at that moment in London, he planned to conduct the queen back to Carlisle. Queen Mary told Lowther calmly that she had come to England to solicit the assistance of the queen of England against her rebellious subjects. She had already in her brief space of freedom in Scotland sent John Beaton to Elizabeth in London with the famous diamond to which Mary attached such importance; she had written to Elizabeth from Dundrennan; now Mary wrote a third letter from Workington asking for help. The queen was taken to Cockermouth the next day, where she lodged in the home of Master Henry Fletcher, and by 18th May was installed in semi-captivity at Carlisle Castle. On her route she encountered the French ambassador to Scotland, Villeroy de Beaumont, on his way back to France after having had his train plundered by Moray's followers. The news he gave Mary of the fate of her own supporters in Scotland was discouraging: Mary was confirmed in her gloomy supposition that she would need English aid if she was ever to make her own way back to Scotland.

Lowther had reported that the attire of the Scottish queen was 'very mean':[11] once more in Mary's history a hurried escape from danger, in disguise, had left her with nothing in the way of a change of clothes. However, Fletcher, who was a merchant, is said to have presented her with a length of velvet for her wardrobe and a black dress was made for her on credit. Also Lowther, noting that the Scottish queen had so little money with her that it would scarcely cover the costs of clothing she so sadly needed, gallantly ordered her expenses at Cockermouth to be defrayed, and provided geldings of his own accord, to convey the queen and her train to Carlisle. Lowther was evidently genuinely puzzled as to exactly how he should treat this strange bird of rare plumage which had so confidently flown into the English aviary; but he was determined to err if anything on the side of courtesy, not knowing from one minute to the next whether his guest might not be summoned to London and there received with every honour by Queen Elizabeth herself. As a result, at this point Mary's own confidence in the rightness of her decision was unshaken, and in a letter to the earl of Cassillis dictated from Carlisle on 20th May she described herself as 'right well received and honourably accompanied and treated' in England; she expected to be back in Scotland at the head of an army, French if not English, 'about the fifteenth day of August'.[12]

Puzzled as Richard Lowther might have been as to how to treat his royal visitor, whether as queen or captive, or a nice combination of both, his bewilderment was as nothing compared to the perturbation of Elizabeth's advisers in London. Here Queen Mary's arrival, romantic foolish gesture as it might be, had caused a flutter from which the English court would take time to recover. After all, how was Queen Elizabeth to treat the royal fugitive? She had not captured Queen Mary, nor sought to do so. Mary had arrived of her own free will, expressly seeking English assistance, as her own letters immediately before and after her arrival testified. It is a point worth emphasizing, since it was to be raised by Mary again and again during the years as an English prisoner, last of all, with pardonable bitterness, at her own trial in England. Yet Queen Mary's request to be restored to her own throne posed Elizabeth a whole series of problems which she could hardly ignore. It was unthinkable in fact for the Protestant English queen to take arms against Scotland on behalf of her Catholic cousin; on the other hand if Elizabeth did not do so, there was nothing to stop Mary making the same request of the French, who might seize with enthusiasm upon this new opportunity for entry on to the British mainland. Therefore, to allow Mary to pass freely through England to France was hardly good politics from the English point of view.

Was the Scottish queen to be received at the English court, and permitted to enjoy full liberty in England? The Venetian ambassador in Paris sanguinely reported that a palace was being specially prepared for Mary in London, with great pomp;[13] but this was an equally obnoxious prospect from the angle of English statecraft. Mary Stuart at liberty might prove an unpleasant focus for the loyalties of the English Catholics. Mary herself might have forgotten that ten years before as dauphiness of France she had claimed to be rightful queen of England, rather than heiress-presumptive to the throne. But Elizabeth's principal adviser, Cecil, had not forgotten her pretensions, and there was no guarantee that the English Catholics had either. Mary at this point knew nothing at first hand of the remarkable character of these people: their obstinacy, their heroism, their fineness of spirit which made them, paradoxically, for all their attitude to the new official religion of the country, among the most admirable of the Elizabethans. But to the prudent Cecil, the possible reactions of the English Catholics to Mary had to be taken into account.

Taken all in all, the most politic course from the English point of view was to temporize, until sufficient assessment had been made of the interior situation of Scotland. In the long run, Elizabeth felt, it would probably be wisest to dispatch Mary back to her difficult subjects, rather than let her loose in either England or France, and furthermore there was that other consideration that subjects should not be encouraged to rebel against queens. But of course there was no question of restoring Mary by the force of an English army; the terms on which the Scots would accept Mary back would have to be discovered by cautious inquiries – and, if possible, negotiated to Elizabeth's own advantage. In the meantime it would be best to keep Mary in the north not exactly a prisoner, but not exactly free, not exactly debarred for ever from Elizabeth's presence, but certainly not welcomed into it.* The only course which was emphatically to be debarred to Mary was that of seeking French help: as Elizabeth's instructions of 18th May stated, Mary was to be told plainly that as Elizabeth intended to assist her herself, any attempt on the Scottish queen's part to bring in the French as well would be regarded as merely renewing old quarrels.[14] Fortunately Mary had not arrived in England with an unbesmirched reputation: there was that unresolved matter of Darnley's death, and the scandal she had caused by marrying the chief suspect. The cloud of old scandal round Mary's head now provided a convenient excuse for putting her off from Elizabeth's presence, until she should have been cleared of all guilt. And in such a work of arbitration, who would be more suitable to act as judge between Mary's cause and that of her nobles than the English queen herself?

Queen Elizabeth's next move was to send her trusted counsellor, Sir Francis Knollys, north to treat with her guest-captive along these delicate lines. Knollys was the husband of Catherine Carey, Lord Hunsdon's sister, who was Elizabeth's first cousin through the Boleyns, as well as being her intimate friend. The Knollys had an enormous family, to whom Sir Francis was a punctilious father. He was now about fifty-five, a man of the highest honour, and a leading Puritan, who had fled to Germany during the reign of Mary Tudor. Despite their religious differences, Mary made an immediately favourable impression upon

---

* From the point of view of the succession, there was something to be said for having Elizabeth's nearest relative under lock and key; acting on this principle, the emperors of Ethiopia used to incarcerate all the princes of blood royal on a mountain near Gondar, until the time came for one of them to succeed.

this experienced courtier. He discovered in her a woman of innate intelligence, blessed with an eloquent tongue and full of practical good sense; to these qualities, she also joined considerable personal courage. A little later, when he felt he knew her better, Knollys ventured on a further and even more favourable character sketch of the Scottish queen:[15] to begin with she was a 'notable woman' because she had no care for ceremonies beyond the acknowledgement of her royal estate (possibly a sly dig at Queen Elizabeth); then she spoke freely to everyone, whatever their rank, and 'showeth a disposition to speak much and to be bold and to be pleasant to be very familiar'. Furthermore not only was she brave herself, but she was also delighted by valour in others, 'commending by name all approved hardy men of her country, although they be her enemies, and she concealeth no cowardice even in her friends'. In short, 'For victory's sake pain and peril seem pleasant to her and in respect of victory, wealth and all other things seem to her contemptible and vile'. Knollys metaphorically scratched his head as he concluded by wondering what on earth was to be done with such a spirited creature. Was 'such a lady and princess' to be nourished in the English bosom? He questioned his correspondents in London whether it was indeed 'wise to dissemble with such a lady'.

The answer came back from the south that it was indeed wise to dissemble, since it was for the moment the most politically advantageous course open to the English. Knollys was therefore instructed to tell Queen Mary that she could not be received at the English court until she had been purged of the stain of her husband's murder, and this purgation could only be achieved if she submitted herself to the judgement of Elizabeth. Tears flowed from Mary's eyes at the news; in a passion of rage at the injustice, she pointed out that both Maitland and Morton had assented to the murder of Darnley 'as it could well be proved, although now they would seem to persecute the same'.[16] Knollys himself was impressed by her arguments: he wrote to Elizabeth that as Mary had easily convinced those around her in the north of her innocence, it might be better for Elizabeth's honour to offer her the choice of remaining in England (to be cleared by Elizabeth of complicity in the crime) or returning once more to Scotland of her own volition. The worst that could happen, thought Knollys, was that Mary would decide to go to France, and in any case Moray would probably put a stop to that from Scotland. But in London Queen Elizabeth found it wiser to concentrate on Mary's honour than on her own – and this honour, she persisted in pointing out, had been too besmirched for her cousin to be released before the formality of an English investigation. Mary and Knollys were left together at Carlisle, with Knollys under orders to get his captive to agree to submit herself to this process.

On 30th May they argued on the subject of Mary's deposition; when Mary inveighed against Moray for his behaviour, Knollys maintained that if princes could be deposed for being mad so they could also for common murdering. Both crimes were the result of evil humours, he continued, with characteristic six-teenth-century preoccupation with the subject, one coming from melancholy (madness) and the other from choler (murder). Poor Mary wept and tried to excuse herself. But Knollys only seized the opportunity to press her further and say that she should now allow herself to be tried by Elizabeth, and thus officially purged of her crimes.[17]

Mary's state within Carlisle Castle was on Knollys's own admission far from luxurious. Her chief lack was of waiting-women: she who had been surrounded all her life by ladies of the highest rank to attend her now had only two or three to help her, and they were 'not of the finest sort'. Her gentlemen included the romantic-minded George Douglas who had fol-lowed the queen into exile: he was one of the three or four allowed to sleep within the precincts of the castle, the rest of the gentlemen leaving the castle at sunset and sleeping within the town, with the rest of her train, down to cooks and scullions, making a total of between thirty and forty. Another serious lack was of horses – for the queen had of course arrived without any at all, and with her enthusiasm for physical exercise she felt the deprivation keenly. There were heavy iron gratings across

Mary's windows and a series of three ante-chambers packed with soldiers led to her own chamber. Although Mary was able to attend football matches organized by her own retinue on the green – Knollys noted with surprise that there was no foul play – whenever she walked or rode she was attended by a guard of a hundred men, lest George Douglas's fancy should once again turn to the subject of escape. Her one attempt at hare-hunting was her last: it was thought too risky to let her ride abroad even under the pretext of sport.

The arrival of Mary Seton, the remaining unmarried Marie of happier times, provided a welcome relief, more especially as Mary Seton was an expert hairdresser: Knollys noted with admiration her skill in the art of 'busking', as he termed it, excelling anything he had seen previously – 'among other pretty devices, yesterday and today she did set such a curled hair upon the Queen that it was like to be a periwig that showed very delicately; and every other day she hath a new device of head dressing, without any cost, and yet setteth forth a woman gaily well'.[18] Such feminine skills were all the more necessary since the queen had chopped off her own hair during the flight from Langside; it never grew again in its old abundance and in any case was frequently cut to guard against persistent headaches; it seems that for the rest of her life Mary was dependent on wigs and false-pieces. Despite Mary Seton's endeavours, the queen's clothing remained a problem. Queen Elizabeth, appealed to for some help out of her own copious wardrobe, responded with gifts of such mean quality – some odd pieces of black velvet and old dresses – that the embarrassed Knollys tried to explain them away by saying that they had been intended for Mary's maids. Moray was scarcely more generous: when he dispatched three coffers of his sister's clothes from Scotland the queen noted angrily that there was but one taffeta dress amongst them, the rest merely cloaks, and 'coverage for saddles' – ironically useless to a captive. She had to send for sartorial reinforcement from Lochleven. In July she did receive from her own chamberlain in Scotland a number of belongings, mainly accessories including gloves, pearl buttons, tights, veils, coifs of black and white, and twelve *orillettes* or bandages, to place over the ears when asleep, no doubt to cut out from the royal consciousness the heavy tread of the hagbutters in the three rooms outside.[19]

To Mary these feminine considerations of dress and hair, and even the conditions of her confinement (which shocked Montmorin, the French ambassador), were secondary to her grand design to reach the presence of Queen Elizabeth. From her arrival at Workington towards the end of May until the end of the conference at York and its removal to London, Queen Mary wrote over twenty letters to Queen Elizabeth, most of them extremely long, well thought out, intelligent pieces of pleading, all elaborations on the same theme of Mary's need for succour to regain her Scottish throne, and her trust in Elizabeth to provide it. Mary even summoned her poetic gifts to her aid: she wrote a poem to her '*chère soeur*' of which both an Italian and a French version survive, expressing the mingled pleasure and pain which the subject of their meeting produced in her heart, torn as she was between hope and doubt. She likened herself to a ship blown backwards by contrary winds just as it was entering the harbour, the poem ending with a prophetic fear that Fortune might once more turn against her in this as in so many things:

> Un seul penser qui me profficte et nuit
> Amer et doux change en mon coeur sans cesse
> Entre le doubte et l'espoir il m'oppresse
> Tant que la paix et le repos me fuit...
>
> J'ay veu la nef relascher par contraincte
> En haulte mer, proche d'entrer au port,
> Et le serain se convertir en trouble.
> Ainsi je suis en souci et en crainte
> Non pas de vous, mais quantes foir a tort
> Fortune rompt voille et cordage double.*

---

* A longing haunts my spirit, day and night
Bitter and sweet, torments my aching heart
'Twixt doubt and fear, it holds its wayward part,
And while it lingers, rest and peace take flight...

Other variations on the theme in letters were the evil plight of her supporters in Scotland under Moray's cruel persecution, and the monstrous nature of her subjects' rebellion against her, a tendency which surely no sovereign queen would encourage. One of the most poignant of the pleas, on 5th July, expostulated: 'Alas! Do not as the serpent that stoppeth his hearing, for I am no enchanter but your sister and natural cousin. If Caesar had not disclaimed to hear or heede the complaint of an advertiser [soothsayer] he had not so died. . . .' And with still more anguish, on the subject of the personal interview: 'I am not of the nature of the basilisk and less of the chameleon, to turn you to my likeness.'[21] Mary was of course writing not only to Elizabeth, but also to France, to Catherine de Médicis, to Charles IX, to whom she protested that she was suffering for the true religion, the duke of Anjou, and her uncle the cardinal. Some of these letters touched naturally on the vexed subject of money, the perennial preoccupation of exiled royalty: Mary now desperately needed the income of her French estates to provide for herself and her household, having arrived without a penny. But her instructions of 30th May to Lord Fleming, whom she dispatched to London, made it clear that if Elizabeth did not agree to help her, then help was to be sought immediately from France, and that Mary herself in these circumstances would arrange to depart thither as soon as possible.[22] Fleming, however, was not allowed to proceed from London to France, and the instructions were never able to be carried out. On 8th June Mary received a visit from Middlemore, Elizabeth's emissary to Scotland, on his way north. Middlemore handed her a letter in which Elizabeth promised to restore Mary if she consented to have her innocence proved by Elizabeth's inquiry. Mary wept and stormed. In vain she tried to tempt Middlemore with the notion of the confidences

Ah! I have seen a ship freed from control
On the high seas, outside a friendly port,
And what was peaceful change to woe and pain:
Ev'n so am I, a lonely trembling soul,
Fearing – not you, but to be made the sport
Of Fate, that bursts the closest, strongest chain![20]

she would make personally to Elizabeth if only she was allowed to meet her: 'I would and did mean to have uttered such matter unto her as I would have done to no other. ... No one can compel me to accuse myself, and yet if I would say anything of myself, I would say of myself to her and to no other.'[23] To such beguilements, Elizabeth was deaf.*

In Scotland Middlemore found that Moray and his supporters had quite independently reached the same conclusion as Elizabeth, to which they had been working since the previous winter: Mary's guilt over Darnley's death and her subsequent marriage to Bothwell were the points to be stressed if Mary was to be kept where Moray would most like to see her – in an English prison. The difference between Elizabeth and Moray was that Elizabeth at this point intended ultimately to restore Mary to Scotland, and only wished to delay the process; Moray on the other hand had no wish to see Mary back on the throne on any terms whatsoever. To Moray, the viciousness of his sister was no moral issue, it was a question of his own survival as governor of Scotland. Moray was therefore determined to go much further than the English and make the mud already thrown at Mary stick so hard that there could be no question of this besmeared figure returning to reign.

It was significant that Cecil himself, in one of those private memoranda he was so fond of drawing up for his own guidance giving the *pros* and *contras* of any given situation, could find Mary's alleged moral turpitude the only true excuse for keeping her off the Scottish throne, and in an English prison.[24] In favour of setting Mary at liberty were the following arguments: that she had come of her own accord to England, trusting in Elizabeth's frequent promises of assistance; that she herself had been illegally condemned by her subjects, who had imprisoned her and charged her with the murder of Darnley, without ever allowing

---

* It has sometimes been conjectured from these words that Mary intended to reveal to Elizabeth the full truth about the murder of Darnley. But Mary's words have the unmistakable ring of the captive, to be heard increasingly from now on in her utterances and letters, who will make any promise, hold out any lure, in order to achieve liberty.

her to answer for her crimes either personally or through a lawyer in front of Parliament; that she was a queen subject to none, and not bound by law to answer to her subjects; lastly there were her own frequent offers to justify her behaviour personally in front of Queen Elizabeth. It was indeed a hard case to answer; it was certainly not answered by Mary's opponents at the time, nor has the passage of time and the unrolling of history made it seem any less formidable as an indictment of England's subsequent behaviour. The case which Cecil put *contra* Mary's liberty was entirely based on the assumption that she had been an accessory to the murder of her husband, and gone on both to protect and to marry the chief assassin, Bothwell — apart from a somewhat dubious argument that since Darnley had been constituted king of Scots, and by Mary herself, so he was 'a public person and her superior', and therefore her subjects were bound to search out his murderer. This argument ignored the fact that Darnley had never in fact received the crown matrimonial, without which, despite his title of king, he could scarcely claim to be Mary's equal, let alone her superior.

It was under these circumstances that, shortly after Mary's flight to England, the first salvos in the new campaign to blacken her reputation once and for all were fired by the men who now occupied the throne from which they had ejected her. The queen's 'privy letters', of which nothing had been heard since the Parliament in the previous December, and which had apparently lain the while untouched in Morton's keeping, now made a new appearance on the political scene. It was interesting to note that these letters seemed not only to swell in importance, but also actually to grow in number as the campaign mounted in fervour. In England at the end of May, Lennox presented his own supplication to Elizabeth, wildly inaccurate in many details and poisonously accusatory of his former daughter-in-law; it referred to one letter only written by Mary by which she was supposed to have lured Darnley to his death. On 27th May Moray commissioned George Buchanan, Lennox's feudal vassal, to prepare a *Book of Articles* to denounce Mary. These articles, to whose inaccuracies reference has already been made in

Chapter 15, were originally in Latin, and contained a short reference to Mary's 'letters'. But this term did not necessarily imply that there was more than one letter: the Latin word was *litterae* which was used to denote one letter as well as several, and in sixteenth-century English, also, the term 'letters' was always used to describe a solitary letter. The Latin *Book of Articles* was ready by June. On 21st May, five days after Mary's flight, Moray dispatched his secretary John Wood to London, gnawingly anxious to prevent Elizabeth showing favour to Mary; Wood's instructions were to 'resolve' Elizabeth's mind of anything she might 'stand doubtful to'.[25] A little while later, translated copies of an unspecified number of the queen's writings were sent on to Wood from Scotland; as copies of letters said to have been written originally in French and now translated into Scottish they were, of course, of little value as evidence. But Wood was to show them secretly to the English establishment, in order to hint what big guns Moray might be able to bring against his sister, if only the English would encourage him to do so.

The encouragement which Moray needed was an assurance from Elizabeth that she would not restore Mary to her throne in the event of her being found guilty of the murder. On 22nd June, therefore, Moray dispatched an extraordinary letter to Elizabeth in reply to her request to explain his rebellion; he virtually asked to be assured in advance that the verdict of Elizabeth's judges would be guilty *if* Moray was able to produce some of Mary's own letters, and *if* he could prove they were genuine. The English were asked to make up their minds on the basis of the translated copies of the letters now in London in order to resolve Moray's dilemma for him. Moray continued the letter on a note of near indignation at his difficulties: 'For what purpose shall we either accuse, or take care how to prove, when we are not assured what to prove, or, when we have proved, what shall succeed?'[26]

Moray's letter was a remarkable document. It may be thought to show more regard for the principles of statecraft than those of justice; it certainly outlined the problems of Moray and his supporters. For it was of no avail to accuse Mary of murder, and even prove it by fair means or foul, if she was subsequently to be restored to her throne, whatever the English verdict. Her vengeance might then be expected to be fierce upon those who had accused her. At this critical juncture, it seems likely that in response to Moray's anxious inquiries, Cecil did in fact give some private unwritten assurances to John Wood in London, to pass on to Moray: whatever Elizabeth might say in public, in order to lure the Scottish queen into accepting her arbitration voluntarily, it was not in fact intended to restore Mary to Scotland if she was found to be guilty.[27] At all events, Moray received some sort of satisfactory answer to his problems at the end of June, for he now began to endorse the plan of an English 'trial' with enthusiasm.

While Mary's emissary in London, Lord Herries, treated with Cecil and Elizabeth over the possibility of the English holding such a 'trial' if Mary would agree to it, Mary herself suffered a change of prison. It was decided to remove her to Bolton Castle in Yorkshire. Carlisle was dangerously near the Scottish border. From the moment of Mary's arrival there, other more secure places of confinement for her had been discussed, including Nottingham and Fotheringhay. The move was complicated by the fact that Mary was still not officially a prisoner. When the suggestion of a change was first broached to Mary, she quickly asked Middlemore whether she was to go as a captive or of her own choice. Middlemore tactfully replied that Elizabeth merely wished to have Mary stationed nearer to herself. To this Mary countered with equal diplomacy that since she was in Elizabeth's hands, she might dispose of her as she willed.[28] But when the actual moment came to leave Carlisle, Mary showed less composure. She began to weep and rage with a temper which was rapidly quickening with the frustrations of her unexpected imprisonment. Knollys had to exercise all his patience to get Mary to agree to proceed, since he did not wish to practise duress. Eventually Mary saw the threats and lamentations were achieving nothing, whereas gentleness might win her some advantage. She therefore withdrew her objections to departure, like a wise woman, said Knollys, and allowed herself to be removed quite placidly, on condition that she should be permitted to dispatch messengers to Scotland. The journey took two days, with a night at Lowther Castle and a night at Wharton. On arrival, Mary was pronounced by Knollys to his satisfaction to be very quiet, tractable, and 'void of displeasant countenance'.[29]

There was, however, much to displease Mary's countenance in the intrigues which were now being spun between Edinburgh and London. In spite of her incarceration, she had some inkling of what was taking place, and her knowledge of Scotland led her to guess more. Some messages from Wood in London to Moray fell into her hands by chance in June and uncovered some of the regent's plotting. The news that some of her own letters were to be used against her reduced her to a state of nervous collapse, and she ended one letter to Elizabeth with a plea to excuse her 'bad writing, for these letters, so falsely invented, have made her ill'.[30] The move away from Carlisle proved to be a severe handicap. Carlisle was at least the capital of the western portion of the English borders, a frontier town with administrative connections, easy of access for travellers. Bolton was an isolated castle in a remote corner of the North Riding of Yorkshire, looking over the broad pastoral valley of Wensleydale; it had no town of its own to surround it, and lay forty miles from York and over fifty miles from Carlisle. The castle itself was comparatively unfurnished on her arrival, and hangings and other belongings had to be borrowed from Sir George Bowes's house some distance away. Far more serious to Mary's cause than these minor discomforts was the fact that she was from now on placed physically outside the mainstream of political life, although mentally she remained very much part of it. Mary had never been well-endowed with advisers, although she was a woman who wished by nature to lean upon others for advice; for the next nineteen years she was deprived of any sort of proper worldly contact by which to judge the situations which were reported to her. Her own servants, although loyal, were no match in intelligence for the English politicians with whom they had to deal. A Herries certainly could not hope to worst a Cecil: in any case the mistress of one presided at liberty over an illustrious court, whereas the mistress of the other pined in enforced seclusion.

Herries came to Bolton from London at the end of July and put the English proposals to his queen; it is easy to understand how Mary, lit up by false hopes of restoration at Elizabeth's hands, agreed at last to the prospect of an English 'trial'.* The fact that the English had no right to try her seemed now less important than the fact that Elizabeth had promised to restore her whatever the outcome, although if the lords proved her guilt, it was stipulated that the lords themselves should go unpunished for their rebellion. If the lords brought no evidence against Mary, on the other hand, or if their evidence was not held to be valid, then Mary was to be adjudged innocent in any case and restored as before, on condition that she renounced her present title to the crown of England during the lifetime of Elizabeth and her lawful issue. Other conditions made were the abandonment of the alliance with France, and the substitution of an alliance with England, the Mass in Scotland to be abandoned by Mary and common prayer after the English form to be practised instead and the ratification at last of the Treaty of Edinburgh. Believing herself to be on the eve of liberty, Mary even bade her partisans in Scotland cease fighting on condition that Moray's would do the same.

The climate in the outside world was harsher than Mary, within her prison walls, remembered. Whether or not Mary's partisans did lay down their arms – at any rate at the Parliament of 16th August Moray swiftly declared the forfeiture of the Hamiltons, Fleming and the bishop of Ross, before ever the boasted English trial had taken place. More damaging still to Mary's cause, on 20th September Elizabeth wrote privately to Moray promising him what Cecil had already divulged in secret:

---

* The English were careful to avoid using the word 'trial', aware that they had no possible right to try the queen of another country, for a crime said to be committed there. But of course the proceedings were a form of trial, and the word is used hereafter without inverted commas.

whatever impression Elizabeth might have given Mary, the Scottish queen would not in fact be restored to her throne if she were found guilty in England. This letter, following on Cecil's hints to Wood, was crucial to the development of Moray's behaviour. On 23rd September Cecil repeated the same information to Sussex.[31] Moray had now every impetus to prepare the blackest possible case against his sister. The queen's 'privy letters' had therefore become the central plank of his accusatory edifice.

The English translation of Buchanan's *Book of Articles*, prepared for the coming trial in September or October, contained a much expanded reference to these letters. Instead of the brief phrase in the Latin version written in June, there was now a long postscript specially devoted to the subject. Mary's own supporters also began to appreciate that these writings were to be the testing-point not only of her own guilt or innocence, but also of the whole future government of Scotland. The Marian nobles, gathered together at Dumbarton, took the opportunity to declare publicly that '... if it be alleged that her Majesty's writing, produced in parliament, should prove her Grace culpable, it may be answered, that there is in no place mention made in it by which Her Highness may be convicted, albeit it were in her own hand-writing, as it is not'.[32] Only Mary herself, wrapped in 'her little prisoner's world', believed, trusting Elizabeth, that the trial was a mere formality, and that she would be set free in any case.

Under these inauspicious circumstances, the conference of York was set up. It was decided that the trial should take the form of examination of the evidence by an English panel, headed by the duke of Norfolk. Both Mary and Moray were to be allowed commissioners. Moray's commissioners included himself and Maitland; Mary's included among others John Leslie, bishop of Ross, and Lords Livingston, Boyd and Herries. Her instructions to her commissioners illustrate Mary's personal conviction that the conference was only being held in order that Elizabeth might in the future restore her to her throne, having accomplished 'the reduction of our said disobedient subjects to their dutiful obedience of us'. With such rising hopes to illuminate her horizon, even captivity at Bolton seemed tolerable to Mary. She occupied herself learning to write English under the tuition of Knollys. It is obvious from his letters that propinquity led Knollys to fall a little in love with his glamorous prisoner. Exercising her arts of fascination on those around her in charming little ways was second nature to Mary Stuart: to Knollys she wrote her first letter in English when he had been absent from Bolton for two or three days. The letter, which is indeed exceedingly misspelt and scarcely intelligible as English at all, announces that she has sent him a little token, asks after his wife, and ends touchingly: 'Excus my ivel vreitn thes furst tym...'[33]

Knollys also applied himself enthusiastically to trying to persuade his captive of the delights of the English religion which he himself practised. Knollys reported happily that Mary was now at Bolton growing to a 'good liking of English common prayer', had received an English chaplain, and had listened to his sermons which had happened to deal severely with the pharisaical justification of works by faith, as well as all kinds of papistry, with 'attentive and contented ears'. Her replies were gentle and weak and Knollys reported complacently that 'she does not seem to like the worse of religion through me'.[34] Mary was by now surrounded by Protestants: her cousin Agnes Fleming, Lady Livingston, joined her in August and both Livingstons belonged to the reformed Church, as did Herries; they may have added their influence to that of Knollys. It is possible also that she felt some genuine and laudable intellectual curiosity concerning the doctrines which the majority of her subjects practised, and that her inquiries helped to while away the captive hours. But the true motive behind this suspicious docility was now as ever her desire to win the good opinions of Elizabeth, for whom Knollys was merely a stalking-horse. At the end of August Knollys put his finger on the point when he reported how marvellously polite Mary had been of late 'as though she conceived I could persuade her Highness to show her great favour'.[35] The *beaux yeux* of Knollys, that good family man, who worried over the welfare of his daughters in London ('experience teaches what foul crimes youthful women fall into for lack of orderly maintenance' he pronounced in an anxious letter), were quite incidental to Mary Stuart's plans.

Mary's apparent Anglicanism did not pass unnoticed in England. Towards the end of September Mary heard that the local Catholics believed she was turning away from the old religion, and were very upset by the news; immediately in the great hall of Bolton, in front of a full assembly, she professed herself as fervently Catholic as ever before, her arguments, according to Knollys, being 'so weak, they only showed her zeal'. To Knollys alone she attempted to make capital out of the incident, saying pointedly that she could scarcely be expected to lose France, Spain and all her foreign allies by seeming to change her religion, and yet still not be certain that Elizabeth was her 'assured friend'. But her letter to her girlhood friend, Elisabeth de Valois, queen of Spain, at the end of September shows that her heart was evidently as Catholic as ever beneath its convenient show of Anglican interest.[36] Mary invokes the memory of their common childhood, the food they had shared in the past which had nourished an indissoluble friendship, to plead for Spanish aid. She tells Elisabeth that she has been offered *'de belles choses'* to change her religion, but whatever Elisabeth may hear to the contrary, Mary will never abandon the Faith, but merely try to accommodate herself to her changing circumstances. In the meantime Mary hoped somehow to smuggle out her little son James from Scotland to marry one of Elisabeth's daughters. By the time this letter reached Spain, Elisabeth was already dead in childbirth (incidentally leaving Philip II, that ever recurring prospective bridegroom, once more free to marry). But in November Mary wrote angrily in the same vein to Philip himself, saying that she was considered too closely related to the queen of England to enjoy the services of a Catholic priest, but that it should not be believed on that account that she had given up the beliefs of her religion, as well as the practice.[37]

The point was a good one. It was perfectly true that on her

first arrival in England Mary had asked Lord Scrope for a Catholic priest to attend her and he had replied firmly that there was none left in England. It was also true, as Mary told Philip, that if Knollys introduced a Protestant preacher into her chamber, she could hardly prevent him. Nevertheless Mary always felt somewhat sensitive in later life on this point of her alleged Anglicanism, not so much out of intellectual distaste – for her own strong but primitive faith seems to have remained perfectly unaffected by all the assaults made upon it – but for the good practical reasons she outlined to Knollys. By such aspersions on her Catholicism, she feared to forfeit the support of her Catholic allies. On the eve of her death, she still took trouble to justify herself for having listened to Protestant sermons when she first came to England. One may perhaps detect in these protestations the murmur of a faintly guilty conscience; possibly Mary did feel later that she had compromised herself a little in this respect in her desire to please Elizabeth. This very minor essay into the realms of Protestantism on the part of Mary may be ascribed in part to the wishful thinking of the ardent Puritan Knollys, in part to the natural curiosity of the captive cut off from contact with her own religion, but mainly to Mary's devouring obsession with the subject of Elizabeth.

Knollys worried himself constantly over the prospect of his prisoner escaping: he even sent a map of the castle down to London so that his security arrangements could be approved. The royal train at Bolton now consisted of Leslie, Herries, the Livingstons, the Flemings, Gavin Hamilton, the master of the household of John Beaton, Bastian Pages and his wife Mary Seton and young Willy Douglas, a corps of loyal supporters. Bolton was only sixty miles to the southwest Scottish border as the crow flies. Escape might or might not have been possible. Knollys's forebodings indicate that Mary might with luck have eluded her captors. But at this point there were positively no attempts at escape, no disguises as a laundress, no stolen keys, no corrupted guards; Mary herself made it clear that this was at her own wish. She saw no reason to try and escape when she hoped for so much from Elizabeth. It suited her too to pretend to be a guest, not a captive. At the beginning of October Mary warned Knollys that things might be very different in the future: 'If I shall be holden here perforce, you may be sure then being as a desperate person I will use any attempts that may serve my purpose either by myself or my friends.'[38]

In the meantime, with the prospect of the successful conference of York in front of her, Mary was content to stay where she was. Knollys really had no need to fear those hare-hunting expeditions across the moors – 'the wind never so boisterous' which made him feel so nervous because he constantly imagined a dozen or so Scots would ride over the moors and carry off their queen. In his mind's eye he saw them riding over mountains and heaths with spare horses, avoiding villages and towns, and rescuing this Diana – 'for she hath an able body to endure to gallop apass'. Knollys believed that the country folk would certainly not stop her: they would laugh in their sleeves to see her go.[39] Mary on the other hand no longer saw herself in this romantic and impulsive light. In mid-September she wrote proudly to the king of France, saying that the fact she had had no response to any of her letters to him pleading for assistance no longer worried her, since now Queen Elizabeth her good sister had promised to do all things to her honour and grandeur and restore her to her estate.[40] In October Mary pinned all her hopes on that conference to open at York, the result of which she believed, win or lose, guilty or innocent, could not fail to be her restoration to the throne of Scotland.

CHAPTER TWENTY

Her Privy Letters

~~~

'By divers her privy letters written wholly with her own
hand ... it is most certain that she was privy, art and
part of the actual devise and deed of the fore-named
murder of the King, her lawful husband.'

From the Act of the Scottish Parliament, 15th December 1567

The conference of York, which opened in October 1568,
was remarkable from the first for the confusion of
aims among its participants. Elizabeth had already left
conflicting impressions upon Mary and the Scottish nobles as
to what she regarded the desirable outcome of this conference
to be. Their own intentions were equally at variance. Of those
present, only Moray was able to show true singleness of purpose,
in that he intended to prove the queen of Scotland's guilt up to
the hilt in order to prevent her return north; with this object in
view he officially took custody from Morton of the debatable
'privy letters' in their silver casket on 16th September, before
setting out for England. However, the incriminating documents
had signally increased from the solitary letter of Lennox's
supplication, and the briefly mentioned *litterae* of Buchanan's
June *Book of Articles*. They were now named in the receipt as
'missive letters, contracts or obligations for marriage, sonnets or
love-ballads, and all other letters contained therein'.[1] Buchanan's
English translation of his *Articles*, prepared at the end of
September for use in front of the commission, also contained
an additional long postscript on the specific subject of the
letters, in contrast to the single phrase used three months earlier.

Moray's supporters were much less single-minded than their chief in their aims; Maitland in particular still dangled after his old scheme of Anglo-Scottish union, in which a restored Mary could play her part. Nor were Mary's own commissioners, including John Leslie, bishop of Ross, and Lord Herries, as resolute in their determination to prove her innocence as was the queen herself; having lived through the troubled times of the queen's marriage to Bothwell, they conceived their role as rather to secure some sort of compromise by which Mary could be brought back to Scotland, than to shout out Queen Mary's freedom from guilt from the house-tops. As for the English 'judges', the earl of Sussex, Sir Ralph Sadler and the duke of Norfolk, it soon transpired that they too were not immune to private considerations. Norfolk had recently been widowed; he was England's leading noble, and himself a Protestant, although he had many Catholic relations; the queen of Scots was now generally regarded as once more marriageable, despite the fact that divorce from Bothwell was not yet secured, and Norfolk's name had been mentioned in this context, even before the opening of the conference. As a 'judge', therefore, Norfolk might be supposed to be somewhat *parti pris*.

Under these circumstances, it was hardly surprising that the conference at York seemed at first to achieve but little. On 11th October Moray decided to make a bold essay to resolve matters. Copies of the 'privy letters' were secretly shown to the English commissioners. Maitland, however, seems to have leaked the news to Mary's own commissioners for the next day they rode over to Bolton and informed her of this development, although they had not actually seen the letters themselves. Moray was still acting cautiously: Norfolk reported back to London that the letters had not been shown to them officially as commissioners, but merely 'for our better instruction'.[2] Moray asked Norfolk to find out how Elizabeth would react to the letters, and whether they would be considered sufficient proof to condemn the queen of Scots of murder. Despite the judicial irregularity of Moray's behaviour, Norfolk professed himself to be horrified by the contents of the letters; although he had only seen copies, he expressed the view that so many letters could hardly be counterfeited; in asking Elizabeth's advice on how to proceed next, he gave the opinion that conviction of the Scottish queen would scarcely be avoided, if indeed the letters were written in her own hand.

Elizabeth's reaction to this communication was to send for the whole conference to start again at Westminster. It was felt that away from the frenetic atmosphere which seemed to have developed at York, calmer counsels might prevail, and some solid solution emerge from out of this morass in which, as Sussex truly pointed out, the crown of Scotland was being tossed about on wave after wave of private feud and interest. Elizabeth was as yet unaware that only five days after Norfolk wrote in such shocked terms concerning Mary's letters, he had had some private conference with Maitland in which it seems likely that Maitland held out to him the bait of Mary's hand in marriage. From Maitland's point of view, the marriage of Mary with a leading English Protestant noble was an excellent step forward in his plans. It had been suggested that at this point Maitland must also have revealed to Norfolk that the so-called Casket Letters were not all they seemed, and that the allegations against Mary as a murderess were not really to be taken too seriously. After all, in this strange quasi-judicial world of a trial which was not a trial, guilt might also be considered non-guilt. At all events, Norfolk now allowed himself to be involved secretly in certain schemes for a marriage between himself and Mary.

Sussex, another English commissioner, did not seem to take the letters particularly seriously himself. In a letter back to London, he neatly summed up the course future developments might be expected to take, if Mary was allowed to appear before the tribunal at Westminster:[3] she would obviously deny the authenticity of the letters *in toto* as a result of which she could never be convicted on their evidence; after this Elizabeth would be compelled to acquit her, and set her free. If on the other hand Mary was not allowed to appear personally, the whole matter could probably be 'huddled up' with some show of saving Mary's honour, and yet without exposing the Scottish lords as forgers; after this Mary could still be kept in prison. It was a shrewd summary, and with its emphasis on the need to prevent Mary making a personal appearance at Westminster, a prophetic one. Knollys, from Bolton, put his finger on the same urgent necessity to condemn Mary somehow or other, if she was to be kept in captivity: he could not see how Elizabeth could with honour and safety detain Mary, unless she was utterly disgraced to the world and 'the contrary party [Moray] thoroughly maintained'.

Knollys's solution to the problem of Mary was to marry her off to his wife's nephew, and Queen Elizabeth's own cousin, young George Carey, Lord Hunsdon's son. This handsome young man had called on Mary at Bolton in September, on his way north to join his father, the newly appointed governor of Berwick. The visit was probably prompted by Knollys's match-making. Carey was courteously received by Mary, although her mind seems to have been more on politics than on dalliance: she spent most of their conversations retailing to him a list of messages to give to his father about border matters, where conditions were by now exceptionally turbulent, as always during a period of governmental unrest in Scotland. Mary was still blithely unaware of the cool conclusions which Sussex had drawn concerning the paramount need to prevent her appearing personally in London. To Cassillis in Scotland she wrote quite confidently on 23rd October of the 'good procedure' at York where nothing had been proved against her. At first puzzled by the transference of the conference, she then consoled herself with the thought that from the first she had always wanted Elizabeth to take personal control of the whole matter, and now she was achieving her wish. Her letter to Elizabeth of 22nd October was a model of docility: 'Since you, my good sister, know our cause best, we doubt not to receive presently good end thereof; where through we may be perpetually indebted to you.'[4]

The commission of Westminster opened officially on 25th November. It was a considerably enlarged body from that of the three commissioners at York, and now included both Leicester and Cecil. Shortly before its opening, on hearing that Elizabeth was constantly receiving her rival plaintiff Moray into her presence, Mary wrote commandingly to her own commissioners saying that they were on no account to take part in the conference if she, Mary, were not allowed to attend it on exactly the same footing as Moray; nevertheless she still does not seem to have believed that this right could actually be denied to her throughout the proceedings.' On 29th November, Moray presented his 'Eik' or list of accusations, followed by the presentation of a personal accusation by Lennox. It was not, however, until 1st December that Mary's commissioners put in their first protest, that Mary also should be allowed formal access to the court, since Moray was personally appearing in it; they demanded that Mary should be allowed to speak in her own defence in front of the English Council and the foreign ambassadors. Elizabeth, however, refused the request on the ingenious grounds that no proofs had as yet been shown against Mary (the Casket Letters had not yet been produced in court); there was therefore no point in her appearing at this juncture, when as far as Elizabeth knew, it might never be found necessary at all, and Mary might be able to be declared innocent *in absentia*. Winter had come early that year. Thick snow piled the ground between London and distant Bolton, 250 miles and days of hard riding away. Mary's enforced isolation proved once more a disastrous hindrance to her cause. For without consulting her, her commissioners continued to try and bring about some sort of compromise to restore her to Scotland, in spite of the fact that Moray in his Eik had openly accused the queen of murder. They thus acted in direct contradiction of Mary's specific instructions to break off from the conference if she personally was not allowed to appear on the same terms as Moray: 'since they have free access to accuse us'.

On 6th December Mary's emissaries made their first protest on the subject; but the English still retained the Marian commissioners within the conference, by the expedient of arguing over the condition of withdrawal. Moray was now asked to produce additional proofs to his Eik; he exhibited the December 1567 Act of Parliament, and Buchanan's *Book of Articles*. Finally, on 7th December the casket itself was produced by Moray and his supporters in front of Mary's own commissioners. According to the Journal of the Commission for that day, the tribunal saw 'a small gilded coffer not fully one foot long, being garnished in many places with the Roman letter F. set under a royal crown'.[6] The circumstances of its finding, outlined earlier in Chapter 18, were now solemnly declared by Morton. Before the casket's contents were exhibited, however, the tribunal were shown two marriage contracts which were not included in it: after this the first two letters from the casket were produced. The next day seven letters out of the casket were displayed, all said to be in French, written in the Roman hand. The English tribunal, according to their account, duly had the letters copied out for themselves, collated the copies with the originals, and then, at Moray's own request, handed him back the originals. This done, Moray produced the cases against Bothwell's servants, Hepburn, Hay, Powrie and Dalgleish, including their depositions.

The next day, 9th December, while Mary's commissioners made renewed attempts to withdraw from the conference, which had for them become a travesty of justice, since they were not even admitted to the proceedings, the tribunal continued to examine the copies of the letters they had taken and the sonnets 'written in French, being duly translated into English'. Morton made a further official declaration about the finding of the casket, and the evidence of Darnley's servant Nelson, and one of Lennox's servants, Thomas Crawford, was also produced. It was now decided to enlarge the tribunal still further with other leading English nobles including Northumberland, Westmorland and Shrewsbury. On 14th December the new tribunal was given a *résumé* of proceedings up to date. In the meantime Elizabeth gave Mary at Bolton three choices: she could answer the accusations through her own commissioners, in writing herself, or personally to some English nobles sent expressly to Bolton for that purpose. To all these alternatives Mary returned an indignant negative: she could hardly be expected to answer accusations based on evidence she was not allowed to see, or surrender the traditional right of the prisoner to face her accusers. But Elizabeth said that if Mary refused these three alternatives 'it will be thought as much as she were culpable'.[7]

At last Mary was beginning to have some inkling of the treacherous nature of the quagmire into which she had so unwarily walked. Her frantic state of mind at this point, cut off at Bolton, dependent on slow-moving letters for news from London, may be judged from her letter to the earl of Mar in Scotland, in which she begs him to guard the infant James well at Stirling, and not allow him to be either brought by agreement to England, or snatched away from him by surprise: Mary adds a postscript in her own hand, reminding Mar that when she handed her son over to him, '*comme mon plus cher joiau*', he promised never to hand him over to another without the queen's consent.[8] On 19th December she belatedly drew up her own Eik for the accusation of Moray, presented on 25th December. Naturally she waxed especially furious over the accusation that she had planned the death of her own child to follow that of his father: the nobles 'cover themselves thereanent with a wet sack; and that calumny should suffice for proof and inquisition of all the rest; for the natural love of a mother towards her bairn confounds them'. Beyond that Mary dwelt on her previous troubles with the lords – the murder of Riccio when they would have 'slain the mother and the bairn both when he was in our womb', and the manifest illegality of Moray's regency.[9]

Despite Mary's counter-accusations, and despite her continued requests to be shown the writings which were said to arraign her, the conference at Westminster was officially ended by Elizabeth on 11th January without either Mary or her commissioners being allowed to glimpse these debatable documents. The verdict of the tribunal was indeed as ambivalent as the rest of the proceedings: it was decided that neither party had had anything sufficiently proved against them. Mary had not proved that her nobles had rebelled against her – 'there has been nothing deduced against them as yet that may impair their honour and allegiances'. But on the other hand, all the prolonged inspection of the so-called Casket Letters had not apparently convinced the tribunal of the guilt of the Scottish queen. Elizabeth pronounced on the subject of the evidence brought forward by the Scottish nobles that 'there had been nothing sufficiently produced nor shewn by them against the Queen their sovereign, whereby the Queen of England should conceive or take any evil opinion of the Queen her good sister, for anything yet seen'.[10] In short, neither side was adjudged guilty at the end of the 'trial', the only difference being that whereas Moray was now allowed to depart for Scotland, after a personal interview with Elizabeth – and incidentally with a £5000 subsidy in his pocket – Mary was still held at Bolton, with preparations afoot to move her to a still more secure prison.

Now at last Elizabeth offered to let Mary have copies of the writings produced against her, provided she would promise to answer them. (The originals had of course gone back to Scotland with Moray.) But at this point Mary's commissioners, who all along had shown themselves so little match for the English politicians, rallied sufficiently to point out that since Moray had by now left England for Scotland, and the conference had no other judicial basis except in so far as it was supposed to judge between Mary and Moray, it was far too late for Mary to answer Moray's accusations. Mary's commissioners were themselves allowed to return to Scotland on 31st January. Thus ended what was surely one of the strangest judicial proceedings in the history of the British Isles, with a verdict of not proven given to both parties, yet one plaintiff allowed to return freely to rule in the place of the other plaintiff, who in the meantime continued to be held a prisoner.

It is time to consider the Casket Letters themselves, those debatable documents, and see how much if anything they genuinely prove against the moral character of Mary Stuart – her adulterous liaison with Bothwell before the death of Darnley, and her guilty foreknowledge of his murder. It is an interesting point that Mary Stuart's contemporaries apparently attached a great deal less importance to the Casket Letters than has been given to them ever since by the studies of historians. In the four hundred years since their appearance, more ink has been spilt on the subject – textual difficulties, language difficulties, theories of authorship, theories of interpolation – than on almost any other textual mystery. Yet at the time when the actual letters were exhibited it has been seen that not only Norfolk took a sufficiently *dégagé* view of the whole matter to pursue marriage to Mary ardently thereafter, but Sussex, another Englishman, was of the opinion that as proofs, the letters alone would never be sufficient to condemn the Scottish queen. Subsequently, due to yet another revolution in Scottish internal politics, Maitland himself became one of Queen Mary's most ardent champions in Scotland, apparently undismayed by the depths of villainy she was said to have revealed in the letters. Despite this contemporary reaction, succeeding generations of historians have attempted to do what Elizabeth's tribunal specifically did not do, and give a verdict on Mary's character based on these letters. Yet every modern argument concerning the Casket Letters, and indeed every argument on the subject since the conference of Westminster in 1568, has of necessity to leave out of account the most important consideration in any discussion of letters said to be forged – the question of handwriting – for the Casket Letters now disappeared from sight as mysteriously as they had appeared.

In January 1569, they were taken to Scotland by Moray, to whom they had been redelivered by the tribunal. On 22nd January, 1571, they were handed over once more to Morton, although what should have been twenty-two documents (eight letters, two marriage contracts and twelve sonnets making up one poem) had mysteriously become only twenty-one, raising a doubt that one document might have been left behind in England. Copies were once more made, but these copies vanished immediately and have never been seen since. After Morton's execution, the letters passed to the earl of Gowrie, who was executed in turn in 1584, after which the original letters were never seen again from that day to this, despite repeated efforts on the part of Elizabeth to get hold of them, ranging from bribery to suggestions of theft.*

Today, in order to consider the authenticity of the Casket Letters, we are dependent on two sources: firstly those contemporary copies made by the clerks at Westminster which have survived. Some of these copies are in the original French, others in the English translation made for the use of the tribunal; all of these contemporary copies (with the exception of one) are in the Elizabethan 'secretary' hand in marked contrast to Mary's infinitely more legible Roman or Italian hand. There are four of these contemporary copies in the Public Record Office, and four others among the Cecil Papers at Hatfield House; a contemporary copy of one of the marriage contracts is among the Cotton MSS at the British Museum.[13] These are the only 'original' manuscripts available for the study of the Casket Letters – all of them purporting to be only contemporary copies. Otherwise we are dependent on the secondary published sources – and in the case of two of the letters, the twelve sonnets, and one of the marriage contracts, for all of which not even a contemporary copy survives totally dependent on them. The contemporary published versions consist of Buchanan's Latin 'Detection' which appeared in 1571, and gave three of the letters; in the same year a Scottish version of the 'Detection' also appeared, giving all eight letters, with the first sentence in the original French; the next year an Anglicized version of the

---

* The only link with the Casket Letters which remains to be seen in Scotland is the beautiful silver casket in the Lennoxlove Museum; although not garnished all over with the Roman letter F. under a crown, as the Journal of the Commission described it, it is the right size, and a French work of the early sixteenth century; its lock is also stricken up in the manner Morton described. There is room for two crossed Fs and a crown where the Hamilton arms are now engraved; alternatively the Journal's description may have been misleading, and the Fs may have been embroidered on the velvet cover of the box, as in another velvet coffer sent to Mary on Lochleven.[11] The Lennoxlove casket has a long provenance: it was purchased some time after 1632 from 'a Papist' by the marchioness of Douglas, daughter of the 1st marquess of Huntly. After her death, her plate was sold but her daughter-in-law Lady Anne Hamilton, later duchess of Hamilton in her own right, purchased it back, and, at her husband's request, had the Hamilton arms engraved on the casket, in place of those of Douglas.[12]

Scottish translation appeared, following the same principle. In 1573 a French edition was published giving seven of the letters; this was not the original French (as can be seen by comparing it with the contemporary manuscript copies) – merely a French version retranslated out of the Scots or English. This retranslation leads to considerable differences between the two French versions.

Quite apart from the lack of originals, the situation over the letters is complicated by the fact that none of them has any dates attached to it and none has any proper beginning or ending or signature; the fact that none is signed by the queen makes the letters particularly remarkable, compared to the rest of Mary's correspondence, since Mary, in all her other letters, always took especial trouble with her endings, and the individual phrase before the characteristic signature MARIE was always carefully suited to the recipient. Furthermore there is not one letter which does not have some internal problem of its own, either of dating or of sheer sense, so far as one can judge from the copy. As forgeries, then, if forgeries they were, these were no smooth and expert job, but botched up – even patched up – efforts, done in a hurry by men who were trying to prove something, and because they had to prove it quickly, were not too particular about details, so long as the broad facts of the case appeared as they wished. These are of course exactly the sort of results which might be expected to emerge from the events of the summer of 1568 – Queen Mary's unexpected flight to England, Moray's desperate need to keep her there, his anguished inquiries to the English as to what sort of evidence they would accept, and his final secretive, deliberately 'unofficial' production of the letters at York to Norfolk. The Casket Letters were to be regarded then as a collection of accusing briefs in a trial: in this context it is significant that the contemporary copies are all endorsed at the top in an English hand, sometimes that of Cecil himself, with a sentence giving the exact point they were said by the lords to prove. But regarded as a bundle of love letters, the Casket Letters are not only quite incomprehensible, but also in places manifestly absurd when applied to the relationship possible between Queen Mary and Bothwell.

Letter I,[14] of which no contemporary French copy survives, only a contemporary English translation, is marked at the top 'proves her disdain against her husband'. It is, however, not a love letter, but a calm and practical communication, from its style evidently written by Queen Mary herself at some point, although not necessarily 'From Glasgow this Saturday morning', as it states at the head of the letter – a phrase easily added. In it, Queen Mary refers to 'the man' who is 'the merriest that ever you saw, and doth remember unto me all that he can to make me believe that he loveth me. To conclude: you would say that he maketh love to me, wherein I take so much pleasure that I never come in there but the pain of my side doth take me.' This 'man' is to be brought by Mary to Craigmillar on Wednesday. From the endorsement, it is clear that the lords maintained this 'man' was Darnley whose advances at Glasgow, when Mary went to fetch him towards the end of January, were causing Mary a pain in her side. But the dates do not fit with Darnley's journey: he could never have expected to reach Craigmillar on the Wednesday; the person whom Mary did take on a journey also in January from Stirling to Edinburgh, arriving there on Wednesday, 15th January, was her son James. And it has been pointed out that Mary's language makes it at least possible she was talking of her baby son, 'the merriest that ever you saw … you would say that he maketh love to me …'; just as the term 'the man' makes more sense as a mother's fanciful term for a little boy, than as Mary's description of Darnley, to whom in all other letters even to her most intimate relative she refers impersonally as 'the King'. However, these details were not likely to bother the English tribunal. At a rough inspection, prodded on by the Scottish lords' explanations, such a letter could easily be held to prove the queen's disdain of Darnley at Glasgow nearly two years back. It was easy to add the phrase 'From Glasgow …' at the head of the letter to give verisimilitude; and a phrase about Paris being commanded to bring back medicine was probably interpolated in the middle of the letter for good measure – Paris being by now a notorious guiltinferring name in the history of Mary–Bothwell relations. But of course, in the absence even of a French contemporary copy of this letter, it is impossible to be certain about this.

Letter II,[15] the famous 'Long Casket Letter', is an extra-ordinary document which must have baffled the English judges if they had ever considered it in detail almost as much as it has baffled historians ever since.* Once again, no contemporary French copy survives to guide us, only the contemporary English copy and the Scottish version later published by Buchanan. The English copy was endorsed by the clerk: 'The long letter written from Glasgow from the Queen of Scots to the Earl Bothwell.' This letter is susceptible of almost any interpretation except that of being one single letter, written on a single occasion from Mary Stuart to Bothwell. It is extremely long – over 2000 words altogether. The contemporary English copy runs to seven pages of manuscript with a long unexplained gap on the fifth page. As before, it begins without any salutation: 'Being gone from the place where I had left my heart; it may be easily judged what my countenance was . . .', but after these first few affectionate but not amorous sentences, it turns into a long account of Mary's journey to Glasgow to fetch Darnley, her meeting with a gentleman of Lennox's, and other meetings *en route* with James Hamilton and the laird of Luss. The letter now gives a long intimate account of Mary's interview and relations with Darnley while at Glasgow: Darnley pleads with Mary to lodge 'nigh' unto him, blames his sickness for Mary being 'so strange unto him', and attacks Mary for her cruelty who will not accept his 'offers and repentance'. These phrases ring very true of what is already known of Darnley's character, and Mary's relations with him, especially when he begs Mary to forgive him on grounds of his youth and inexperience; 'May not a man of my age, for want of

---

* See the Appendix, p. 693, for the two versions of this letter. The full text of all the letters has most recently been published in *The Casket Letters* by M. H. Armstrong-Davison, London 1965, to which the reader is recommended for a more prolonged survey of this complicated subject. The full text is also to be found in A. Lang, *The Mystery of Mary Stuart*, London 1901, and T. F. Henderson, *The Casket Letters*, London 1890.

council, fail twice or thrice, and miss of promise, and at the last repent and rebuke himself by his experience …' The words echo the phrases, related by Nau, which Darnley used to Mary after the death of Riccio.

Mary now taxes Darnley with his plans to depart in an English ship, and the rumours of his plotting spread by Hiegate – matters which we know from her letter to Beaton just before she left for Glasgow were very much on her mind. The conversation ends with Darnley pleading with Mary to spend the night in his lodging, and with her refusing to do so until he is 'purged' of his disease; Mary then offers to bring Darnley to Craigmillar where he can be cured, and she can be near her son – an offer which we know did take place. She also promises to resume physical relations after he is cured. To this Darnley asserts that he knows Mary will never harm him, and as for the others, he will sell his life dear enough – sentiments which again fit neatly with Darnley's character and with his continued trust of Mary, proved by the fact he did accompany her to Edinburgh. Up to now it is evident that we are receiving from Mary a frank report on her relations with Darnley at Glasgow, written to some close confidante. But in the next phrases the tenor of the letter changes and the sense becomes more obscure. Mary writes of Darnley's attempts to win her: 'Fear not, for the place shall continue till death. Remember also in recompense thereof not to suffer yours [Bothwell's heart] to be won by that false race that would do no less to us both …' Later she writes: 'We are tied to two false races; the goodyeere untie us from them. God forgive me, and God knit us together for ever for the most faithful couple that ever he did knit together. This is my faith. I will die in it.'

These phrases which, on quick reading, seem to show that Mary was cold-bloodedly planning Darnley's murder with Bothwell, her lover, with a view to marrying him, make no sense on a second reading, if applied to the Mary–Bothwell relationship. Who was the 'false race' which might win Bothwell's heart, and to which he was tied, to the exclusion of Mary? Not the Gordons surely, who were now among Mary's most faithful adherents; Huntly, Bothwell's brother-in-law, had been Mary's loyal supporter over the Chaseabout Raid, and the Riccio murder, and was to continue as such throughout his sister's divorce proceedings (to which he agreed with alacrity) up to and beyond Carberry Hill. As for the rest of his family, after July 1565 Mary had no more devoted adherents; his mother was one of her chief ladies; his sister Jean allowed herself to be divorced with incredible speed in order that Bothwell might marry the queen. Yet throughout the rest of the letter, there is a theme of constant, agonizing jealousy on the part of the writer for some other woman in Bothwell's life, who from the angry references to Huntly as 'your false brother-in-law' is clearly Bothwell's wife Jean Gordon. This 'false brother-in-law' is making mischief between the writer and Bothwell, and is to be given no credit 'against the most faithful lover that ever you had or shall have', to please whom the writer will 'spare neither honour, conscience, nor hazard nor greatness'. It would have been quite impossible in January 1567, or indeed at any other date, for Mary to have referred to Huntly in those terms.

It becomes apparent therefore that some letter, or draft of a letter, written by Mary herself, has been loosely and not particularly skilfully run together with a love letter written to Bothwell by some other woman. There is more than one possible candidate for the role of the other woman: Anna Throndsen in particular had every reason to consider herself badly treated by Bothwell and tricked out of a promise of marriage; but as she had left Scotland by the date of Bothwell's marriage it seems that the charge of writing these tortured jealous letters cannot be laid at her door, although they fit with what we know of her character. However, Bothwell had many mistresses previous to his marriage: in the autumn of 1565 Randolph referred to some mysterious French mistress imported by Bothwell to Scotland. Bothwell did not marry Jean Gordon until the spring of 1566, and the match could well have aroused the most poignant jealousy in some discarded mistress, seeing herself passed over in favour of the rich and powerful Huntly connection. Whereas it is highly unlikely that Bothwell would have retained an incriminating letter from Mary written before Darnley's death among his papers, he might easily have preserved a bundle of love letters of no political implications, from an insignificant but passionate mistress; these could have been seized either in June 1567 from George Dalgleish, or at any other point after Bothwell's departure from the Scottish scene and before October 1568, during which time the lords were totally in power in Scotland.

The interpolation of a love letter from the other woman makes sense not only of the inordinate length of this letter – and Mary, who was only at Glasgow two nights, was already supposed to have written one letter from thence to Bothwell – but also of the strange activities she described herself as doing there: she writes on two separate occasions in the same letter of a bracelet she is making for her lover, a bracelet which she is staying up late to finish in secret, an amazing occupation for Queen Mary to adopt in the course of her critical mission to Glasgow. The pleading tone of the latter half of the letter is also strangely at variance with Mary's character: 'Alas, and I never deceived anybody but I remit myself wholly to your will, and send me word what I shall do, and whatever happens to me I will obey you. ...' Bothwell is said to be almost making Mary a traitor – an odd phrase for a queen to use, who could hardly be accused of treason towards herself. Still more puzzling, if the whole letter had indeed been written by Mary, is the concluding sentence: 'Remember your friend and write unto her and often.' For not only have no love letters from Bothwell to Mary survived (it is surely strange that the allegedly reckless Mary should have been so much more prudent than the theoretically cold-blooded Bothwell), but also Mary was about to return to Edinburgh, where she would actually sleep under the same roof as Bothwell at Holyrood; Bothwell being here in constant attendance on her, she would surely have no need for these constant communications for which the writer cravenly begged.

If parts of this long letter are dismissed as interpolations of another hand, this still leaves the problem of Mary's own highly confidential letter, and to whom it was addressed. One piece of internal evidence points to the fact that it might have been Moray: the queen compares Darnley's evil breath (due in fact to syphilis, although she did not know it) to 'your uncle's breath'. Bothwell had no uncles; and only one great-uncle, the bishop of Moray, whom Mary had met once over four years ago. His personal hygiene can scarcely have been so vividly in her mind. But Moray's uncle, the earl of Mar, was a prominent courtier, had been so over a number of years, and was now guardian of the queen's son. Mary would have every reason to know such an intimate detail about Mar. Another piece of internal evidence suggests even more strongly that the queen's part of the letter was not intended for Bothwell: at the very end of the published Scottish version of the letter there follows a mysterious list of headings: 'Remember you ... of the purpose of Lady Reres, of the Inglismen, of his mother, of the Earl of Argyll, of the *Earl Bothwell*,* of the lodging in Edinburgh.' These headings were clearly intended to remind the writer of certain points she was to raise: but Mary would hardly remind herself to raise the subject of the Earl Bothwell in a letter written to Bothwell himself. These are not the only headings in the letter: half-way through the letter occurs a further list of headings, referring back to subjects already discussed. The existence of two such groups of memoranda lead one to suppose that Mary's part of the Long Casket Letter might have been only a draft for a letter which was never in fact sent. As a draft, it would have remained in her possession, and might therefore have been seized among her other papers when she was taken to Lochleven.

Whether such a draft was intended for Moray, or possibly even one of Mary's French relations, who would all have uncles known to her, to follow up her letter to Beaton the day before is less relevant than the light this letter casts on Mary's state of mind at Glasgow. The report of the Spanish ambassador in July 1567, the statement in Parliament in December of the same year, Lennox's supplication to Elizabeth in May 1568, and

* Author's italics.

Buchanan's early mention of *litterae* applicable to a single letter, show that quite early on in their rule of Scotland, the lords did feel they possessed some sort of written evidence against Mary – to be distinguished from the actual Casket Letters themselves. It is quite possible that this evidence was the draft of Mary's letter from Glasgow, in which she discusses her relations with Darnley with such candour, and relates her own promise to renew their married life once he was cured. It is significant that Crawford's deposition to the English tribunal was apparently tailored from the Marian parts of this letter, to the extent of virtually copying it.

Darnley's docile acceptance of his removal from Glasgow, into what he must have known was danger, is one of the more puzzling aspects of the Kirk o'Field tragedy. It has been seen that Mary more or less certainly suspended physical relations with her husband from the late summer onwards: perhaps the promise of renewal was made to bring the invalid to Edinburgh. This still incidentally provides no proof of Mary's adulterous liaison with Bothwell, merely of her own desire to get Darnley to Edinburgh, by promise if not threats, and under her influence once away from his own conspiracies. When the lords came to present their evidence to the English tribunal, they too did not find this draft letter sufficiently damning, and therefore laced it with a few classically villainous phrases – such as a suggestion that Darnley's 'physic' at Craigmillar should be poisoned – as well as interpolating, very roughly, another love letter to Bothwell.

Letter III,[16] of which a copy in the original French survives, is marked 'to prove the affections' in a clerkly hand. No attempt was made by the lords to date it, which would indeed have been very difficult, and it is of course not signed. It is quite inconceivable that it should have been written by Mary to Bothwell at any point in their relationship: the writer appears to have followed Bothwell's fortunes over a long period (as he is said to know) and have been brought into 'a cruel lot' and 'continual misadventure' as a result. Nothing was less true of Mary, to whom Bothwell brought good fortune up to the last moment, after which she was not able to write love letters to him. There is a reference to a secret 'marriage' of bodies, which the writer hugs to her bosom until their marriage can be made in public – the classical delusion of the girl who has been seduced. For all Bothwell's unkindness, the writer will in no way accuse him: 'neither of your little remembrance, neither of your little care, and least of all of your promises broken, and of the coldness of your writing, since I am so far made yours, that that which pleases you is acceptable to me'. This is hardly the pattern of Bothwell's relations with Mary: he broke no promises to her, was never cold, but acted for many years as a loyal servant and lieutenant before he aspired – his aspirations, not hers – to become still more powerful as her consort. Letter III, on the other hand, comes from the pen of someone who has had a long, passionate and unhappy love affair with Bothwell, over many years – in short, the other woman. If it be true that in all love affairs, *il y a un qui baise et l'autre qui tend la joue*, with the other woman and Bothwell it was always she who kissed and he who extended the cheek. Mary Stuart's relations with Bothwell took place on the less fanciful plane of politics: and it was Bothwell, as the seeker after power, rather than Mary as the fount of it, who was the aggressor in their relationship.

Letter IV[17] refers to that mysterious incident which Buchanan also mentioned in his 'Detection' (but to which Moray never referred although said to be a witness of it) in which Mary was supposed to have incited Lord Robert Stewart to quarrel with Darnley, with a view to getting him neatly killed in the course of the dispute.[18] This letter was marked by the English clerk 'Letter concerning Holyrood House' – a mistake for the house at Kirk o'Field. Apart from backing up Buchanan's dubious story which seems to be its main point in the lords' scheme of accusation, it is an extraordinarily obscure letter, despite the existence of both French and English contemporary copies, suggesting that the copyist found the original difficult to decipher, or else that the original was somewhat clumsily forged. It is a long letter – which makes it implausible that Mary should have written it to Bothwell on 7th February, two days before Darnley's death, during a week when Bothwell was in constant attendance on her both at Holyrood and at the provost's lodging. Again, many of the references are quite out of keeping with Mary at this point, including the reiterated theme of the 'ill luck' of the writer (quite inconsistent with Mary's fortunes at this date) and her jealousy of some rival who has not 'the third part of the faithfulness and voluntary obedience that I bear unto you'. Who was the rival who in February 1567 had the advantage over Mary in Bothwell's affections? The only possible answer was his wife Jean Gordon. Yet the writer of the letter deliberately compares herself to Medea, the first wife of Jason, whom he deserts to marry Glauce – the implication being that the writer, unlike Queen Mary, had been first in the field with Bothwell.

The letter concludes with the most enigmatic phrase in the entire Casket documents: in the French copy it reads, '*Faites bon guet si l'oiseau sortira de sa cage ou sens son per comme la tourtre demeurera seulle a se lamenter de l'absence pour court quelle soit.*' This translates literally as 'Beware lest the bird fly out of its cage, or without its mate like the turtle-dove live alone to lament the absence however short it may be.' The only possible implication is that the writer is the bird who may fly out of her cage, if badly treated, or else go into a decline out of melancholy. But, of course, such a sentiment could hardly be applied to Mary. Therefore the contemporary English translation, presumably at the instruction of the Scottish lords present, tries to make Darnley the bird who may fly out of the cage, and by mis-translating *per* (mate) as father (*père*), implies that the absence of Lennox is making Darnley mourn like the dove. The published Scottish version, on the other hand, while making Darnley the bird who may fly out of the cage without his mate, makes the writer the dove who will remain alone to mourn his absence, an interpretation which fits neither the French nor Mary's alleged disdain of Darnley – since there was no reason why she of all people should mourn the absence of Darnley.

Letter V,[19] of which the contemporary French copy survives, is endorsed 'Anent the dispatch dismissal of Margaret Carwood; which was before her marriage; proves her affection.' This endorsement is indeed essential to explain the production of this letter, which is otherwise of little guilty import in the history of Mary's relations with Bothwell. The writer – whose style one has now come to recognize as that of the other woman – expostulates against the folly and ingratitude of a certain woman who has made trouble between her and her lover: 'I beseech you that an opinion of another person be not hurtful in your mind to my constancy ...' and whom she now detests in consequence. There is as usual no signature and no proper names are mentioned. In point of fact Margaret Carwood was never in any disgrace with Mary: she was married from her service and as has been seen her wedding was attended by Queen Mary herself on the Tuesday after Darnley's death, a mark of signal favour; the queen also paid for her wedding-gown as the inventories show. There was certainly no question of her 'dispatch' from Mary's service. These facts were either forgotten or ignored by the lords presenting the ladies, in their inspiration at fitting this particular letter into the scheme of things, or else they rightly banked on such details of Scottish court life nearly two years before being unknown to the English tribunal.

Letter VI[20] is ostensibly written from Stirling where Mary went on 22nd April to visit Prince James. It was on her return journey that she was abducted by Bothwell, and the letter is thus endorsed 'From Stirling before the ravishment – proves her mask [pretence] of ravishing.' It exists in the contemporary French copy, and the English translation among the Cecil MSS at Hatfield House. Once again this love letter contains many internal references which make it impossible to have come from the pen of Mary. The external theme of jealousy on the part of the other woman for her rival is once again present: Bothwell is accused of having 'two strings to his bow', and Huntly is once more described as 'your false brother-in-law' who has come to the writer and warned her that Bothwell will never marry her 'since being married you did carry me away'. Yet Huntly at this point had just signed the Ainslie bond, backing Bothwell's marriage to the queen, and he certainly never seems to have been morally troubled by the abduction in any way. Furthermore, the other woman repeatedly reproaches Bothwell with being a negligent suitor, who has promised to resolve everything, but in fact: '*Vous n'en avez rien fait.*' Yet Bothwell in April 1567, as far as Mary was concerned, was a man of consummate vigour and resource, as the organization of the Ainslie bond itself goes to prove. Clearly the lords were struck by the coincidence of the phrases concerning Bothwell carrying his mistress away, referring in fact to some other earlier adventure, and adapted the letter to their own purposes.

There is, however, one interesting point to note about the contemporary copies of this letter: the original French copy at Hatfield is in an italic hand, in contrast to the 'secretary' hand of all the other copies. This hand, while clearly distinguishable from Mary's on close inspection (the c's and d's are completely different, the writing is smaller and neater), is nevertheless of the same Roman type, and might even be taken for it at a quick glance, particularly by a group of men used to dealing with a very different type of handwriting. Why should this one letter survive in the Roman hand? No explanation has ever been offered. But its existence does seem to argue that it may quite possibly be one of the original Casket Letters, masquerading as a clerk's copy; perhaps the prudent Cecil took one of the originals away with him, in place of a copy, as a piece of wise reinsurance bearing in mind always Queen Mary's close relationship to the English throne, which might at any minute, by the premature death of Elizabeth, make her his sovereign. The fact that the twenty-two documents had mysteriously sunk to twenty-one by the time they were handed over to Morton in 1571 may be explained by this piece of abstraction, which was not noticed at the time.

It is a fascinating, if speculative, thought. If this Hatfield letter is accepted as one of the original documents shown to the English tribunal, it still leaves us no nearer knowing whether this Roman hand was that of a Scottish forger, or that of the other woman, who, being brought up on the Continent, happened to write in very much the same manner as Mary herself.

The Hatfield group of Casket documents were only discovered at Hatfield House in 1870 by Mr R. Gunton, private secretary and later librarian to the 3rd marquess of Salisbury. They were first published in the Calendar of the Historical Manuscripts Commission in 1883. If any further copies of the text were ever discovered in French, in this same handwriting, akin to Mary's but not hers, or in any other Roman hand, fresh light might yet be cast on the whole complicated subject of the Casket Letters.

Letters VII and VIII,[21] for which no contemporary copies exist, are like Letter VI supposed to have been written from Stirling during the day and two nights Mary spent there before her abduction. Letter VII has a genuine Marian ring: the tone is regal in contrast to the self-abasement of the others, and Bothwell is here addressed very much as the faithful servant – the role which he occupied also to outward eyes in April 1567. If Letter VII is accepted in its entirety as being written by Mary from Stirling, then it certainly proves that she had foreknowledge of the abduction. Mary writes that she leaves 'the place and the time' to Bothwell. As for marrying her afterwards, Mary believes that Bothwell will deserve a pardon for his behaviour through 'your services and the lang amities ... if above the duty of an subject you advance yourself', especially if he gives as his motive the need to preserve the queen from a foreign marriage. This need to save her from the arms of a foreign-born prince was one of the arguments Mary always gave afterwards for believing that Bothwell was the nobles' own choice of consort. This letter also stresses another point on which Mary was known to be anxiously concerned at the time: Bothwell is firmly adjured to make sure of the support of the lords, and to take particular trouble to smooth down Maitland (Bothwell's known antagonist). This eminently practical letter, which Bothwell would have good reason to preserve among his most important papers, lest he could be accused of treason in that he had abducted the queen against her will, is another possible candidate for the queen's incriminating 'privy letters' which the lords might have discovered in the summer of 1567.

Letter VIII, on the other hand, although also said to have

been written from Stirling, must have been written by Mary at some other date, since it refers to Huntly as 'your brother-in-law that was'. The divorce of Bothwell and Jean Gordon did not take place until after the abduction; at Stirling Huntly was still very much Bothwell's brother-in-law; it was a mistake which Mary could not possibly have made. Letter VIII is once more a Marian letter, calm, without words of passion, warning Bothwell of various problems, and hoping in unemotional terms to see him soon: 'pray God send us an happy interview shortly'. The letter would seem to have been written to Bothwell some time after their marriage, the most likely date, as Dr Armstrong-Davison suggests, being 8th June when Bothwell had gone to Melrose to raise help against the rebels, and Mary was in Edinburgh. It won a place in the dossier, however, through the wording of this passage: 'there be many folks here, and among others the Earl of Sutherland who would rather die, considering the good they have so lately received of me, than suffer me to be carried away'. Although the apprehensions of the 'folks' applied to Mary's probable fate at the hands of her rebels, the lords tried to interpret the words as applying once more to the abduction, ignoring the erroneous description of Huntly.

The twelve love sonnets, as they were termed, consist in fact of one long love poem of twelve verses. We are dependent on the published French and published Scottish version for their text, since no contemporary copies have survived.[22] Brantôme and Ronsard, who both had intimate knowledge of Mary's earlier verses, indignantly denied that these poems could have been by Mary Stuart. These long, rather turgid verses are certainly remarkably unlike Mary's known poetic efforts, her early simple poems and her later more complicated poetry, which tends to be extremely courtly in phrase and analogy, as might be expected from the atmosphere of the High Renaissance in which she had been educated. But style apart, these verses contain sufficient material to convince one once more that they are the works of the other woman. This unhappy poetess has abandoned all her relatives and friends for her lover, unlike Mary who neither did nor was asked to do any such thing. There are references also

to Bothwell's wealth, which were unthinkable for Mary to make.
To her, Bothwell was a comparatively poor man, who had to
be subsidized with grants of money from their earliest meeting;
it was she who encouraged the profitable Gordon marriage on
his behalf, and finally she gave him grants of money after their
marriage. Furthermore, the habitual theme of jealousy pervades
the whole long poem. The only lines in the total of 158 which
might seem to apply to Mary, and Mary only, are those in which
she describes how she has subjected herself, her son, her country
and her subjects to Bothwell:

> Entre ses mains & en son plein pouvoir
> Je mets mon fils, mon honneur, & ma vie,
> Mon pays, mes subjects, mon ame assujetie
> Et tout à lui, & n'ai autre vouloir.

Apart from the fact that Mary neither placed nor tried to place
James in Bothwell's hands (it was a favourite accusation of
her enemies but untrue: throughout the Bothwell marriage he
remained in the care of the earl of Mar), the third line has an
odd ring, as if the words '*mes subjects*' (so pointedly applicable to
Mary, so inapplicable to any other woman) had somehow been
substituted for another shorter word in a line which already
ended '*mon ame assujetie*': '*mon coeur*', for example, fits the rhythm
much better. Although erasions and substitutions are impossible
to describe with any certainty in a poem of which only a
published version survives, the natural inference is that here
once again the interpolator has been at work. In order to apply
a melancholy, rather verbose love poem to the particular case
of the queen of Scots and Bothwell, the interpolator has altered
one small word – not difficult to do – on the same principle as
the words 'From Glasgow this Saturday morning' were added
to the head of Letter I, to adapt it to the fatal fetching of
Darnley.

There remain the two marriage contracts which the lords
produced. One of these, in French, is a manuscript from among
the Cotton MSS in the British Museum.[23] It has been argued in

the past that this is the original document, which was somehow never redelivered to Moray, using the previously cited alteration in the number of documents handed over to Morton in 1571. But the Journal of the Commission specified that this contract was 'written in a Roman hand in French';[24] unless the Journal was mistaken, the Cotton contract cannot possibly be the original, since it is in an Elizabethan not Roman hand, whose salient feature is the thick backward strokes given to certain letters. Moreover, the signature MARIE R at the end of the contract is a manifest forgery, if indeed this is the original contract shown to the tribunal. The most marked characteristic of Mary Stuart's signature, seen on letters and documents throughout her life, is the even level of all the letters, including the first letter M; there is sometimes a slight rise in the level of the word towards the end, on the R or I, but M is never of greater height than the A. The Cotton signature on the other hand is conspicuous for its capital M, which is twice the height of the other letters.

The lords themselves exhibited this French contract with some doubts and the explanation: 'although some words therein seem to the contrary, they suppose [the contract] to have been made and written by her before the death of her husband'. Certainly some words do seem to the contrary, for the queen specifically refers in the text to 'my late husband Henry Stuart called Darnley', before declaring herself once more free to marry, in consequence of which she chooses Bothwell. If an original French contract in her own handwriting, signed by her, did ever exist, this might well have been a document written and signed by the queen at Dunbar at Bothwell's dictation, shortly after her abduction; in which case, Bothwell would certainly have pre-served it among his papers. The absence of any date would be explained by the fact that the lords lopped it off, thus opti-mistically hoping to incriminate the queen by pretending the contract had been signed before Darnley's death, despite the wording of the contract which states to the contrary. The fact that Mary, in the contract, says that she makes her promise to marry Bothwell 'without constraint' does seem, on the principle of *qui s'excuse s'accuse*, to suggest that this document was drawn up at Dunbar.

The second contract does not survive in a contemporary copy but was printed by Buchanan.[25] It is said to be a marriage contract signed on 5th April at Seton, between Mary and Bothwell, at a time when he was not yet 'cleansed' of Darnley's murder. It is a long document in official language, quite unlike the other contract, said to have been witnessed by Huntly and Thomas Hepburn, parson of Oldamstock: the fact that Huntly should have witnessed such a contract made nonsense of many of the other letters, but these details were obviously considered unimportant. It is reminiscent of Queen Mary's actual wedding contract, signed on 14th May, and binds the queen to marry Bothwell, rather than some foreign prince, once Dame Jean Gordon, his 'pretended spouse', shall have been removed from his matrimonial path. Although Mary, Bothwell and Huntly were all at Seton on 5th April, it seems highly unlikely that she would have signed such a document before Bothwell had been divorced. It has been suggested that the clerk, as sometimes happens with official documents, mistook the month, and this contract really dated from 5th May, when marriage preparations were very much under way. If this coincidence is dismissed, the most likely explanation of the contract is that Bothwell and Huntly drew it up at Seton, but only presented it to the queen for signature at Dunbar nineteen days later; otherwise her signature might have been quite plainly forged, as on the copy – this being impossible to tell without a sight of the original document.

So much for the Casket Letters on which Mary's reputation was so thoroughly blasted in later centuries, although Queen Elizabeth herself understandably found nothing in them which was proof against her dearest sister. Compounded of Bothwell's previous love letters, some textual interpretations from other letters and a certain amount of inexpert forgery, all glossed over by a great deal of optimistic explanation on the part of the lords who presented them, they were plainly never intended to be exposed to the fierce glare of criticism and discussion which has been directed on to them ever since. The intensity of this discussion results from the fact that they are the only direct proof – inadequate as they are – of Mary's adultery with Bothwell before Darnley's death. Yet a rational consideration of the letters, in so far as is possible from mere copies, shows that at most Mary can be accused of two 'crimes', neither of them anything like as serious as the murder of her husband. In the first place it is likely that she induced Darnley to leave Glasgow for Edinburgh with the promise of resuming physical relations with him once he was cured of his pox; but this does not in itself constitute a proof of adultery with Bothwell, and Mary's partisans might even point out in her defence that there was no proof that she would not have implemented her promise if Darnley had lived. Secondly, and much more cogently, she can be accused of foreknowledge of her own abduction by Bothwell. Once more this is not criminal so much as unwise behaviour and has no specific bearing on the death of Darnley six weeks earlier. It reflects much more acutely on Mary's total inability at this point to deal with the internal politics of Scotland without leaning on some sort of support, and in the event she chose the wrong sort of support. These aspects of Mary Stuart's behaviour in the first half of 1567 are certainly not enough to brand her as a murderess or even as a scarlet woman, deserving the vengeance of society.

As to the hand of the forger, the finger of accusation must inevitably point in the direction of Maitland. He, who had been Mary's secretary for so many years, must have known her handwriting by heart; it would have been an easy task to produce something of sufficient verisimilitude to convince men who were not in themselves experts on handwriting. The collation of the writings does not seem to have been particularly prolonged: the passage in the Journal is in any case ambiguous and it is just possible that the collation refers to Morton's two declarations rather than the queen's handwriting;[26] even if such a hasty collation were made, Leicester and his company were certainly inexperienced in the delicate science of judging forged handwriting. Furthermore, as Queen Mary herself stated, her handwriting is a particularly easy one to forge for anyone who had made a study of her letters.* Of course, if it is accepted that Maitland performed the forgery, he still should not be blamed utterly for the ruin which fell upon the queen as a result of the use made of the letters: Maitland, like his contemporaries, certainly did not foresee the enormous prominence which history was to give to these botched-up documents; the mere fact that he subsequently supported Mary shows what a swift temporary expedient was the production of the famous letters. On the other hand, even if Maitland is acquitted of performing – or directing – the forgery, he cannot be acquitted altogether of participation in the fraud: from the first moment he set eyes on the letters he must have realized that they had not in fact been written by his mistress, since of all the Scottish nobles it was Maitland who had the most profound and sympathetic know-ledge of Mary, from the years of service spent with her.

It has been further adduced against Maitland as being the forger that he was married to one of the queen's ladies, Mary Fleming, who would have been able to assist him in the task. Once again Mary Stuart herself hinted, in her declaratory statement on the subject before the conference at York, in September 1568, that her ladies might be able to counterfeit her handwriting[27] – 'There are divers in Scotland, both men and women, that can counterfeit my handwriting, and write the like manner of writing which I use, as well as myself, and principally such as are in company with themselves,' she pronounced, before going on to add (surely with truth), 'I doubt not, if I had remained in my own realm, but I would have gotten knowledge of the inventors and writers of such writings before now. …' All her Maries had been educated like herself in France and therefore wrote in different forms of the italic hand. The hand-writing of Mary Beaton is the most similar to that of the queen; furthermore Mary Beaton was at this point involved in a dispute with her former mistress over some jewels. This dispute has led some students to suggest in turn that Mary Beaton was the

---

* Lang prints some examples of modern forgeries of Mary's handwriting impossible to tell from the originals printed beside them, in *The Mystery of Mary Stuart*.

actual forger. It would be sad indeed if Mary Stuart, who always loved and nourished her attendants with a quasi-maternal passion, was rewarded by this ultimate treachery at such a critical moment in her fortunes, by one of those who had once been nearest and dearest to her. But there is no proof against Mary Beaton or indeed Mary Fleming except the merest supposition: Mary Fleming like her husband Maitland subsequently became one of Queen Mary's keen advocates in Scotland itself; furthermore it would surely have been highly indiscreet to have involved one of the Maries in such a confidential business, when ancient loyalties might so easily have prevailed later and unloosed the tongue of the forger at some future date to reveal her own villainy and that of her confederates. There were those much closer to home, in the heart of the nobles' party, foremost among them Maitland, who could do the job as well as any former Marie. In any case, as Queen Mary herself was never shown the letters, she at least never knew for certain the answer to that classic conundrum of history – who wrote the Casket Letters? Had she seen them, the result would surely have been, as she herself put it, 'to the declaration of my innocence, and confusion of their falsity'.

My Norfolk

〜

'Our fault were not shameful: you have promised to
be mine and I yours; I believe the Queen of England
and country should like of it.'

Mary Queen of Scots, to the Duke of Norfolk

As the last farcical acts of the conference of Westminster
were taking place, preparations were already afoot in far-
away Yorkshire to move Queen Mary to a more secure
prison at Tutbury in Staffordshire. This time Mary could hardly
persuade herself that she was no longer a prisoner, or that
restoration to her throne was imminent, since the news that
Moray had been allowed to return to Scotland unscathed
represented an undeniable blight to even her most timid hopes.
In December Mary had told Knollys that she would have to be
'bound hand and foot' rather than be removed from Bolton.[1]
In January Knollys was still her jailer, although arrangements
were being made to hand the queen over to the earl of
Shrewsbury, owner of a magnificent string of dwellings across
the midlands of England; here it was felt that Mary could be
contained in safety, equally distant from the London of her
desire and the dangerously Catholic northern counties. In the
meantime Knollys had his own troubles: his wife was sinking
fast in the south, and died in the midst of all the commotion
involved in the removal.

The journey itself, in icy winter weather through the north of
England, was frightful. Lady Livingston fell ill *en route* and had

to be left behind; two days later the queen herself also collapsed between Rotherham and Chesterfield, and the cortège had to be halted while she recovered. Then a message was received by Knollys to say that as Tutbury had not yet been made ready for the queen of Scots' arrival, they would have to lodge temporarily at Shrewsbury's own house at Sheffield. But before they could reach Sheffield, another bulletin arrived to say that since all the Sheffield hangings had already been sent to Tutbury, Sheffield itself was uninhabitable – so it was once more on to Tutbury.

This medieval castle, which Mary finally reached on 3rd February, 1569, was of all her many prisons the one she hated most. She always maintained afterwards that she had begun her true imprisonment there,[2] and this in itself was sufficient reason to prejudice her against it; but Tutbury quickly added evil associations of its own to combine with her innate distaste. The castle, which was large enough to be more like a fortified town than a fortress, occupied a hill on the extreme edge of Staffordshire and Derbyshire from which the surrounding country could be easily surveyed. Although Plot in his *History of Staffordshire* written a hundred years later waxed eloquent on the subject of Tutbury's view, comparing the castle to Acrocorinthus 'the old Castle of Corinth whence Greece, Peloponnesus, the Ionian and Aegean seas were semel and simul at one view to be seen', it is doubtful whether the weary royal party and the mourning Knollys would have appreciated the comparison when they finally arrived: for since the early sixteenth century, the structure originally built by John of Gaunt had been virtually falling down, and as a Dutch surveyor reported in 1559, 'only indifferently repaired',[3] hence the powerful need to bring hangings and furnishings from Sheffield. Not only was Tutbury in many parts ruined (as the English government from the vantage point of London never seem to have realized), but it was also extremely damp, its magnificent view of the Midlands including a large marsh just underneath it from which malevolent fumes arose, unpleasant enough for anyone and especially so for a woman of Mary Stuart's delicate health. Later on, when Mary had reason to know full well the evils of Tutbury, she wrote of its horrors in winter, and in particular of the ancient structure, mere wood and plaster, which admitted every draught – that *'méchante vieille charpenterie'*, as she put it, through which the wind whistled into every corner of her chamber. As for the view, Mary herself, in words very unlike the raptures of Plot, described Tutbury as sitting squarely on top of a mountain in the middle of a plain, as a result of which it was entirely exposed to all the winds and *'injures'* of heaven.[4]

Nevertheless Mary had perforce to make the best of her new accommodation – her comfort not increased by the fact that her jailers had not even any money to provide for her, and Knollys wrote desperately to London for an immediate grant of £500, since they were destitute.[5] She now made the acquaintance of George Talbot Earl of Shrewsbury, and his famous or infamous second wife, known to history as Bess of Hardwicke. Shrewsbury, who was to act as the queen's jailer, with only short breaks, for the next fifteen and a half years, was a man of about forty. He himself was a Protestant although his father had been a fervent Catholic and he had many Catholic relations. He was immensely rich and possessed an enormous range of properties across the centre of England; but like many rich men he was obsessed with the need to preserve his inheritance, so that in the course of his wardship of Queen Mary, his letters to the English court began to sound like one long complaining account book of rising prices, servants' keep and inadequate subsidies. But Shrewsbury had long proved his loyalty to Elizabeth, and his character, fussy and nervous, constantly worrying about the reactions of the central government to his behaviour or that of his prisoner, made him in many ways an ideal jailer, for a state captive. Despite these suitable attributes of a public servant, Shrewsbury was not a strong character; at the time when he took charge of Mary, he was totally dominated by the redoubtable Bess.

Bess was now forty-nine, eight years older than her husband, and over twenty years older than Mary. She had been married three times previously, and by her second husband Sir William Cavendish of Chatsworth had had eight children. It was no mere flight of fancy that led her third husband Sir William St Loe to address her in letters by the name of this Cavendish mansion, which she herself inherited – the salutation which he often used of 'my honest sweet Chatsworth' gives a more realistic indication of the attention which this remarkable lady bestowed upon material possessions than of her actual qualities of nature. Bess's practical streak led her to marry off two of her Cavendish children, Henry and Mary, to Shrewsbury's heir Gilbert Talbot and his daughter Grace, in order to preserve as much wealth as possible within the bounds of the family. She was also, in the words of Lodge, 'a builder, a buyer and seller of estates, a money-lender, a farmer and a merchant of lead and coals and timber'.[6] Apart from this financial acumen, in private life the 'honest sweet Chatsworth' occupied the role of a termagant, for as Lodge painted her, she was 'a woman of masculine understanding and conduct, proud, furious, selfish and unfeeling'. In short, Bess was in character the exact opposite of her new charge, Mary Stuart, who was so feminine in both brain and intuition, and, if proud, was also full of generosity and feeling towards others.*

However, at first meeting, the queen and her new captors got on agreeably enough. The queen spoke 'temperately' to Shrewsbury, and Shrewsbury spoke *de belles paroles* to her, as each graciously admitted. Mary was allowed to set up her cloth of state to which she attached such importance, and a certain Sir John Morton was introduced into her *ménage*, who was in fact a Catholic priest, a fact of which Shrewsbury was either ignorant or agreed to turn a blind eye; in any case Mary must have been pleased by the innovation. The queen and Bess were even described by the fond husband Shrewsbury as sitting peacefully together embroidering in Bess's own chamber where, with Agnes Livingston and Mary Seton, they delighted in 'devising' fresh works to carry out. 'They talk together of

---

* A letter from Bess in the unpublished Bagot papers illustrates her attitude to those who stood in the way of her schemes: an elderly widow who is failing to agree to some project which is to Bess's advantage (but not her own) is described as 'behaving very badly'.[7]

indifferent trifling matters,' reported Shrewsbury happily, 'without any sign of secret dealing or practice, I can assure you.'[8] It was during this first visit to Tutbury and the early honeymoon period of Mary's relations with Bess that much of the joint embroideries attributed to them, at Hardwicke Hall, Oxburgh Hall and elsewhere, must have been completed.

Embroidery was to prove the great solace of Queen Mary's long years of captivity. It was a taste she had already acquired as a young queen, and it has been seen that one of her first actions on Lochleven was to send for her sewing materials. Now, with all too ample leisure at her command, the taste was to become a passion and almost a mania. Pieces of embroidery, lovingly and hopefully done with her own hand as though the needle could pierce the stony heart where the pen could not, were to prove the basis of the gifts which Queen Mary sent to Queen Elizabeth; Norfolk was similarly honoured with an embroidered pillow. An inventory of her belongings six months before her death included many items of embroidery not yet finished, including bed hangings and chair covers, as though the captive had set herself the Penelope-like task of ornamenting every object in her daily life. Into her embroidery the queen put much of herself, including her love of literary devices and allusions, which she had first acquired at the French court, and which had led her during her first widowhood to adopt two anagrams of her own name as devices: TU AS MARTYRE and TU TE MARIERAS (both of which were in a manner of speaking prophetic). This enthusiasm for devices was also shared by Elizabethan society, having reached England from Italy, where it had been introduced by the French invasions at the beginning of the century;[9] thus Mary's passion was able to find an answering echo in the heart of Bess – she who was to have E S (Elizabeth Shrewsbury) so firmly carved round the pedestals of the new Chatsworth. But quite apart from the contemporary delight in such conceits, which today might be satisfied by the more mundane pursuits of crossword puzzles and acrostics, they seem to have appealed to the romantic streak in Queen Mary's nature, a child-like love of intrigue and secrecy. This was a strain only encouraged by captivity and her attitude to codes, secret messages and the like can be compared to her love of emblems and devices; it is as though having been captured at the age of twenty-four, and cut off from outside society before she had fully reached maturity, Mary remained in some ways frozen in curiously youthful and even naïve attitudes.

In 1614 William Drummond of Hawthornden gave a full and marvelling description of the joint embroideries of Mary and Bess in a letter to Ben Jonson; these panels, which in most details can be equated with the hangings now at Oxburgh Hall,* contained a series of *impresas*, or allegorical pictures with text, in which the words expressed one part of the meaning, and the emblem another. One panel consisted of a lodestone turning towards a pole and the name MARIA STUART turning into the anagram SA VERTUE M'ATTIRE which Drummond preferred to the other anagram of her name VERITAS ARMATA. A phoenix in flames was said to be the emblem of Mary's mother, Mary of Guise, and the words accompanying the device were that now famous motto of Mary Stuart: EN MA FIN MON COMMENCEMENT. About the same date Cecil's emissary White noticed this motto also embroidered on Queen Mary's cloth of state.†[10] Some emblems referred to Queen Mary's past – the crescent moon and the motto DONEC TOTUM IMPLEAT ORBEM for Henry II, the salamander for King Francis I. Others alluded more directly to Mary's recent fortunes and her future hopes from Elizabeth – for example two women upon the wheels of fortune, one holding a lance, and the other a cornucopia with the motto FORTINAE COMITES. A lioness with a whelp and the motto UNUM QUIDEM SED LEONEM referred to Mary and her son

---

* See *Embroideries by Mary Stuart and Elizabeth Talbot at Oxburgh Hall*, by Francis de Zulueta, for a discussion of the authenticity of these tapestries. Also *English Secular Embroidery*, by M. S. Jourdain, for a further discussion of Queen Mary's embroideries.
† These famous words have always been taken to refer to Queen Mary's religious beliefs and the victory of the soul after death; but if Drummond is correct in reporting that they were attached to the emblem of Mary of Guise, they originally had the more philo-progenitive meaning that in the end of the mother was the beginning of the child.

James. At Oxburgh, one panel just below the centrepiece, which is yet another monogram of Mary Stuart, has a large monogram GEORGE ELIZABETH beneath a coronet, and is surrounded by the legend GEORGE ELIZABETH SHREWSBURY in full – representing a unity later to be crudely disrupted by the marital disputes of Mary's jailers, just as the unity between Mary and Bess, embodied in these hangings, was also to be torn asunder by Bess's venomous accusations. It seems also that Mary's early French life was never to be forgotten: the cipher combining the Greek letter Phi and M – for Francis and Mary – which the queen had used on her own signet ring after her return to Scotland, is also to be found in the corner of at least four of the Oxburgh panels, yet it was now half a generation since the death of Francis.

In captivity Mary's health was her most obvious problem, apart from her desire for freedom. It was often the old pain in her side which put a final end to a day's embroidering. Her health was only worsened by the discomfort of Tutbury. In March Shrewsbury noted that she was once more severely ill from what he termed 'grief of the spleen' and which his doctor told him was '*obstructio splenis cum flatu hypochondriaco*'; the queen's symptoms were pains, said to be the result of 'windy matter ascending to the head' strong enough to make her faint.[11] Even a move from odious Tutbury to the more salubrious Shrewsbury dwelling of Wingfield Manor did not effect the desired cure. At the end of April, the queen went into such a decline at hearing of the dreadful fates of some of her friends in Scotland that her whole face swelled up, and she sat weeping silently and uncontrollably at supper. By 12th May the queen was critically ill once more; at Chatsworth – 'my wife's house', as Shrewsbury put it – where she was taken for the cleaning or 'sweetening' of Wingfield, she had to be seen by two doctors.[12] As it happened Shrewsbury's own health suffered that summer, for he had both gout and 'the hot ague', to the extent of announcing that he no longer wished to live; his physician Dr Francis was deeply concerned over the many hot choleric vapours which had apparently found their way up to the patient's head from his stomach, when Shrewsbury took a fever after drinking too much cold water. But whereas Shrewsbury suffered occasionally from bouts of painful ill-health, Queen Mary's health now became a chronic problem for her and her jailers, only exacerbated by the conditions of captivity, and there are few of her letters in the ensuing years which do not refer in some manner to the physical pain she had to endure.

It was at the end of February 1569 that Nicholas White, who was journeying to Ireland on Cecil's behalf, broke his journey at Tutbury in order to report on the state of the Scottish queen. From his letter back to his master, it is clear that he found her as dangerously fascinating as had Knollys nine months earlier – although White, like Knox, had a rather less chivalrous reaction to the spectacle of her beguiling charms.[13] He too observed that the queen spent much of her time embroidering, telling him that 'all the day she wrought with her needle and that the diversity of colours made the time seem less tedious'. They also had a pleasantly intellectual discussion on the comparative artistic merits of carving, painting and embroidering, in the course of which Queen Mary expressed the view that painting was the most commendable of the three. At which White, who had already unpleasantly and most unfairly told Mary that she was responsible for the death of Lady Knollys by keeping Sir Francis away from her side (although there was surely nothing Mary would have liked better than for Knollys's duties to have been ended by her own release), replied rudely that he had read that painting was a false truth – *Veritas Falsa*. Mary understandably drew the audience to a close at this brusqueness, and withdrew to her own room.

Nevertheless for all his churlishness – and he may have feared to be seduced by this famous basilisk – White fully took in the physical appearance of Mary, informing Cecil that he found her hair dark, although Knollys had warned him that she often wore false hair of different colours.* And the percipient White added:

---

* White may have been deceived by false hair in this instance. Mary in youth had light red-golden hair. Although hair darkens with age, it could never have reached a really black tint naturally.

'She hath withal an alluring grace, a pretty Scotch accent, and a searching wit, clouded with mildness. Fame might move some to relieve her, and glory joined with gain might stir others to adventure much for her sake.'

White's words concerning the inducements there would be to rescue Mary were prophetic. Indeed, already the thought of 'glory joined with gain' had led Norfolk to go forward in the negotiations to marry the Scottish queen, the project first mentioned to Mary before the York conference. Mary's captivity in England had after all no legal basis, and even her abdication from the throne of Scotland had been made under duress, which robbed it of its validity; in the meantime her blood relationship to Queen Elizabeth, and her possible succession to the English throne – cast into further prominence by the death in 1568 of the unfortunate Lady Catherine Grey, the main Protestant Tudor candidate – made her a rich prize. Elizabeth's disapproval was by no means a foregone conclusion: after all she herself had suggested Norfolk as a possible bridegroom for Mary before her marriage to Darnley. Under these circumstances the secret moves to marry Mary to Norfolk, and then presumably restore her to the throne of Scotland, neatly linked to a Protestant English bridegroom, proceeded apace. Maitland was involved, and shares with Mary's envoy, John Leslie, bishop of Ross, the possible credit or discredit for having first initiated the plan; many of the Scots were said to look on the scheme with favour, and even Moray himself appeared to play along with the idea of the marriage for the time being, although he soon had an opportunity of publicly showing his strong disapproval of any notions of Mary's restoration. Many of the English nobles, who themselves disliked the dominance of Cecil within the English Privy Council, and in addition felt that his foreign policy, so intensely hostile to Spain, was against England's best commercial interests, saw in the elevation of Norfolk as Mary's bridegroom a convenient way of dealing with Cecil's rising influence. This particular question in English internal politics had been brought to a head in the winter of 1568–9 when Elizabeth confiscated three Spanish treasure ships at Cecil's instigation, and to the violent disapproval of many others within the council.*

The actual part played by Queen Mary herself in all the cobwebs of intrigue and counter-intrigue which followed was negligible: considerations of Anglo-Spanish commercial rivalry became somehow enmeshed with rival considerations of Scottish internal politics; England's foreign policy towards France and the attitude of the Pope towards Queen Elizabeth and the English Catholics were likewise issues which became firmly entangled in the simple topic of Mary's marriage to Norfolk. Yet throughout all these negotiations, whether secret or open, Mary remained a comparatively isolated captive, and her personal role was therefore a minor one, except in so far as her mere existence made her, as Elizabeth angrily wrote at the end of it all, 'the daughter of debate that eke discord doth sow'. But Mary could hardly be blamed for her mere existence, and as for her captivity, which made such an apple of discord in the centre of England, there was no one more anxious to end it than Mary herself. In all the first attempts or conspiracies to procure her release, Queen Mary adopted exactly the same attitude: since her imprisonment was illegal, she would consider herself free to try and achieve her liberty by any means in her power, as she had warned Knollys that she would in October 1568. As a 'sovereign princess' over whom Elizabeth had no jurisdiction, she never considered that any schemes, letters of instruction, however daring from the English point of view, could possibly be fairly held against her by English justice.

This was her personal point of view on the subject of escape. There were refinements to it: for example Queen Mary was strongly predisposed towards any scheme that sounded as if it might have the backing of a major power, and strongly disinclined to consider any hare-brained scheme which had exactly the opposite ring. At the head of her list of major powers who she thought might help her was still Elizabeth – whom Mary

---

* These ships, however, continued to be held, and were not in fact released till 1572.

still hoped would achieve her restoration to Scotland in the end. Beyond that Philip of Spain was one possibility and Charles ix of France another. With the latter in mind she early established a code with which to correspond with the French ambassador in London, Mothe de la Fénelon. But Elizabeth was still, and continued to be so for the next three years at least, the person from whom Mary hoped for the most effective succour. It was the blood tie which joined them, which Mary always felt must surely in the end influence Elizabeth to assist her; and Elizabeth's approval or disapproval, so far as she could guess at it, was something Mary always took into account in any project which was outlined to her. Mary was therefore a catalyst rather than the chief conspirator in the two plots which followed.

Mary's new potential bridegroom, Thomas Howard, 4th duke of Norfolk, now a man of thirty-three and a widower, was not an especially glamorous figure by any standards: an anonymous admirer described him in 1569 as being 'no carpet knight ... no dancer or lover knight', while going on to boast that he came of the race of Howards who could never be made to hide their face from the enemy.[14] Mary never actually met him, and most of her information on the subject of his personal attractions seems to have come from his sister Lady Scrope in whose charge she had been placed at Carlisle, and with whom Mary had become extremely friendly.* In spite of being no carpet knight, Norfolk had other more solid qualities to commend him: he came of ancient lineage (he was in fact the only duke in England) and was a territorial magnate on a grand scale, who was able to tell Elizabeth that he was 'as good a prince in his bowling-alley at Norwich' as Mary would have seen in the midst of her own country of Scotland.[15] He was also an experienced administrator, who had been English lieutenant-general in the north from 1559 to 1560, before becoming chief commissioner at York. Mary's part in the marriage negotiations – conducted

* It is sometimes suggested that Mary and Norfolk did meet briefly while she was at Carlisle, staying with his sister. But there is no proof of this, and if so, it is strange that neither of them ever referred to the incident in their correspondence. Certainly, Norfolk himself was always emphatic that he had never met Mary.

in strict secrecy from Queen Elizabeth whose temper on the subject of any marriage, and especially royal ones, was notoriously uncertain – was confined to writing a series of affectionate and even loving letters to Norfolk; yet since she had never met their object, these letters belonged very much to the world of pen-friendship and dreams rather than to that of reality. He was now to Mary 'my Norfolk', to whom she emphasized her unhappiness and the desire for liberty. 'My Norfolk', she wrote charmingly on occasion, 'you bid me command you, that would be beside my duty many ways, but pray you I will, that you counsel me not to take patiently my great griefs. ...'[16] She also underlined the fidelity she would show to him: 'I trust none that shall say I ever mind to leave you,' she wrote, 'nor to anything that may displease you, for I have determined never to offend you, but remain yours. I think all well bestowed for your friendly dealings with me, all undeserved.' The famous pillow which Leslie later revealed Mary had sent to Norfolk was embroidered with the motto VIRESCIT IN VULNERE VULTUS, and the arms of Scotland, to signify Mary's courage. Norfolk himself sent Mary a fine diamond, which was brought to her by Lord Boyd, and Mary prettily vowed in a letter of thanks to keep it hung round her neck unseen 'until I give it again to the owner of it and me both'.[17]

Yet it is clear that despite these affectionate demonstrations, in the Norfolk negotiations Mary was very much following the line of conduct presented to her by her advisers, rather than leading them forward; this was in part due to her captivity, and the conditions which made her dependent on the reports of others to estimate any other situation. It was also due to her natural suspicion of the whole state of marriage which had brought her into such a parlous condition at the time of her marriage to Bothwell. She had believed Bothwell to be the choice of her nobles and he had turned out to be their bane; she had believed Darnley to be the choice of Elizabeth, but she had been rewarded for marrying him by the virulent fury of the English queen. It was hardly surprising that she greeted the first approaches over the Norfolk match with considerable doubts. When she finally gave her consent, it was on the strict understanding that Elizabeth's approval would be secured: 'she wished them first and foremost to get the Queen's assent, lest the matter might turn to her hurt and the Duke's whereof she had had experience before in her marriage with Lord Darnley contracted without her (Elizabeth's) assent.'[18]

But Mary managed to convince herself in her prison, or was persuaded by John Leslie, bishop of Ross, that Elizabeth did approve these negotiations, or would approve them when she was informed. As late as January 1570 (when she had had considerable evidence to the contrary), she wrote confidently to Norfolk that their marriage would be generally approved: 'Our fault were not shameful: you have promised to be mine, and I yours; I believe the Queen of England and country should like of it.'[19] In the following August Leslie told the Spanish ambassador that Mary had been much importuned over the marriage, but had been driven to it by necessity, since she believed Elizabeth wanted her to marry an Englishman. Therefore, despite Mary's formalized sentimental attitude to Norfolk, her wearing of the diamond which he sent to her, for which Mary sent in exchange a miniature of herself set in gold, it is evident that Mary was seeking an honourable exit from her cage approved by Elizabeth rather than involvement in a life-and-death conspiracy.

In the summer of 1569 Elizabeth showed further encouraging signs of favour to Mary by testing out a series of restoration proposals with the Scots. There were three possibilities: that Mary might ratify her abdication, and live in England; that Mary and James should rule jointly; and, thirdly, that Mary should be restored with certain religious guarantees, and a promise for the security of Moray. The English nobles and Leslie also secretly imagined that the Norfolk marriage would fit neatly into this third solution, the only one, as Leslie proclaimed, which would be tolerable to his mistress. Already in the previous October Mary had expressed herself willing to be divorced from Bothwell, and messengers had been sent to him in Denmark to sign the necessary documents. Now, with a view to proving that there had been no marriage, emissaries were sent to Rome to institute a suit of nullity on two grounds: firstly, it was said that Bothwell had never been properly divorced from Jean Gordon, so that Bothwell could not have rightly married Mary; secondly, it was suggested that Bothwell had used force to effect his marriage to Mary, which was in itself a cause of nullity. In June 1569 Lord Boyd was given authority by Mary to treat with Moray on the subject, and a written mandate to apply for the divorce.[20] Such negotiations made it clear not only that passion for Bothwell had well and truly waned – if indeed it had ever existed – but also that Mary was prepared to suit her marital situation to anything which she imagined might lead to her restoration in Scotland.

These restoration proposals, to which Elizabeth herself seems to have been genuinely well-disposed, were turned down by the Scots themselves, led by Moray, at the Perth convention at the end of July, when the idea of Mary's return was rejected by forty votes to nine; among the nine who voted for Mary's return on certain conditions were Atholl, Huntly, Balfour and Maitland. Six weeks later Moray's position was made still more secure when Queen Elizabeth discovered the Norfolk marriage plot. Her rage was extreme. Mary found herself moved back to the hated Tutbury, and given an additional jailer in the shape of Huntingdon, the man whom she particularly disliked and even feared because she always believed his own pretensions to the English throne (he had Plantagenet blood) might lead him to do away with her. Her suite was cut down, and Elizabeth angrily ordered that Mary should neither give nor receive messages to the outside world; Mary complained to Elizabeth that her rooms had been roughly searched by men armed with pistols. Norfolk was imprisoned in the Tower. Elizabeth even turned, through his servant John Wood, on Moray, amazed to discover that he too had apparently been favourable to the notion; but Moray quickly informed Elizabeth's Governor Hunsdon at Kelso that he had never done more than tell Norfolk that if Bothwell were dead or Mary divorced, and if Elizabeth agreed to the match, then he would approve.*

The northern rising in November, under the Catholic earls of Northumberland and Westmorland, did nothing to improve Queen Mary's lot. This rising, ill-prepared and ill-organized, was more in the nature of a separatist movement on the part of northern Catholics than a revolt on behalf of Mary Queen of Scots. Queen Mary herself disapproved of it, not only on the grounds that she hated violence and wished to avoid the risk of the slaughter of innocent people, but also on the very sensible grounds that she did not believe it would do her cause any good, since the moment was hardly ripe for such a demonstration. Leslie later testified that she had asked him to try and get Northumberland to stop or stay the rising. Yet whatever her own wishes, a Catholic queen was the inevitable rallying-point for such an enterprise. Mary was hastily taken to Coventry for the time being in order to be geographically still further away from the rebels; here she had to be temporarily lodged in an inn, since Coventry Castle had been uninhabited since the Wars of the Roses and was therefore destitute of furniture – the government in London being as usual in ignorance of conditions in the Midlands. The idea of the inn infuriated Elizabeth when she learned of it, since she thought it implied too much dangerous social life for the queen of Scots. Mary was then removed to a house in the centre of the town;† here she in turn was annoyed to hear that Huntingdon, her jailer, had been listening to some sermons containing 'lewd preachings' against her, which she herself understandably refused to attend. Yet the see-saw nature of English noble attitudes and alliances at this time may be judged by the fact that Huntingdon now took the opportunity to press the suit of his own brother-in-

---

* It is difficult to believe that Moray ever really countenanced the match, which would have been dangerous to his prospects. Moray's biographer, Lee, suggests that all along Moray relied on Elizabeth to prevent the marriage once she heard of it – as indeed she did.[21]

† Local legends suggest that she was kept in the upper room of the building known as 'Caesar's Tower' (now rebuilt) which adjoined St Mary's Hall.[22]

law, Leicester – Mary's former suitor Robert Dudley under a new name – on the grounds that Queen Elizabeth was now considering the duke of Anjou as a husband, which left Leicester free for Mary; Mary, reporting this back indignantly to Norfolk, said that Huntingdon's next proposal was that his own claims to the throne of England should be recognized in return as being next to those of Mary and James.[23]

In the meantime events in troubled Scotland were about to take another dramatic turn: on 11th January, 1570, the regent Moray fell dead, struck down by the bullets of an assassin in the main street at Linlithgow; the story that he fell a victim to the vengeance of a poor man whose wife he had driven out into the snow, to meet her death, has long since been exploded. In fact his assassin was a Hamilton, and the Hamilton archbishop of St Andrews had at least foreknowledge of the plot. The death of Moray drew to an end the career of one who had aimed high: it will never be known exactly how high, or whether the pretensions by which his enemies accused him of aiming at the throne itself had any substance.* Mary certainly came to believe that he had aimed at the throne, and paid his assassin a pension. At all events, under Moray's brief regency Scotland had not more, but much less stability than in the early years of Mary's rule, and there was nothing in his conduct of affairs to justify his ejection of his sister from the throne on administrative grounds. It was no coincidence that he was struck down by a Hamilton, a member of a rival family: Scotland was by now, and continued to be throughout the minority of James, a hotbed of warring factions; Scots with long memories might have looked back to the minority of James's mother Mary and seen that little outward progress had been made.

The death of Moray meant the search for a new regent, to whom most parties would agree. It was not until the summer that the choice finally fell upon James's grandfather, Lennon,

---

* A popular rhyme current at the time of the conference of Westminster suggested that Moray was a traitor trying to seize the Scottish crown on the pretence of his mother's lawful marriage.[24]

largely as a result of the favour of Elizabeth, who supported him as being a likely tool for English policy. In the meantime Mary herself made frantic efforts to maintain some sort of maternal contact with her little boy, now three and a half. Just before Moray's death she sent him a little pony of his own, and a saddle, with a pathetic little note to accompany them: 'Dear Son, I send three bearers to see you and bring me word how ye do, and to remember you that ye have in me a loving mother that wishes you to learn in time to love know and fear God.' Mary wrote in vain, for neither her letter nor her presents were allowed by Elizabeth to pass to Scotland, to the son who could not remember Mary; and James himself, far from being taught to remember his duty 'anent her that has born you in her sides' as his mother hopefully put it, was being instructed by George Buchanan and others that his mother had cold-bloodedly murdered his father to marry her lover. These teachings did not augur well for Mary's future relationship with James.

In the summer of 1570 there was some scheme promoted by Elizabeth for bringing James to England (that old desire of the English to acquire a Scottish princeling); the Scots never agreed to it, but Mary was enthusiastic at the opportunity of bringing her child a little nearer. She swallowed her pride and even contacted her former mother-in-law and established enemy, Lady Lennox, on the subject, seeking her grandmotherly advice about James. 'I have born him and God Knoweth with what danger to him and to me both, and of you he is descended, so I mean not to forget my duty to you,' she wrote. But this scheme came to nothing. In the autumn of 1571 Mary was still pleading with Elizabeth to let her correspond with her son, or at least find out how he was faring, in her own words, from the point of view of a 'desolate mother whose solitary child has been torn from her arms'.[25]

In May 1570 Mary was once more taken back to Chatsworth, and here a fantastic plot was hatched on the part of some romantic local squires to rescue her. At the time of the northern rising, Mary had been offered a possible chance of escape by Leonard Dacres, Northumberland's cousin, and had refused the bait, because she felt herself committed to Norfolk and her plans in that direction; Norfolk had pointed out that an escape would ruin everything, and leave no chance of Elizabeth's approval. By May the papal bull *Regnans in Excelsis*, which had been promulgated by Pope Pius v in Rome in February, had reached England, and had been posted up on the door of the bishop of London by a Catholic hand. This bull was to have an enormous effect on Mary's future, since it formally excommunicated Elizabeth and declared that her Catholic subjects were released from their loyalty to her. But at Chatsworth this summer Mary still remained damping towards the ardour of her supporters who wished to compass her escape.

The fabric of the plot was revealed in the examinations of those involved after they had been arrested; it seemed the protagonists were Sir Thomas Gerard, a local Catholic squire (father of the future Jesuit missionary John Gerard), two brothers, Francis and George Rolleston, one John Hall and two Lancashire magnates, the brothers Sir Thomas Stanley and Sir Edward Stanley. But the most searching cross-examinations could never make the actual practical details of the plot amount to very much, and Sir Edward Stanley strongly denied that he had had any effective part in it, giving the ingenious excuse that he had been away in the north at the time courting a Mrs Strickland. Gerard's idea was that the queen of Scots having escaped from Chatsworth should be shipped away to the Isle of Man by the good offices of Thomas Stanley; but he put his finger on the main trouble with any private rescue plot to do with Mary Stuart during all her years of captivity when he said that he had 'feared to make any man privy thereof for danger of discovery, and unless many were made privy, the thing could not be done'.[26]

Finally Hall and Rolleston did manage to have a cloak-and-dagger meeting with the master of Mary's household, John Beaton, on the high moor above Chatsworth at the conspiratorial if chilly hour of 5 a.m. Beaton told them he would have to consult the queen herself, but he could give them in advance her general answer to such proposals: 'So would she wish that no man should go about that matter, unless they were assured to put her in surety.' The plot was finally betrayed by George Rolleston, and Thomas Gerard was arrested and spent two years in the Tower. Francis Rolleston in his examination showed how frail the structure of conspiracy had been when he said that Chatsworth had been chosen as a good escaping ground because the queen could be carried off as she took the air on the moors, but it was never decided what to do with her next 'because the matter never grew to any determination or likelihood' since everyone had been in doubt of everyone else.[27] Hall's examination was especially significant on the subject of Mary's attitude to the whole project: Beaton had thought that the escape should take place at night, despite the fact that the queen's servants were then locked into rooms, but he admitted that Mary herself remained distinctly unenthusiastic since 'she nothing doubted but that the Queen's Majesty [Elizabeth] at the request of the Kings of Spain and France would restore her to her former dignity hereafter, the which she rather minded to expect, than to adventure upon a mere uncertainty, by such means to work her own delivery which might if the matter miscarried turn her to confusion and all her partakers'.[28]

This was a commendably prudent reaction. Beaton was never able to be arraigned for his part in the conspiracy since by the time it was uncovered he was dead, and buried (a sad expatriate Scot but a loyal servant) in the parish church at Edensor, close by Chatsworth. Mary's words showed that her eyes were sternly fixed on where the power lay, on the help of monarchs, not a handful of local lords, whose number of horsemen varied from 100 to 200 to 'a few', and at times apparently intended to ship her beyond the seas and at other times imagined 'they might keep her in some secret place undiscovered, if she could not have ready passage'. She showed no more interest when there was an attempt to revive the plot the next year. Mary was by now a woman of nearly thirty, on the verge of middle-age by the standards of the time; the old impetuosity of her youth was gone. She was chronically sick, alone in a country she did not know; it was a different matter to elude the bars of her own palace of Holyrood and ride to Dunbar through her own kingdom of Scotland, than to travel in disguise through unknown England, a foreign queen among foreigners. Under the circumstances Mary preferred to pin her hopes to more substantial targets.

In August 1570 Norfolk was released from the Tower. His release proved the signal for a further and much wider conspiracy, in which he was once more involved, under the inspiration of an Italian banker based in London, named Roberto Ridolfi. The Ridolfi plot, as opposed to the earlier plan, which merely proposed marrying Norfolk to Mary, had distinctly dangerous objectives if its widest aspects were taken seriously. Ridolfi himself was a man with an Italian love of intrigue but unfortunately with little of the Italian Renaissance skill at diplomacy; he understood little of the workings of the English mind, or indeed the workings of England itself. His aim was apparently to secure an invasion of England from the Netherlands by Philip II's general there, the duke of Alva, which invasion was to be supplemented by a rising of native Catholics within England. This combination of invaders and internal rebels would free Mary and, having seized Elizabeth, place Mary on the throne of England, side by side with her consort Norfolk. These were rash and treasonable schemes indeed. There were many difficulties in the way of their being carried out – the principal one being, as Philip II was quick to notice, that there was no proof that there would be another Catholic rising within England. Yet Philip stipulated that there should be no Spanish invasion until the English themselves had risen. In the meantime Alva formed the lowest opinion of Ridolfi, whom he termed a *gran parlaquina* or chatterbox, and a lightweight; as late as September 1571 he wrote to Philip from the Netherlands with a sarcastic lack of respect for Ridolfi's ability to carry out any sort of practical scheme, that even if Philip and Elizabeth jointly agreed to the invasions it still would not be sure that Ridolfi would be able to carry it through! Alva also analysed with terrible correctness the danger, to both Norfolk and the queen of Scots, if such a scheme was discovered or miscarried: either or both might lose their lives.[29]

Mary's attitude to, and personal involvement in, Ridolfi's schemes is open to question. She had not lost interest in Elizabeth's projects for her restoration to Scotland, which still dragged on. In October 1570, Cecil and Mildmay paid Mary a personal visit at Sheffield Castle, possibly spurred on by the king of France's representations to Elizabeth on the subject of Mary. They put before Mary a long list of articles proposing an alliance between herself and Elizabeth. Many of these articles reiterated the familiar English position since the abortive Treaty of Edinburgh: Mary was to give up her unlawful claims to the English throne. In addition Mary was to give up bargaining over her remarriage without Elizabeth's consent, and the question of James coming to England as a hostage if Mary was restored to Scotland was officially incorporated. In the course of their discussion, Cecil showed himself not immune to the famous charm of the queen of Scots: in a memoir of 1569 he had already referred to 'her cunning and sugared entertainment of all men', whereby she won many to her cause; now a personal experience of this sweetness led him to agree with Maitland: 'The Queen of Scots was of a clement and gentle nature, and was disposed to be governed by counsel of them in whom she reposed her trust.' Leslie, who reported this favourable verdict, even thought that Cecil had promised to bring Mary at last into Elizabeth's presence. Yet nothing concrete ever actually happened as a result of these articles, and by the spring of 1571 Mary was writing wearily to Sussex that she seemed to have been looking for a happy resolution to her affairs for so long 'which has been so many times delayed for every light matter that did occur, that we are for our own part in doubt if finally there shall be any good succeed unto us therein'.[30]

It is possible that under these circumstances of three years' onerous English captivity, Mary did allow herself to be persuaded to write the incriminating instructions and letters to Ridolfi quoted against her at Norfolk's trial. The original of the credentials said to be given to Ridolfi by Mary and Norfolk have mysteriously disappeared.* In these instructions Mary wrote wildly concerning the miserable state of England, the cruelty of her own position, the persecutions of the Catholics, the fact that Huntingdon and Hertford (Catherine Grey's son) were threatening her rights to the English throne, the need for the Pope to press ahead with her nullity suit, and how she intended to send James to Spain to marry him to a Spanish princess. Norfolk was described as being the head of the enterprise, and a keen guardian of the rights of the Catholics. All practical details were to be left to him; furthermore Mary castigated the French who had, she said, done absolutely nothing to help her.[31] However, the evidence of Mary's other letters, written at the same time to Mothe de la Fénelon, the French ambassador, show that she was, to say the least of it, trying to keep all the options open. She had, for example, far from given up all hopes of French assistance and in October twice approached the ambassador begging him to continue to help her and to interest the king and queen of France in her cause 'because she had no means to help herself'.[32] Nor had Mary in any way despaired of Elizabeth's assistance: for at the same moment as her approaches to Mothe de la Fénelon, Mary was writing to the English queen, stating the full confidence she felt in Elizabeth, and her desire to have her (Mary's) succession rights discussed in the English Parliament.[33] Subsequently Mary did admit to having given some sort of financial commission to Ridolfi, but she always denied that it had been anything so specific and dangerous to England as Cecil suggested.

The main architect of this unrealistic conspiracy, on Mary's side, other than the serpentine Ridolfi and the irresolute Norfolk, was Mary's envoy Leslie. Mary Stuart like most human beings was inclined to trust increasingly those whom she had trusted for a long time. Since the bishop of Ross first came to France in the spring of 1561 – when he incidentally propounded the

---

* See Francis Edwards, *Dangerous Queen*, London 1964, and *The Marvellous Chance*, London 1968, for a detailed consideration of the validity of the various documents in these intrigues.

foolish scheme for a northern Scottish invasion which Mary wisely rejected – Leslie had been an assiduous if not especially tactful servant of the queen; although he had managed to have good relations with both Darnley and Bothwell. As Mary's ambassador in England after her imprisonment, he was certainly in a position of enormous difficulty: the point has been well made that he was expected to act as the 'representative of a foreign ruler powerless to protect her servants but strong enough to attract discontented elements',[34] but Leslie was endowed with an unfortunate combination of energy and application – unfortunate in the sense that he lacked the essential *finesse* which would have enabled him to judge not only the right action to take on Mary's behalf but also the right time to do it. His anonymous publication in London in 1569 of the *Defence of the Honour of Queen Mary*, which asserted her old rights to the succession, was scarcely diplomatic when the favour of Elizabeth, so famously touchy on this particular subject, was all-important to Mary.

For all his erudition, which enabled him to write his long history of Scotland during this vital period of his stay in England, as Mary's ambassador, Leslie never quite appreciated the point which Alva quickly perceived: a plot in favour of Mary which miscarried could be far more dangerous than no plot at all. He was also, like his mistress in certain moods, a man of impulse with a quick rash temper. Yet Mary had perforce to put enormous faith in the bishop and his summing-up of situations, as well as in his capacity to amplify her own written communications by personal interviews. Many of Mary's letters at this period ended by promising that the bishop of Ross will further enlighten the recipient. It was unfortunate under the circumstances that by March 1571 Leslie, Mary and Norfolk were all cut off from each other, with the dubious Ridolfi acting as a go-between. Mary deeply regretted the loss of Leslie's news bulletins, which she regarded as her window on the outside world: by the summer, the lack of 'the daily intelligence she was wont to receive from the bishop' was mentioned as being the thing which troubled her most.[35]

If the incriminating documents are genuine, it is possible that Mary gained such a falsely rosy picture of the situation that she allowed herself to be committed on paper to an extremely hazardous venture. Such a false picture would not necessarily have been painted on purpose by Leslie to confuse Mary: it is more than likely that Leslie himself was also bewildered and muddled in his intrigues. He was not after all able to confront Mary face to face to discuss the situation verbally; dependence had to be made on letters, and letters could all too easily be intercepted. Although Maitland's son later made harsh comments on Leslie's character, and accused him of aiming at his own glory, and the enrichment of his bastard offspring, the situation was wide open for Cecil if he wished to lure the intriguers to their downfall by misrepresenting what each had said to the other; with Mary in prison, cut off from her servant, Leslie showed himself at first to be impetuous and later cowardly; but these qualities did not necessarily make him a villain.

News of what was afoot began to trickle through to the English government in the late spring. Elizabeth received a private warning from the grand duke of Tuscany, who had learnt only too easily of Ridolfi's hazardous plans. Finally and most disastrously, a certain Charles Bailly was arrested at Dover with a whole packet of books and letters sent from Ridolfi to Leslie. The connection of Leslie and Ridolfi was a fatal one for Mary, because Leslie in turn led directly to the Scottish queen, whose official envoy he was. The next step was to uncover Norfolk's association with the whole plot, which proved easy enough when Norfolk was found to be sending money to Queen Mary's supporters in Scotland. On 7th September Norfolk was arrested once more and placed in the Tower. More harmful still was the arrest of Leslie himself, for he produced a series of most damaging confessions, under threat of torture, which mentioned not only the foreign troops which were going to be imported into England, but also the use of papal money in the affair, some of which had been sent to the Marians in Scotland.

On 3rd November Leslie attributed the rising in the north to continuous communication between Mary and Norfolk, and between Norfolk and the northern earls – an injurious if inaccurate diagnosis. On 8th November his interrogator, Dr Wilson, the Master of Requests, described to Cecil how Leslie had said that Mary was not fit for any husband, for she had first poisoned Francis, then consented to the murder of Darnley, and thirdly matched with the murderer Bothwell, and after that she had brought Bothwell to Carberry Hill in the hopes that he would be killed in his turn; now she was pretending marriage with the duke of Norfolk, whom Leslie believed would not have survived long in the embraces of this female Bluebeard. Such confessions, however much promoted by physical fear, hardly pointed to Leslie as a stable and loyal servant. Even Wilson, shocked at this manifestation of what he took to be Scottish ingratitude, exclaimed: 'Lord what a people are these, what a Queen, what an Ambassador.'[36] But Leslie through all his tribulations did not lack self-confidence. On 8th November, the very day on which Leslie had outlined Queen Mary's marital career in such amazing terms, he wrote to her himself and said that he had been forced to confess everything since her letters had been produced in front of the Privy Council; nevertheless he could not help discerning the hand of providence in the discovery of the 'design', since Mary and her friends would be taught a sharp lesson against seeking relief by such means in the future![37] This egregious commentary on the outcome of the Ridolfi plot did not prevent Leslie from urging Mary to use all means in her power to get him released, and at the least to help him financially.

In January 1572 the duke of Norfolk was tried for high treason. Shrewsbury was specially imported from the Midlands to take part in the trial as one of the judges, leaving Sir Ralph Sadler temporarily in charge of Queen Mary. Norfolk was condemned, and finally executed in the following June. When Queen Mary heard of the execution of 'her Norfolk', she cried bitterly and kept to her room. Bess, finding her prisoner 'all bewept and mourning', asked her rather tactlessly what ailed her. Mary replied with some dignity that she was sure Bess knew what the cause of her grief was, and would sympathize with her in it; as for herself, she feared lest anything she herself had written to Norfolk might have brought him to such a pass. To these modest apprehensions, Bess replied ungraciously that nothing Mary had written could have done either good or harm, since Norfolk had been tried by a fair committee of his peers – including, of course, Shrewsbury.

Despite the snub administered by Bess, Mary had by her mere existence led Norfolk to conspiracy and death; in the same way Norfolk's trial and execution, and the revelations of the Ridolfi plot, were of acute relevance to Mary's position in England. It was not so much that she had lost a suitor – for there were many suitors in Europe of varying eligibility – as that her character in the eyes of the English nobility and the English Parliament now underwent a change. Popular opinion has a loud voice but a short memory. The circumstances of her arrival, now four years away, were quite forgotten in the tide of popular hatred which spread against her – this 'monstrous dragon' as one Member of Parliament termed her. Mary was now seen as a foreign-born Catholic spider, sitting in the centre of England spinning her webs in order to depose the English Protestant queen. The fact that she was an isolated prisoner with very little money was ignored in the light of the dangerous possibilities which the Ridolfi plot seemed to expose. It was at this point that Elizabeth herself seized her pen and wrote the famous lines on the subject of Mary, the 'daughter of debate', which ended:

No foreign banished wight shall anchor in this port;
Our realm it brooks no stranger's force,
    let them elsewhere resort
Our rusty sword, with rest, shall first his edge employ
To poll their tops that seek such change,
    and gape for joy.

But although Elizabeth's sword, rusty or otherwise, did eventually and reluctantly poll the top of Norfolk in June, despite the most ferocious baying for blood on the part of her faithful Commons,

Elizabeth refused to consider the execution of Mary. In mid-June the English commissioners Shrewsbury, Delawarr and Sadler visited Mary at Sheffield and solemnly accused her of her heinous part in the Ridolfi plot as well as a list of other crimes: of having taken up arms against England, approving the papal bull of ex-communication of Elizabeth (*Regnans in Excelsis*), and actually claiming the crown of England. To all these charges Mary replied firmly that as a sovereign princess she could not recognize their jurisdiction over her; she requested to appear before the English Parliament to justify herself, and once more demanded to be taken into the presence of Elizabeth. In detailed answer to the charges, the queen freely admitted that she had written to the king of France, the king of Spain and the pope and others asking for help, in order to be set at liberty and restored to her own country. She admitted the original offence of bearing the English title, when she had been a girl of seventeen, but denied ever bearing it since the death of Francis, over eleven years ago, which was correct. Over the Norfolk marriage, she reiterated her genuine belief that the match had been to the general liking of England. She admitted having given a commission to Ridolfi but said that it had been of a financial nature, and strongly denied any more compromising schemes with the Italian.[38]

Despite the Scottish queen's dignity, it was the will of Queen Elizabeth, not the answers of Queen Mary, which stayed the hand of the Commons against her in the summer of 1572. Elizabeth personally prevented the Commons from passing a bill of attainder on the Scottish queen; instead a bill was passed merely depriving Mary of her right to succeed to the English throne, and declaring her liable to a trial by peers (peers of the English realm, rather than her own peers, or equals, who would be sovereigns), should she be discovered plotting again. Most unfortunately the publication of the papal bull, *Regnans in Excelsis*, although not sought by Mary, and not even intended by Pius v to assist her personally, since he disapproved of her marriage to Bothwell, had begun the process of presenting her as a foreign traitor in their midst to English patriots. The massacre of the

Huguenots on St Bartholomew's Day, 24th August, 1572, at the hands of the French Catholics, led by the Guises, although once again hardly any fault of the prisoner of Sheffield Castle, only increased Mary's unpopularity in England. 'All men now cry out of [against] your prisoner,' wrote Cecil ominously to Shrewsbury. But Elizabeth would not allow this tide of xenophobia to sweep away her 'good sister and cousin', in spite of all the revelations of Ridolfi.

In the strange tortuous map of Mary's relations with Elizabeth, and Elizabeth's with Mary, Mary's feelings are much better charted than those of Elizabeth, since she gave many open declarations on the subject. But just as Elizabeth's incarceration of Mary on evidence she herself declared to be insufficient is greatly to her discredit, her preservation of Mary Stuart's life in 1572 by personal intervention must be allowed to be to her credit. Elizabeth, like Mary, had a constitutional dislike of spilling blood. Perhaps both of them were reacting against their blood-thirsty Tudor ancestors. Elizabeth was also conscious that Mary was by now by far her closest adult relation, since the sons of the dead Catherine Grey were still boys, and James was not only a mere child, but a child in control of the Scots; Elizabeth may have had some reluctance to abandon her kingdom to the care of young children (which had proved so fatal in the case of Scotland) if the assassin should find her as he had found Moray. Most of all, however, she was aware that Mary like herself was a sovereign princess: the death of one princess might strike at them all.

Too little is known of Elizabeth's inner feelings for Mary, since the English queen had learnt in childhood to hide all inner feelings, those dangerous traitors, within the breast. That closeness which two queens and near cousins should feel for each other, so often chanted by Mary, may have found more echoes in Elizabeth's heart than she ever admitted. In the meantime this merciful strain, this sneaking affection, could not fail to be noticed by Elizabeth's advisers: the point was taken that if ever the execution of Mary Stuart was to be secured,

Elizabeth would have to be thoroughly convinced that her good sister had repaid her clemency with flagrant and harmful ingratitude.

The Uses of Adversity

~

'Tribulation has been to them as a furnace to fine gold – a means of proving their virtue, of opening their so-long-blinded eyes, and of teaching them to know themselves and their own failings.'

Mary Queen of Scots on the lives of rulers,
Essay on Adversity, *1580*

B y the summer of 1572 the public cause of Mary Stuart seemed lost indeed; she was left to discover for herself in the private life of captivity the uses of adversity, sweet or otherwise. This outward decline in her circumstances was due in great measure to the fact that the fickle wheel of fortune had rolled away from her direction in Scotland. Argyll, for example, had remained a Marian supporter after Langside, despite his failure at the scene of the battle. Mary harangued him with anxious letters from her prison, addressed at times to 'our Counsellor and Lieutenant', at times to 'our dearest cousin' and rising in a crescendo of supplication to 'Brother' (a relationship based on his marriage to her half-sister Jean Stewart) to whom she signed herself in a fevered personal postscript 'your right good sister and best friend forever'.[1] These frantic missives did not manage to dissuade Argyll from deserting Mary's side for that of Moray in April 1569; he leagued once more briefly with the pro-Marian Hamiltons after the regent's death in 1570 before, finding Mary's cause hopeless, he abandoned it once more. The attitude of Lord Boyd – the royal servant who had brought the fatal diamond from Norfolk – was typical of that of many of Mary's more stable former supporters:

in the summer of 1571 he too began to despair of her cause. The death of the regent Lennox during a raid on Stirling in August 1571 led to the substitution of Morton as effective leader, under Mar as a nominal regent; Boyd agreed to Mar's election and was once more enrolled in the Privy Council. Mar's death in October 1572 confirmed Morton as regent in name as well as deed, and Morton was not only no friend to Mary at any time, but also an Anglophile, whom it suited Elizabeth to support. The final blow to Mary's prolonged hopes for restoration at English hands came in the following spring when the castle of Edinburgh, so long held by Kirkcaldy and Maitland on behalf of the Marians, and officially on behalf of Mary herself, was at last effectively besieged by heavy cannon brought north from England manned by English gunners under Drury. This lethal English intervention proved decisive: in May 1573 the castle fell.

The gallant Kirkcaldy was executed. Maitland either died naturally or, as Melville suggested, committed suicide 'after the old Roman fashion', before the executioner's axe could reach him. In any case his health had been deteriorating with a form of creeping paralysis: by March 1570 Randolph noted that his legs were 'clean gone', his body so weak that he could not walk, and even to sneeze caused him exquisite pain. Randolph commented spitefully: 'To this hath blessed joy of a young wife brought him.'[2] But Mary Fleming, for all Randolph's gibes, acted the part of a loyal wife after her husband's death. It was her moving personal plea to Cecil which saved Maitland's wasted corpse from the humiliating treatment accorded to Huntly's body after death in the shape of the traditional Scottish treason trial. In a firm letter to Morton, Queen Elizabeth pointed out that such barbarous habits were extremely distasteful to the English way of thinking: 'It is not our manner in this country to show cruelty upon the dead bodies so unconvicted, but to suffer them straight to be buried and put in the earth.' As God had shown His intentions towards Maitland by allowing him to die naturally and thus escape execution, so Maitland should be buried naturally and well and not 'pulled in pieces'.[3] Thus thanks to his wife, the foremost of the Maries, Maitland escaped the fate of Huntly.*

Mary kept her feelings to herself on the subject of Maitland's death: 'She makes little show of any grief,' reported Shrewsbury. 'And yet it nips her very near.' In the last years of his life since his quarrel with Moray, Maitland had energetically promoted Mary's interests; and he had died a loyal Marian. But he had not always lived as one. Queen Mary may well have reflected that if more years had been granted to him, he might have used them for further changes of allegiance. Nevertheless the death of Maitland brought to an end an era in Scotland; under Morton, a brutal man but one who showed himself to possess a certain administrative talent, the beleaguered country even enjoyed a period of comparative calm. Its quondam queen, Mary Stuart, also entered a phase of enforced tranquillity, in which the minor pains or pleasures of her prison routine became temporarily more important than European or Scottish politics.

The actual conditions of her captivity were not in themselves particularly rigorous during the 1570s by the standards of a state prisoner, except during moments of national crisis. In the first place Queen Mary was officially allowed a suite of thirty, which was enough to make her adequately comfortable if not a large number to one who had lived as queen her whole life. At the time of her first committal to Shrewsbury and Huntingdon in 1569 this thirty included Lord and Lady Livingston and their own attendants, Mary Seton, who had her own maid and groom, three other ladies of the bed-chambers, Jane Kennedy, Mary's favourite bed-chamber woman, John Beaton, her master of the house, her cupbearer and her physician; then there were her grooms of the chambers, one of them being that witty masque-maker Bastian Pages, Gilbert Curle, her secretary, Willy Douglas, now described as her usher, and her chair-bearer. There were four officers in the pantry, and three officers in the kitchen

---

* Mary Fleming lived on for many years after her husband's death. She obtained the reversal of the forfeiture of his possessions in 1583. She seems to have brought up her children, including that son James Maitland who was to publish a defence of his father's honour, as Catholics.

including a master cook and a pottager. Most of these were Mary's tried and loyal servants who made up the official thirty, but beyond this figure had crept in others, bringing the total up to forty-one. This proliferation, due not only to the infiltration of such further aides to the queen as Bastian's wife and some stable grooms, but also to the introduction of further attendants to look after the attendants, was tolerated by Shrewsbury out of kindness, as he himself admitted.[4]

But as the royal suite happily escalated through Shrewsbury's laxity, its increase in numbers inevitably reached the ears of the government in London, who took a much less generous view, especially when outside events seemed to threaten the safety of the queen of Scots. In times of danger there would be an outcry against this burgeoning suite – 'too much enlarged at the present time' wrote Elizabeth angrily in September 1569, at the time of her discovery of the first Norfolk marriage negotiations. There would be demands from London that numbers should be cut; this would result in tears and protests from Mary, coupled with guilty denials from Shrewsbury to London that he had ever allowed the number to rise.

More servants, quite apart from the danger of official complaints from London, meant more mouths to feed. Here Shrewsbury was less indulgent. His allowance from the government for the feeding of the queen was the subject of agonizing solicitude on his part throughout all his long years as her guardian, and as late as 1584 he was still complaining about the number of dishes the attendants consumed – eight dishes at every meal for the queen's gentlemen, and five dishes for the ladies. When Mary was first committed to Shrewsbury, he was allowed £52 a week to maintain her, but in 1575, without any reason being given, this allowance was cut to £30 a week. Shrewsbury squeaked with protest but all to no avail: it was an economy which the careful Elizabeth was determined to make. Shrewsbury's seventeenth-century biographer Johnston estimated that he was actually spending £30 *a day*, and was thus nearly £10,000 a year out of pocket; yet not only were his complaints disregarded, but he frequently had much difficulty in extracting the allowance which remained from the government.*[5] Eventually, on the advice of Walsingham, Shrewsbury applied to Queen Elizabeth for a fee farm to try and get back some of the expenses in a manner that would not hurt the royal pocket; even this request took a long time to be granted. In the meantime Walsingham reflected that cutting Shrewsbury's allowance might turn out to be a false economy if it meant that the queen of Scots was allowed to escape through lack of guards – 'I pray God the abatement of the charges towards the nobleman that hath custody of the bosom serpent, hath not lessened his care in keeping her'.[6]

In fact the care which Shrewsbury showed in keeping Queen Mary, like the numbers of her suite which he tolerated, varied very much with the attitude of the central government, and this in turn depended on the state of national security. Shrewsbury was not a cruel man and strictness generally had to be imposed from above. Even when the government resolved that the queen should be kept more 'straitly', its wishes were not always implemented very speedily; Derbyshire and Staffordshire were a long way from London, and travelling, especially in winter, from houses like Chatsworth set amidst the mountainous area of Derbyshire represented considerable difficulties. This worked both ways. In the first place Shrewsbury, like all ambitious Elizabethans, constantly pined for the royal sunshine of the court, and bewailed the duties which kept him so long away from it: he felt he was being excluded from the glorious possibilities of the queen's favour, as well as an opportunity to make his case about his allowance. In 1582, in the autumn, deprived at the last minute of permission to make a longed-for visit to London, Shrewsbury commented sadly to Walsingham

---

* It is difficult not to sympathize with the unfortunate Shrewsbury in his frequent moans of penury; he was certainly not justly treated by the Elizabethan government over the allowance. At the same time, it should be pointed out that it was at this same period that Shrewsbury felt himself able to embark on the major building-scheme of a new house – Worksop – although he was already amply endowed with residences. It does seem to argue that he was bankrupted more by his building-schemes than by the diet of the queen of Scots.

that neither the weather nor the time of the year would have prevented him arriving. Shrewsbury had to content himself with bombarding his friends at court with letters and gifts reminding them of his existence – such as some tasty 'red deer pies', made from his own deer, and posted off to London to win the favour of Cecil.*[7] But just as Shrewsbury was often tortured by the thought of the delights of London and the court, so the government who occupied this delightful city were themselves from time to time agonized at the idea that the Scottish queen in the far-off Midlands was enjoying far too much liberty, seeing people, receiving visitors, holding a virtual court, riding about on horseback in conditions tantamount to liberty ... such rumours, untrue as they were, spread by those recently arrived in London from the Midlands, caused Elizabeth to choke with fury and fire off indignant reproaches to Shrewsbury for neglecting his duty.

Although Shrewsbury never failed to write in return protesting his extreme loyalty to Elizabeth and his eternal vigilance as a jailer, there was no doubt that the question of access to the Scottish queen was a delicate one, and whatever he swore to Elizabeth Shrewsbury did not always interpret the rules in the harshest possible light. In April 1574 he wrote down to London, in answer to some accusation that he was showing too much kindness to his captive: 'I know her to be a stranger, a Papist, my Enemy. What hopes can I have of good of her, either for me, or for my country?'[8] But of course there was a simple answer to Shrewsbury's question, as to what he – leaving out his country – could hope for from the queen of Scots, and Cecil and his fellows were well able to supply it for themselves: if Elizabeth died suddenly, who knew but that Mary's fortunes might not be dramatically reversed? If the captive were to be transformed overnight into the queen, and Mary were to ascend the throne of England, as would have been a possibility at least, had Elizabeth died while James was still a child, then Shrewsbury

---

* Cecil was created Lord Burghley in February 1571, but for the convenience of the present narrative, he will continue to be referred to by his original name.

could expect much from his former charge if he had shown himself a sympathetic host to her in her times of distress. This consideration of Mary's potential as queen of England, which died away in the 1580s after James grew to manhood, was very much present in the minds of the English statesmen in the 1570s; not only Shrewsbury but also Cecil and Leicester kept the possibility at the back of their minds in their dealings with the queen of Scots.

From Mary's own point of view she was of course anxious to be allowed to receive as many local people and enjoy as much local life as possible. Such visits helped to while away the tedium of her imprisonment: the great families of Staffordshire and Derbyshire, the Manners and the Pagets, far from being Philistines, had the particular enjoyment of music and musical festivities which Mary shared.[9] These visits also provided an excellent cover for messengers and messages to slip by secretly. By the summer of 1569 irritating reports were reaching London that the Shrewsburys were allowing Mary some sort of social life at Wingfield. Lord Shrewsbury countered such complaints by detailing his extravagant precautions for Mary's safety – how, for example, when a child was born to his son and daughter-in-law, Gilbert and Mary Talbot, in March 1575 he deliberately christened the baby himself, to prevent unnecessary strangers entering the house. Nevertheless Shrewsbury was on some occasions accused of actually showing off his distinguished captive to his visitors – a charge of which one feels he was probably not completely innocent, since the presence of the famous queen of Scots in the Midlands of England must have caused a sensation among the local gentry on her first arrival. Cecil told Shrewsbury that Elizabeth had heard in London of 'a gentleman of Lord B' who, on visiting Shrewsbury at his home, had been asked by him whether he had ever seen the queen of Scots. Cecil's indictment continued: 'Then, quoth your lordship, you shall see her anon.'[10] Such tales made Elizabeth's blood boil and Shrewsbury's run cold.

Mary's access to the baths at Buxton was the subject of a long-drawn-out three-cornered skirmish between Elizabeth,

Shrewsbury and Mary. Buxton, which lay comparatively close to Chatsworth, although cut off from it by rough countryside, was endowed with a well, the healing properties of whose waters had been known even to the Romans. In early Tudor times it had been known as the well of St Anne, and had become a centre of religious pilgrimage, where the people came to be cured as much by their faith as by the waters themselves; as at a modern centre of pilgrimage, Lourdes, the crutches and sticks of the cured were hung up in the little chapel over the springs where Mass used to be said on behalf of the afflicted. During the iron dominion of Thomas Cromwell these innocent pursuits were rudely interrupted: the crutches and sticks and the offerings to the chapel were angrily swept away as manifestations of 'papist idolatry' by Cromwell's emissary; the baths themselves were locked up and sealed. However, by the time Queen Mary reached Derbyshire, the baths were once more unsealed, and were enjoying a considerable vogue even with the courtiers in far-away London for their remedial powers which were thought to be particularly helpful in the case of gout. In 1572 a Dr Jones wrote a thesis on the benefits to be derived from the 'Ancient Baths at Buckstones' which described the commodious arrangements made there for the reception of the sufferers. Bess had apparently already turned her agile mind to the possible profit to be derived from these baths and their tepid, clear mineral waters: Dr Jones's narrative implies that she planned some sort of Buxton Bath Charity, in which it was intended to have a clear scale of charges according to the wealth of the patient – £3 10s. for a duke and 12d. for a yeoman.[11]

To visit these baths became the dearest object of Mary Queen of Scots; again and again she pleaded the near-breakdown of her health in an effort to secure the desired permission. Shrewsbury himself built a special house next to the famous baths, in which it would be possible to house the Scottish queen as she took her cure, without danger of escape. But every time Elizabeth appeared to be on the point of agreeing, she seemed to hear of some fresh plot to rescue the prisoner. These heart-searchings eventually culminated in permission being granted, albeit reluctantly. Mary paid her first visit to Buxton at the end of August 1573 and spent five weeks there. Thereafter it became the outing to which she most keenly looked forward, not only one may suppose for the remedial effects of the waters – considered efficacious also for female irregularities as well as gout – but for the unique opportunity which it gave her to mix with people. The presence of occasional court folk at Buxton was indeed a source of equal joy to both Mary and Shrewsbury. Thus Mary was able to meet Cecil, in 1575, and later Leicester, her former suitor, in 1578 and 1584. Cecil in his cautious way actually turned down a projected match of his daughter with Shrewsbury's son, on the grounds that it might confirm ugly reports that he had become too friendly with Mary while at Buxton. But Leicester went on after his cure at Buxton to be entertained by Shrewsbury at Chatsworth, where Mary was at that moment confined. Mary's keenest hope was of course that Elizabeth herself would succumb to the temptation to visit the baths, so that the longed-for meeting would be brought about. But although Elizabeth visited the town of Stafford and the nearby Essex house of Chartley in the course of a progress in August 1575 – the moment in their lives at which the two queens were geographically nearest to each other – she did not journey on to Buxton.

Such visits gave Shrewsbury an opportunity of lavishing actual presents as well as showing kindness to prominent courtiers, or their wives and relations. Venison, fruit, fowl, meat, wine and ale flowed in a rich stream from the Shrewsbury domains to make the stay of these fashionable figures in distant Derbyshire more palatable. In August 1576 Sir Walter Mildmay, the Chancellor of the Exchequer, thanked Shrewsbury profusely for his kindness to his wife during the period of her cure, without which 'her being at Buxtons, in so could and raw a country, would be very odious to her'.[12] Happy Shrewsbury! The arrival at Buxton of Sir Thomas Cecil, Cecil's elder son, and his lady, my lady Essex, and the earl of Bedford's two daughters all with the clouds of court glory still freshly trailing about them, gave him a magnificent opportunity to load them with five hogs-heads of beer and ale, further wine, sheep, rabbits, and further emoluments to supplement their diet, including 'a fat cow'.[13]

Yet so long as these visits of Mary to Buxton continued, they remained a source of apprehension on the part of Elizabeth. Dreadful rumours that Mary might be endearing herself to the common people there by small acts of charity began to reach London. In 1580 Shrewsbury was once more defending himself against the accusation that Mary was being allowed too much access to the world: he admitted that there had been one poor cripple who had spoken to the Scottish queen at the well, 'unknown to all my people that guarded the place', but he promised it would not happen again. In 1581 Cecil complained to Shrewsbury that Mary was known to have visited Buxton twice that summer, although she only had official leave for one visit. In 1584 Elizabeth apprehensively forbade an assembly of freeholders in the forest of the Peak, three miles from Buxton, on the grounds that the inhabitants were 'backward and for most part ill affected in religion', despite Shrewsbury's protests that these were good men who had been summoned in respect of Elizabeth's rights of vert and venison there, which had fallen into disuse for the lack of such courts.[14] Mary herself spoke the truest word on the subject of such terrors on the part of the Elizabethan government, that her charity might win her hearts. To Paulet, a subsequent jailer, who criticized her for giving a smock to a poor near-naked woman out of pity for her condition, she replied, 'You fear lest by giving alms I should win the favour of the people, but you ought rather to fear lest the restraining of my alms may animate the people against you.'[15]

Apart from these desirable visits to Buxton and the demands of safety in time of crisis, Mary's little household found the locality of their prison changing from time to time in any case, owing to the sanitary arrangements of the time: the contemporary method of cleansing large houses such as those inhabited by Shrewsbury was to empty them totally of their inhabitants, who would be transferred to another house, and then clean the dwelling thoroughly from top to bottom. Not all Mary's prisons were as uncomfortable and hateful to her as Tutbury – whose evil drainage system and notorious 'middens' stinking beneath her own windows became one of her chief sources of complaint during her later years there. Wingfield was a great Derbyshire manor house of considerable style and grandeur, and even Mary approvingly called it a palace. Sheffield Castle and Sheffield Manor lay close together, the castle in the valley and the newly built manor on the hill: one of the reasons why Shrewsbury was anxious to transfer Mary to Sheffield in the first place was that the propinquity of the two houses would make cleaning problems easier, since Mary could be shifted conveniently from one to the other. At Chatsworth Mary could enjoy the beauty of the wild country in which it was set – those moors from which Gerard hoped she could be plucked – or the park itself where Queen Mary's bower still commemorates today the little closed garden where she is said to have taken her exercise.

Within the pattern of these moves, the mimic court and household of the queen had its own tiny excitement and dramas. The queen was allowed to ride when governmental suspicions were not too keen, and even went hawking with Shrewsbury; at one point she had as many as ten horses in her stables, three grooms and a farrier, before this equestrian abundance was brought to an end by angry protests from London. She was allowed the pleasure of archery, which she had enjoyed in Scotland, exercising her long bow with 'her folks', to take her mind off her friends' losses in Scotland, as Shrewsbury told Cecil.[16] She obtained a greyhound which she later tried to persuade Paulet to let her run at a deer. Then there were little pleasures of small dogs, caged birds (sent from France), other birds including barbary fowls and turtle doves, and much lute-playing as in Scottish days. Towards the end of her life Mary introduced a billiard table for the benefit of her house, although she herself does not seem to have used it. Nor did the queen lose all her interest in fashion and dress, being prepared to send off for patterns of dresses, such as were then worn at the London court, and cuttings of suitable gold and silver cloth.[17]

The romances of the chaste Mary Seton provided a positive drama within such a subdued setting. The only Marie to remain unmarried, and the only one therefore to follow her queen into captivity, Mary Seton had a naturally devout nature, and also a certain amount of pardonable family pride – the Setons being among the grandest of the Scottish court families, and her father and brother in turn playing a leading part as magnates, loyal to the crown. But these two aspects of Mary Seton's nature, admirable as they might be in theory, combined in practice to give her a certain spinsterish quality which was not a happy augury for marriage; nor was she herself as beautiful as Mary Fleming and Mary Beaton, or as vivacious as Mary Livingston. Yet in England this pious high-born Scottish lady did find her admirers: at Wingfield the younger son of Sir Richard Norton, Christopher Norton, was said to have fallen in love with her, although he was unfortunately executed at the time of the northern rising. She was no luckier with her next suitor, Andrew Beaton, who succeeded his brother John Beaton, Mary's master of the household, when he died in October 1572. Within the propinquity of the royal family circle, Andrew Beaton fell in love with Mary Seton. But the romance hung fire; there was some question that Mary Seton had sworn a vow of perpetual chastity, but the real trouble seems to have been that Andrew Beaton, although coming of an honourable Scottish family (the Beatons of Creich had given many loyal servants to the Scottish crown), was not quite on an equal social level with the daughter of Lord Seton.[18]

As Andrew Beaton struggled with the combined spiritual and material obstacles of a vow of chastity and family pride, he decided to resolve at least one of the difficulties: in August 1577 he went to France to obtain the nullification of Mary Seton's vow. On his homeward journey he was drowned. Mary Seton was left to mourn her last chance of married happiness, and as no one further attempted to dissuade her from the consolations of religion to which she had clung so long, she was able to die as she had lived under the name of Seton which she prized so much. From 1581 onwards her health declined, and began to interfere with the carrying out of her duties to her mistress, duties she had first incurred thirty-five years before when she had attended the child queen on her first journey to France. In

1583 Mary Seton was allowed to retire to France, and for the rest of her life lived at the convent of St Pierre at Rheims under the aegis of Mary's aunt, Mme Renée of Guise. Yet her devotion to her mistress was not diminished: in the same year a book and a box sent by Mary Seton in France to Mary Stuart via the French ambassador fell under suspicion; it was considered important that they should both be searched, for they would surely contain some secret messages for the Scottish queen.[19] Mary Seton's love of Scotland also remained; in 1586 she wrote sadly to M. de Courcelles, the new French ambassador, on his way to Scotland: 'It is now nearly 20 years since I left Scotland and in that time it has pleased God to take the best part of my relations, friends and acquaintances; nevertheless I presume there remain still some who knew me, and I shall be obliged by your remembering me to them as occasion may serve.'*[20]

Another household event, less poignant than the blighted romance of Mary Seton, but of some significance for the future, was the death of Mary's secretary, Augustine Raullett, in August 1574. Shrewsbury took the opportunity of Raullett's demise to go through his papers where he found 'Nothing of moment', as he reported to London. Mary's difficulty was indeed to replace him: for one problem which she had in common with her jailer, Shrewsbury, was that her finances were causing her great concern. Her accounts were by now in chaos due either to the carelessness or dishonesty of her treasurer, Dolin, a man who brought his mistress no luck, since in 1577 her jewels were actually stolen from his charge in Sheffield Park. The queen's dowry from France was paid irregularly, and all revenues from Scotland were apprehended by the current regent. Mary was now anxious to have above all things a new secretary with a

* The calm of the religious life led to longevity. Mary Seton survived her mistress by nearly thirty years, being last heard of in 1615. In 1602 an elaborate will provided for three High Masses to be said in the church of St Pierre for the repose of the soul of Mary Stuart, queen of Scotland. But her latter end was less glorious than her first beginning: in 1613 James Maitland reported that this once proud daughter of an ancient Scottish house was now 'decrepit and in want', and dependent on the charity of the nuns. Maitland begged James VI to help her, for his dead mother's sake.[21]

good business brain; on the other hand she could only offer little pay in return, as well as the highly restrictive conditions of work.

Claude Nau, the candidate now submitted by her Guise relations, was himself of a good Lorrainer family: one of his brothers had been in Mary's service earlier and had been with her at Bolton. Claude Nau had studied law and practised it in Paris; he was clever and quick-witted, speaking and writing good Italian, accurate Latin and English almost as fluent as his native French. Nau was a self-centred man, fond of personal display as Riccio had once been, and altogether a less engaging character than Mary's other secretary, the melancholy but charming Gilbert Curle. But these faults seemed for the time being outweighed by the fact that Nau was intelligent and zealous: as Mendoza said later, Curle might be good, but he was stupid. It was to Nau that Mary now related the important memorials of her personal rule in Scotland, referred to in earlier chapters. Mary was also able to employ Nau's many gifts in her ceaseless foreign correspondence. His abilities impressed her sufficiently for her to dispatch him in 1579 on a mission to Edinburgh, the principal object of which was to see and report on the young James, now thirteen. Mary sent with Nau some little golden guns of the sort to which young princes of the period were so partial, designed to win the heart of her son.[22] Perhaps she imagined James to be more martial, more Guise-like, than the scholarly creature he had in fact become. But the appeal of the little guns was never even tested, for Nau was not allowed to have access to James. After Mary's transference to Tixall at the time of the Babington plot, one of these little guns was found pathetically back at Chartley; she seems to have given them to her surgeon as a memento just before her death, and her groom of the chamber, Hannibal, received a little golden bow and arrow which was probably originally intended for the same source.

It will be observed that with all these little activities, Mary's day-to-day life during the 1570s and early 1580s was not particularly arduous in itself; but there was one factor which made the whole era intolerably burdensome to her, and that was her own appalling health. This ill-health was grievously exacerbated by the mere fact that she was confined, and few springs, let alone winters, passed without her being subjected to some really severe bout of illness. Her severe illness in the summer of 1569, which she compared later to her near fatal attack at Jedburgh in October 1566, was followed in the autumn by a nagging pain in the side which prevented her sleeping; she was also constantly sick. Norfolk's death brought on a passion of sickness, and through the 1570s the eternal nagging pain in her side reduced her at times to real throes of agony. Apart from this pain, Mary also endured distressing pains in her right arm, which is often mentioned in her letters as preventing her either from writing herself, or from writing properly. A bad fall from her horse at Buxton in 1580 resulted in an unpleasant blow on her spine. In 1581 she had another dangerous illness, which began as gastric influenza, and in November 1582 the same symptoms led the royal physicians to believe that she was actually dying. Her legs were also extremely painful and by the date of her death she was almost permanently lame. Thereafter other different symptoms, thought at the time to be those of dropsy or nephritis (kidney disease), developed. Mary's health must be regarded as by far the heaviest physical burden which she had to bear in captivity, and by the late 1570s it was a sufficiently accepted phenomenon for all those who knew her to comment upon it, not only her friends but even such creatures of lesser sympathy as Bess writing to Walsingham. Babington in his confession mentioned that at the time of his first plotting in the early 1580s the queen of Scots was considered to be an old and sickly woman, who was not likely to live much longer.[23]

Yet apart from the weight of suffering itself, Mary had to endure two additional ordeals with regard to her health. In the first place her captors were extremely reluctant to believe that she was genuinely ill at all, suspecting that she merely invented her symptoms in order to secure further freedom or privileges such as visiting Buxton; such symptoms as they could not deny, they attempted to put down to hysteria. Shrewsbury himself admitted as much: 'I perceived her principal object was and is to have some liberty out of the gates,' he wrote in a covering letter to a report on her health, but added that, being finally convinced she was indeed ill, he had allowed her to walk at least upon the leads in the open air, in the dining-chamber, and also in the courtyard. In this report M. de Castellaune explained that he too had originally put down her illness to the 'painful, importunate and almost constant workings of her mind', but now the unmistakable evidence of constant vomitings, discharges from the brain and 'the greatest debility in the stomach' forced him to realize that her sufferings were all too genuine.[24] Secondly, quite apart from the difficulty of convincing her captors that she was ill at all, Mary was additionally unfortunate in that her whole being craved fresh air, the free physical exercise, the ability to ride regularly every day, which she passionately believed would alone cure her. All her life she had shown a desire for physical exercise, especially riding, bordering on a mania; as a queen it had been all too easy to gratify this wish. Now she found herself totally deprived of regular exercise, except when Shrewsbury's régime became lax enough to permit it, and at the same time her health rapidly deteriorated. Her very muscles seemed to seize up with lack of use. It was no wonder that her letters were permeated with agonizing pleas for more sympathetic regard to her physical needs in this respect, and that she herself attributed her increasing sickness to her deprivation of sufficient exercise and fresh air.

The exact medical causes of Mary's undoubted ill-health have been the subject of several modern investigations. It used to be suggested that her symptoms corresponded most nearly with those of a sufferer from a gastric ulcer.* But recently Drs Ida Macalpine and Richard Hunter, working on a group of diseases known as the porphyrias, have identified the recurrent illness of George III as belonging to it.† An important aspect of this

* By Sir Arthur Salusbury MacNalty, *Mary Queen of Scots*, London 1960, Appendix I, where her symptoms are listed in detail and this conclusion is drawn.

† See *Porphyria – a Royal Malady*, British Medical Association publication, 1968, including articles published in or commissioned by the *British Medical Journal* by Drs I. Macalpine, R. Hunter, Professor Rimington, on porphyria in the Royal

disorder is that it is hereditary, being transmitted as a Mendelian dominant character, showing itself in varying degrees of severity, from individual to individual. In the course of their investigations they have traced back similar symptoms to George III's ancestor and ancestress James VI and I and Mary Queen of Scots. There are of course difficulties in the way of any medical diagnosis made at the distance of four hundred years, if only because the medical language used then was inevitably angled towards the diseases of whose existence the doctors were aware. Sixteenth-century medicine was obsessed by the notion of the four 'cardinal humours' or chief fluids within the human body – blood, phlegm, choler and melancholy, or black choler; their relative proportions within individuals were thought to determine their physical and mental qualities as well as their total temperament. Since the various 'defluxions' or physical substances which proceeded from the unfortunate queen of Scots were always considered by her doctors in the context of this theory, contemporary commentators may well have overlooked clues vital to the modern diagnostician.

The symptoms of porphyria are severe attacks of abdominal 'colicky' pain with vomiting and extreme distress at the time, even transient mental breakdown, which may be interpreted by observers as hysterical. The attacks may be mild or severe and may occur frequently or at long intervals; another feature of the disorder is that often, despite the severity of the attack, the patient recovers quickly afterwards. It certainly seems far easier to relate these symptoms rather than those of a gastric ulcer to the case of Mary; in particular the episodic nature of her sufferings – bouts of severe illness followed by speedy physical recovery – fits better with the known pattern of the porphyria-sufferer than that of the ulcer subject. It is clear that Mary, like her descendant George III, underwent genuine rather than hysterical sufferings, which at times amounted to a complete breakdown, indistinguishable from madness.

Houses of Stuart, etc., and by Professor Goldberg on 'The Porphyrias' as a group of diseases.

The period when she definitely showed every sign of break-down and hysteria to outsiders – after the birth of James until her incarceration at Lochleven – may even have been due to the exacerbating effects of her confinement upon the disease, such as have been traced by Drs Macalpine and Hunter in the case of George III's granddaughter, Princess Charlotte. Mary's gastric symptoms, her 'colicky' pain, which James VI himself noted that he had inherited from his mother, fit with the known symptoms of acute and intermittent porphyria. Even the pains in her arms and legs to which she so often referred in her own letters, which she ascribed to rheumatism, correspond to the painful paresis of the extremities often experienced by the porphyria-sufferer. Her attacks of 'hysterical' distress certainly occurred at irregular intervals, and although they appeared to die away towards the end of her life, since her lifespan was cut short at forty-four it is impossible to tell how her medical history might have developed in later years. As to the hereditary nature of the disease, the mysterious 'hysterical' manner of the death of James V, which has so long puzzled historians, suggests that if Mary did suffer from porphyria, it was from her father that she inherited it.

But to Mary personally it was the intensity of her sufferings, not the origins of her disease, which was of importance; the fact that she was probably a victim of inherited porphyria was unknown to her as it was to her jailers, fascinating as the speculation is to both historians and doctors. For Mary at the time, the important fact was that the nineteen years of her captivity were darkened still further by the black clouds of genuine physical suffering, in which her captors often did not believe, when her horizon was already tragically obscured by lack of liberty.

Sick woman as Mary Stuart might be, she did not abandon hopes of release. Her own correspondence continued to buzz with schemes for assistance from abroad. The fact that she was generally regarded as marriageable meant that despite her cap-tivity she never lost her place as a piece on the complicated chessboard of European politics in the 1570s. Her right on

Catholic grounds of legitimacy actually to occupy – rather than succeed to – the English throne was another factor which gave her prominence as a chess piece; even if she herself was unable to organize any move personally, there was always the possibility that some foreign monarch would step in and help her to move once more on these grounds alone. The excommunication of Elizabeth by Pius v had brought this claim of Mary's into fresh prominence; the new Pope Gregory XIII, who succeeded Pius in 1575, believed strongly in Mary's claims to the English throne, and consequently also interested himself in the question of her future bridegroom. The most likely foreign monarch to help Mary – because he was the natural enemy of England – was of course Philip II. Mary herself was so anxious to court Philip's approval that in 1577 she made a will in which she actually made over her rights to the English crown and elsewhere to Philip, supposing that her immediate son and heir James never returned to the true Catholic Church.[25] However, such a will, made by a captive, had little reality, and was intended rather to please Philip – who was apprised of its sentiments – than to make any serious testamentary innovations.

Encouraged by the Pope, plans were now mooted by which Mary should be married off to Philip's dashing illegitimate brother, the famous Don John of Austria. The problem was of course not so much how to bell the cat as how to rescue the cat from her captivity, before the match could actually take place. The prelude to this marriage was intended to be an invasion of England from the Spanish Netherlands, organized by Philip II, with papal approval and led by Don John, who would be rewarded, as in a fairy story, by the hand of the captive princess; together this romantic pair would then reign happily ever after as Catholic king and queen of England. The idea of a marriage between Mary and Don John, of whom even Walsingham admiringly observed 'Surely I never saw a gentleman for personage, speech, wit and entertainment comparable to him. If pride do not overthrow him, he is like to become a great personage', is a tantalizing one. Unfortunately the scheme, like so many involving the rescue of the queen of Scots, was subject to all the complicated pressure of politics in Europe at this period. The marriage never actually left the realm of dreams to which it belonged, as Spain, England and France and their respective sovereigns jockeyed among themselves to maintain their position or increase it, and Elizabeth allowed her strange courtship by the duke of Anjou to hold out prospects of an Anglo-French alliance. In this situation the Spanish Netherlands, in a state of seething revolt against Spanish overlordship, acted as a perpetual apple of discord among these goddesses. From the point of view of English trade, Elizabeth was anxious to see the stabilization of the Netherlands; yet she was equally concerned that they should not be so stable that Spain should be able to use the provinces as a convenient jumping-off place for the invasion of England; at the same time unrest in the Netherlands at any moment might provide an excuse for France to intervene there, a prospect which horrified Elizabeth. In the meantime Philip continued to maintain his usual caution in considering any invasion schemes, which he was sensible enough to realize might result in the rapid execution of Mary long before her would-be rescuers ever reached her.

The curious fact was that although the Pope continued to take a great interest in the subject of Mary's fourth husband, she was still legally married to her third husband, Bothwell. Despite the report of the English ambassador in Paris, Norris, to that effect,[26] the nullification of Mary's marriage to Bothwell was not secured in the late summer of 1570. The validity of any marriage Mary might have contracted in the past had to be referred directly to Rome, the marriages of royal persons being reserved to the Pope himself as *causae majores*. In Mary's instructions to Ridolfi in February 1571, whether genuine or false, she bewailed the Pope's delay in giving the decree of nullity and asked him to speed matters on: about July 1571, Pius v seems to have authorized a commission to examine the case.[27] But it was not until 1575, when Leslie was freed from his English prison, that some serious action seems to have been taken on the subject. Notwithstanding his temporary betrayal of his mistress, under interrogation in the Tower, Leslie was re-adopted into Mary's service and his liberation was even celebrated by a short poem from her own pen, beginning:[28]

> Puisque Dieu a, par son bonte imence,
> Permis qu'ayez obtins tant de bon heur...*

Leslie subsequently went to Rome on Mary's behalf and in August 1576 a number of depositions were taken on behalf of the Bothwell marriage in Paris, at his instance, before a French judge ordinary.[29] The witnesses included John Cuthbert, Leslie's servant, James Curl, an elderly Scottish Catholic exile, Sebastian Danelcourt, a Frenchman married to a Scotswoman who had abandoned Scotland for France on religious grounds, and Cuthbert Ramsay, brother of Lord Dalhousie, an expatriate Scot, as well as two Scottish priests living in Paris. Leslie's petition for nullity was based on the fact that the marriage of Bothwell and Jean Gordon had been a true marriage; that Bothwell had taken Mary by force; and that in any case Bothwell and Jean had not been properly divorced; he also added the fact – perfectly true – that Mary and Jean were kin. The depositions of the witnesses added little to what was already known about Bothwell's two marriages, but merely confirmed quite straightforwardly that Bothwell had lived with both Jean and Mary in turn as his lawful wedded wives.

Despite the establishment of this evidence, and despite the fact that Mary was obviously regarded as free to marry again by the Pope as by every other ecclesiastic, no decree of nullity was actually proclaimed.† The reason for this was the extreme danger which it felt threatened the queen of Scots if too much publicity was given to plans to free her: a declaration that she was no longer married to Bothwell carried the inevitable corollary that she intended to marry someone else. This would point a finger

---

* Since God, in His wondrous goodness,
Hath given you so much joy...
† There is no record that such a decree was ever made and extensive recent researches in the Vatican Archives on the author's behalf by Dr C. Burns have failed to reveal it.

of suspicion at her. Not only might plots outside miscarry, but also her own head might be struck from its shoulders. A letter from the cardinal of Como in 1576 indicates the papal reasoning: 'As the Queen of Scotland is a prisoner, his Holiness sees not how it will be possible to treat with her as to providing her with a husband without running manifest risk of revealing what should be left secret.'[30] In April 1578 the death of Bothwell in his Danish prison freed Mary in any case from the bonds of matrimony, just six months before the death of Don John himself, probably of typhoid, in the Netherlands, put an end forever to Mary's hopes in this direction.

The conditions of Bothwell's last years were shockingly frightful: nothing he had done in life could justify the incarceration of this once active and vigorous man in a foreign prison for eleven years without trial. At first the Danish king had held him as a possible pawn against Elizabeth; now an Anglo-Danish alliance had put an end to his usefulness in that respect. In vain his Scottish enemies had repeatedly attempted to secure his extradition. Bothwell lingered on in prisons of increasing rigour, until the swift vengeance of his fellow-nobles might have seemed an infinitely preferable fate. It seems virtually certain that he was driven mad in his last years in the cruel fortress of Dragsholm, by the intolerable conditions in which he was held; James Maitland, who wintered in Copenhagen only twelve years after his death, heard this. There is a tradition – without definite proof – that he ended by being chained to a pillar half his height like an animal, so that he could never stand upright. The memoirs of Lord Herries wrote his epitaph thus: 'The King of Denmark caused cast him into a loathsome prison where none had access to him, but only those that carried him such scurvy meat and drink as was allowed, which was given in at a little window. Here he was kept ten years till being overgrown with hair and filth he died.'*[31]

If Mary would scarcely have recognized in this demented and

---

* The mummified corpse of Bothwell is still displayed in the crypt of Faarevejle church, near Dragsholm.

pitiful figure the man to whom she had once looked above all for strength and support, perhaps Bothwell himself might not have easily discerned in the sad, staid captive of Sheffield Castle the features of the young and beautiful queen whom he had first served and then married in the year of her personal rule in Scotland. The 'sweet face' which the good people of Edinburgh had blessed as their queen passed nearly twenty years ago on her first arrival in Scotland had altered much as a result of ill-health and the privations and cares of close confinement. The largest and best known category of the portraits of Mary Stuart date from these later years of her life – being various versions of the picture sometimes termed the Sheffield portrait which shows her standing either full-length or three-quarters, wearing black velvet dress and the white peaked head-dress she immortalized.* The date is often painted in the corner of the picture. A number of versions of this picture were made and circulated about the Continent during Mary's lifetime, as she became increasingly a focus of Catholic respect and devotion. After her death, this Catholic devotion only increased, while after the accession of her son James to the throne of England, versions of this picture also found their way into the possession of grand English families, as part of the general rehabilitation of Mary's memory, as mother of the sovereign.

The origin of all these portraits seems to have been in miniatures, painted without the knowledge of the English government. Even a miniaturist was difficult enough to introduce into Mary's prison: in 1575 she had to ask her ambassador in Paris to have some little pictures of her made up abroad, in order to distribute them to faithful Catholics in England who were asking for them.[32] But by 1577 there was evidently some sort of miniaturist at work, at Sheffield, for Nau mentioned in a letter to Archbishop Beaton in Paris that 'he had thought to have accompanied this letter with a portrait of Her Majesty, but

---

* This 'Marie Stuart hood' consisted of a small white lawn headdress, dipping over the forehead and edged with lace; behind it flowed a lawn veil or head-rail, threaded with wire at the top to frame the head and shoulders in an arch.

the painter has not been able to finish it in time'.[33] Two surviving miniatures in the Mauritshuis and in Blairs College, Aberdeen, are probably to be identified with the work of this unknown painter. The actual miniature from which the whole group of Sheffield portraits derives can, however, be identified: it is by Nicholas Hilliard.[34] It seems likely that Hilliard was one famous painter who did personally penetrate the queen's captivity: not only does the Hilliard miniature show signs of close observation from the life, but Bess of Hardwicke herself is known to have patronized Hilliard, and in 1591 there was some question of his painting a secret miniature of Arbella Stuart.[35] It would have been quite possible for Bess to have allowed Hilliard the privilege of painting her royal prisoner, in the same gambling spirit as she later considered the painting of Arbella, in order to forward Stuart claims. Although most of the later versions of this famous picture date from after 1603, despite earlier dates painted in the corner, for the Hilliard miniature itself a date of 1578 is perfectly acceptable on costume grounds.*

The face in the Hilliard miniature and all versions of this portrait shows how much the queen's youthful beauty had been dimmed by the passage of time, even allowing for the wood-enness of the treatment. Mary is now very far from being the laughing Goujon-like *belle* of the French court: this is a woman with a drawn face, a beaky prominent nose almost Roman in its shape but cut finely at the end, with a small rather pinched mouth; the smallness of the whole face is in contrast to the fullness of the body, which is now matronly in its proportions. It is well attested that by the date of her death nine years later Mary had fully lost that willowy slimness of figure which, combined with her elegant height, had been one of her chief

* This Sheffield portrait used sometimes to be known as the Oudry portrait, after the words P. OUDRY PINXIT painted on the version of it at Hardwicke Hall. It was suggested that the unknown Oudry had been the original artist who painted Mary in captivity. But the Hardwicke Hall version is not listed in the 1601 inventory of the house; an entry in the accounts in 1613 probably relates to payments made for bringing the picture to the house. Since earlier versions of the picture do not have the words painted on them, the legend of Oudry the unknown artist is exploded.[36]

attractions when she was young. It is evident from the Sheffield portrait, as also from the medallion portrait of her *en profil* which was the frontispiece of Leslie's history *De Origine Moribus et Rebus Gestis Scotorum* also published in 1578, that by then this process was at least well advanced. The profile, believed to have been done from a miniature in Italy, shows that the charming and clearly defined oval of Mary's face in youth had by now blurred into fullness round the chin. Health may have been responsible for Mary putting on weight, but the queen was by now presumably approaching the age of the menopause, and this too may have played its part in the process. One beauty remains in these portraits which time could not touch: although the once gay and slanting eyes are now sad and watchful and the mouth with its lips which once curved so prettily in a delicate arch above all other features shows the effect of pain and illness in the way the corners have newly tucked in, yet the hands of Mary Stuart are as beautiful as ever. Long and exquisite, the white fingers splay out against the black velvet gown, or drape themselves in some versions of the portrait on the red table, as romantically as they ever did in the days when Ronsard hymned their beauty.

The outward changes in the appearance of Mary Queen of Scots were paralleled by the inward changes in her character. In 1580 Mary wrote on her own initiative a long *Essay on Adversity* in which she explained that she of all people was most suited to write on this melancholy subject – in any case the mental exercise would save from indolence one who had once been accustomed to rule, and could no longer follow her destined calling. She concluded that the only remedy for the afflicted lay in turning to God.[37] Indeed those long white hands were now often clasped in prayer. It was no mere coincidence that in the portraits a great gold rosary is often shown hanging down from her belt. The woman who had once believed implicitly but unreflectively in the truths of the Catholic religion, and had allowed action not thought to rule her life, now found herself involuntarily forced back on the resources of meditation. It would be true to say that the quality of Mary's religious beliefs had never truly been tested up to the present. In France there had been nothing to try, much to encourage, them. In Scotland she had insisted on the practice of her own religion, but this minor concession had not been difficult to establish in view of the fact that she was the reigning queen, and was herself prepared to show total tolerance to the official Protestant religion of the country. In her early months in England she had seen no particular harm in allowing others to explain to her at their own invitation the truths of the Protestant religion as they saw them. But now to exercise her religion needed cunning and tenacity; she was living in a country where Catholics were not only not tolerated, but often persecuted, and persecuted with increasing severity after Pius v's bull of excommunication towards Elizabeth.

Sir John Mortoun, the secret priest, died and was succeeded by another secret chaplain, de Préau. For a short period in 1571, Ninian Winzet, the Scottish Catholic apologist, entered her service, nominally as her 'Scottish secretary' but in fact acting as her confessor, through the good offices of Beaton; he was subsequently sent away to London to join Leslie in his house arrest.[38] In October 1575 Mary wrote to the Pope asking that her chaplain should have episcopal function, and the power to grant her absolution after hearing her confession. She named twenty-five Catholics whom she asked should be granted absolution for attending Protestant ceremonies in order to divert suspicion. Mary asked for a plenary indulgence as she prayed before the Holy Sacrament or bore in silence the insults of a heretic: with prescience for the future, she asked that in the moment of death, if she repeated the words *Jesu, Maria*, even if she only spoke them with 'her heart rather than her mouth', her sins might be forgiven her.[39] A Jesuit priest, Samerie, managed to visit the queen secretly on three occasions in the early 1580s, to act as her chaplain, disguised variously as a member of her household, including her valet and her physician.[40] Such manoeuvres and the preservation in secret of the rites of the Mass by one means and another demanded courage and the real will to take part in them. But to Mary, as to many others in whom the hectic and heedless blood of youth fades, giving place to a nobler and gentler temperament, her religion itself had come to mean much more to her.

It was not only that the Catholic powers abroad represented her best hope of escape from captivity; it was also that she herself had undergone a profound change of attitude to her faith, and indeed to life itself. It is the mark of greatness in a person to be able to develop freely from one phase into another as age demands it. Mary Stuart was capable of this development. Her whole character deepened. Having been above all things a woman of action, she now became under the influence of the imprisonment which she so much detested a far more philosophical and contemplative personality. Two poems printed in Leslie's *Piae Afflicti Animi Consolationes* of 1574 speak of sad memories, of the world's inconstancy and of the need for sacrifice. Lines written in a Book of Hours in 1579 allude bitterly to false friends, and the need for solitary courage, in face of the fickle changes of fortune.

> Bien plus utile est l'heure et non pas la fortune
> Puisqu'elle change autant qu'elle este opportune*

But in another poem, probably written in the early 1580s, she showed more Christian resignation:

> Donne seigneur, donne moi patience
> Et renforce ma trop debile foi
> Que ton esprit me conduise en ta loi
> Et me guarde de choir imprudence†

And at the end of her *Essay on Adversity*, after discussing a series

---

* Time than fortune should be held more precious
For fortune is as false as she is specious!⁴¹
† Give me, dear Lord, the true humility
And strengthen my too feeble halting faith;
Let but Thy Spirit shed his light on me –
Checking my fever with His purer breath.⁴²

of Biblical, Roman and medieval examples of rulers who had fallen into adversity, Mary quoted the parable of the talents to explain how much would be forgiven to those who had made the best of their lives: 'God, like the good father of a family, distributes His talents among His children, and whoever receives them and puts them out of profit is discharged and excused from eternal suffering.' She certainly put her own philosophy into practice to the extent that the talents she showed in her middle-age were very different from those she displayed in youth. The carefree buoyancy which Mary displayed then, so alluring in a young woman, would have been intolerable and even frivolous in the captive queen. Mary's utterances in her forties show on the one hand an infinitely nobler and deeper spirit, and on the other a serenity and internal repose quite out of keeping with her previous behaviour.

Mary Stuart achieved this serenity and this intelligence at the cost of much pain, heart-searching and suffering. She, who had never been known to exist without an adviser, and had never wished to do so, whether it was her grandmother, her Guise uncles, the lamentable Darnley, her half-brother Moray, Riccio or Bothwell, was compelled in the last years of her life to exist without any sort of reliable advice or support from outside. She was now the shoulder on whom her servants leant, and to whom her envoys, many of them of questionable loyalty, looked for direction. She might even secretly write to the outside world for advice, and receive it, but when it came to taking action, actually within the confines of the prison itself, there was Mary and only Mary to make decisions and inspire their implementation. The pretty puppet-queen of France, the spirited but in some ways heedless young ruler of Scotland, could never have carried through the remarkable performance which Mary Stuart was to display in her last years. The uses of adversity for Mary Stuart, bitter-sweet as they might have been rather than sweet, were to teach her that self-control and strength of character which were to enable her to outwit Elizabeth at the last by the heroic quality of her ending.

CHAPTER TWENTY-THREE

Mother and Son

~

'... nor let thy soul contrive
Against thy mother aught; leave her to heaven
And to those thorns that in her bosom lodge
To prick and sting her...'

*The advice of Hamlet's ghost-father on the subject of
his mother Gertrude (the relationship of Hamlet and Gertrude
is thought to have been founded by Shakespeare on the story of
Mary Queen of Scots and James VI)*

While Mary languished in captivity, the child whom she
had last seen as a ten-month-old baby at Stirling Castle
in 1567 had grown to a precocious adulthood. Mary
still pined for James, or the idea of the infant she had lost. In
return she genuinely imagined that James also longed for her,
prompted by the dictates of natural affection which she believed
must always exist between a child and its mother. No doubt she
allowed herself to be buoyed up with the falsely sanguine stories
of his love for her related to her by kindly courtiers. Such
apocryphal tales were easily spun, and greedily accepted by the
maternal heart of the prisoner, who had no means to check
them, and every reason to hope they were true. One such tale,
from a Catholic source, related how James as a boy had once
been observed to be in an especially happy mood at supper,
and had smiled all over his face; the reason for his genial temper
proved to be that he had secretly obtained a copy of Bothwell's
dubious *Testament of Confession*, read it and from this had realized
that his mother was in fact quite innocent of the murder of his
father. Similar stories must have given Mary a very false impression of the way James's mind was being bent. As late as 1584
Lady Margaret Fleming wrote to Mary from Scotland and told

her that although Scottish court manners had sadly changed for the worse, this was not James's fault, and he himself would certainly always behave as 'a humble, obedient and most loving son' towards her.*[1]

The reality was to be very different; nor did James ever show himself in the light of a loving, let alone obedient, son to Mary. It was Mary's tragedy that she continued to believe that he would do so, and that she had from the first a totally false impression of the mother-and-son relationship. In the first vital years of infancy, James had been looked after by the countess of Mar, a 'Jezebel' of a woman as Knox called her, who hated Queen Mary. From four years onward his education was mainly in the hands of Mary's inveterate enemy and chief traducer George Buchanan. The man, once Mary's respectful admirer, who had allowed himself to concoct the disgusting stories of the *Detection* was scarcely likely to spare Mary's reputation when discussing his mother with the child. Later James imbibed a great deal of Calvinist theology from the one tutor, Peter Young, for whom he seems at least to have felt some affection. James's childhood was an unhappy compilation of long hours of learning – he later commented ruefully that he had been made to learn Latin before he could even speak Scots – with occasional dramatic and bloodthirsty interventions, as terrifying as any pre-natal influence from Riccio's slaughter, as when at the age of five he witnessed the bleeding corpse of his grand-father Lennox being carried past him into Stirling Castle. Not only was he totally cut off from a mother's love in childhood, but he was also trained to regard his mother as the murderess of his father, an adulteress who had deserted him for her lover, and last of all, the protagonist of a wicked and heretical religion.

It was true that James subsequently turned on Buchanan for his libels on his mother; he called the regent Moray that 'bastard

* One version of the Sheffield portrait which was definitely known to the engravers before 1603 is the large double portrait of Mary and James, now at Blair Castle, dated 1583. But although mother and son are here shown tenderly side by side, such a meeting never actually took place outside the realm of the artist's imagination.[2]

who unnaturally rebelled and procured the ruin of his own sovereign and sister'; in 1584 he obtained the condemnation of Buchanan's writing in Parliament. Much later he counselled his own son against reading 'the infamous invectives' of Buchanan and Knox.[3] But the point remained that enough had been done in early childhood to rob James of any natural feeling at all, let alone for his mother. Intellectually he could replace Buchanan's false picture of Mary with one he chose to believe was the true one. But he could never replace in his heart the inborn love of son for mother, since this flickering newly-lighted flame had been extinguished shortly after his birth by Mary's enemies.

James, like Mary herself, had been brought up to believe himself to be a ruling monarch, despite the fact that his mother was still alive. In appearance he had grown up to be a wizened creature with sad eyes, in stature very unlike his tall and god-like parents. Fontenay, who visited him at Mary's instigation in 1584, was impressed by James's intelligence: he found him to have a retentive memory, to be full of penetrating questions and able to conduct a good argument; yet he had three faults which Fontenay listed – overconfidence or an inability to estimate his own poverty and insignificance, an indiscreet love of favourites, and a tendency to pursue pleasure rather than politics which too easily allowed others to seize the reins of the realm.[4] In 1580 Father Robert Abercromby, a Jesuit on a mission to Scotland, gave his own opinion on James: he found the king to be deep in Calvinism, simply because he had known no other religion discussed since adolescence.[5] None of this added up to much possibility of genuine sympathy with Mary; this was not the tender charming boy of Mary's imagination who would make every effort to release his mother from the nightmare of her captivity. Like many people who have had an unhappy and unaffectionate childhood and withdrawn into their own thoughts for security, James was already a practised deceiver by the time he reached his teens. Elizabeth's comment when she heard of the execution of Morton in 1581 probably contained far more important guidance for Mary on the subject of James's character than any of the more optimistic comments to which Mary herself listened: 'That false Scotch urchin!' exclaimed Elizabeth. 'What can be expected from the double dealing of such an urchin as this!'[6]

Mary's picture of her son and of their relations was very different: she had after all carried this child in her womb through manifold dangers and difficulties, and he was her only child – 'One like the lioness' as the motto proudly proclaimed which she had embroidered on her hangings. She had few other objects on which to lavish her affections. The years in which James had grown up from unconscious babyhood to near adulthood had been spent by Mary cut off in captivity; her memories of her child kept green in her heart. Her will of 1577 in which she formally expressed the wish that her son should marry a Spanish princess and embrace the Catholic faith was only one example of how out of touch she had become with her son's true development. In 1561 when Mary returned to Scotland, one of her problems had been that having been brought up in France she had insufficient understanding of the working of the Scots' mind: now, from 1581 onwards, in the course of Mary's schemes for unity with James, her difficulty was not being able to follow the complexities of her son's mind after thirteen years of captivity.

Quite apart from this obstacle to their accord, Mary's position as queen of Scots threatened that of her son as king. Mary had revoked the abdication she made under duress at Lochleven, during her few days of liberty before Langside in May 1568. In her own mind, therefore, and those of her supporters, especially the Catholic powers abroad, she was still the true queen of the country; James, despite his coronation at the age of thirteen months, and the government in his name which had existed ever since, was a usurper. This was Mary's real hold over her son in 1580, rather than the natural ties of affection. There were advantages to James in having his *de facto* kingship recognized as *de jure*: not only would his position with France and Spain be improved, but also his position in the English succession might also be better secured. When James grew up, his letters to his mother struck an uneasy compromise: he addressed her as the queen of Scots, but signed himself James R. It was under these circumstances that, early in 1581, Mary outlined her own plan for 'Association' – or the joint rule of mother and son – through a Guise emissary, a scheme which naturally involved the restoration of Mary to Scotland.

The project naturally commended itself vividly to Mary, who had suggested it: once more she envisaged the prison gates opening and her own return to her throne. James himself was sufficiently attracted by the idea of the recognition of the Catholic powers at least to write a pleasant letter in return. The key to the whole project in James's mind was of course the attitude of Elizabeth: English approval was still in the reign of James, as it had been in the reign of Mary, very much a factor of Scottish politics; the same considerations of an English alliance, English subsidies, the shared Protestant religion, and the involvement of the Scottish monarchy in the English royal succession, still obtained. In 1581 the emergence of James's first favourite, his cousin Esmé Stuart whom he created duke of Lennox, in alliance with the bold swashbuckling Captain James Stewart,* led to the downfall of the pro-English regent, Morton. Morton was tried and executed for the murder of Darnley (who, like Banquo's ghost, seemed to play a much more effective part in Scottish politics once he was dead than when he was alive). Mary had never forgiven Morton, and exulted over his death from her prison – 'of whose execution I am most glad', she wrote firmly.[7] The new duke of Lennox did not long enjoy the power which this denouement gave to him; in August 1582 a palace revolution in the shape of the kidnapping of the king's person by the Ruthven family, headed by the earl of Gowrie, placed the government of Scotland once more in pro-English hands. Esmé Stuart, duke of Lennox, retired to France after the raid of Ruthven and there died. A year later, however, James eluded his captors, and power was once more in the hands of the apparently anti-English Arran (James Stewart). James therefore

---

* Now created earl of Arran by James despite the continued existence of the wretched, mad, true incumbent of the title, Mary's former suitor.

professed himself to the Guises ready to entertain the notion of the Association, at the sacrifice of Elizabeth's favour. Arran's position was further strengthened when an unsuccessful attempt to unseat him on the part of pro-English lords including Mar and some Hamiltons, in the spring of 1584, ended with their flight to England, as Moray had once fled after the Chaseabout Raid in 1565; there was a further parallel – these lords had expected English aid in the project but had not received it.

James might be prepared to toy with the idea of the Association – since it temporarily fitted with his plans – but Mary herself was enthusiastic on the subject; into her service in this cause she now enlisted Patrick, master of Gray. Gray, a young man of Lucifer-like beauty, had also all the mingled potentialities of talent and treachery of the former archangel within his breast. In France Gray had entered the service of Mary's ambassador, James Beaton, archbishop of Glasgow, and on being received into the inner circle of Mary's supporters in Paris had become extremely friendly with the Guises; the esteem in which he was held in these circles may be judged by the fact that he was presented with silver plate to the value of five or six thousand crowns. Gray had paid one visit to Scotland, either with Esmé Stuart, or after the fall of Morton, during which his ostensibly Catholic faith had wavered, and he had promised to renounce it in favour of the reformed religion. His second visit occurred in November 1583, when he brought back Esmé Stuart's young son, at James's request, to be brought up at the Scottish court. Although entrusted by Mary to represent her counsels at the Scottish court, and push forward the notion of the Association, Gray quickly appreciated that it would be far more profitable personally to ally himself with the son, a king on a throne, than the mother, a prisoner without a kingdom. He became the friend and confidant of Arran, and from here reached the ear of James himself. From the first, Gray was in possession of enough of Mary's secrets, and those of her little clique of supporters in France, to be able to betray both parties to James whenever he wished to convince him anew that, in a case of mother versus son, it would always be the son whom he would serve. Yet

Mary, under the illusion that Gray was her emissary, continued to trust him to work for her, as she continued to believe in the affections of James.

It was now that the attitude of Elizabeth became so vital to the future, if any, of this plan of the Association. On mature reflection it was only too easy for James to see that the return of a released Mary to Scotland would be at least a serious nuisance to his own position; they were of different religion, to say nothing of different generation; how much better to secure the benefit of the Association, in the shape of Elizabeth's favour and foreign approval, without the release of Mary. In an extreme case, it would still benefit James more to have an alliance and subsidy from Elizabeth than the official recognition of France. Yet such negotiations had to be conducted with enormous delicacy, since Elizabeth's attitude could only be ascertained by secret probing, and in the meantime Mary had to be encouraged lest after all the Association might turn out to be advantageous to James. In the summer of 1584 it was Gray who was sent down to London to conduct these negotiations on behalf of the king. In the meantime not only was Mary specifically assured of James's welcoming attitude towards her proposals by a letter from James himself in July, but she was also further informed that Gray's mission was merely to treat with Elizabeth over the subject of the rebel lords who had fled to England.[8]

Mary had reluctantly to accept this story; from her prison there was little else she could do. Her own emissary Fontenay believed the season would never again be so favourable – *'jamais si belle'* – to bring about the Association since both James and the Scots were now inclined towards Mary.[9] Nevertheless, in a series of letters written during October to Gray, and to Castelnau de Mauvissière, the French ambassador in London, she showed herself highly conscious of the dangers of her position should James ever try to negotiate separately; Mary, with the keen perception of the captive, saw that her only hope of eluding her prison was if James made her release one of his conditions of treating with Elizabeth. She emphasized to Gray the importance of not letting Elizabeth think that there were divisions between

James and herself; furthermore Gray must demand Mary's liberty as one of the conditions of an Anglo-Scottish *rapprochement*. Mary, still believing herself to be employing Gray, gave him a series of very explicit instructions as to how he was to negotiate while in London, and although her eventual destination after her release was left vague – either England or Scotland – the importance of the release was underlined.[10] Yet from the first moment Gray arrived in London, it was immediately realized by the English that he would now serve the interests of James and Elizabeth rather than those of James and Mary: indeed, in view of the excellent knowledge Gray had acquired of Mary's organization and her secrets while in her service, Elizabeth had acquired a valuable potential ally and Mary a dangerous potential traitor. In London Gray was given lodging by Sir Edward Hoby who had known him in France: Hoby, commenting to Cecil on Gray's keen personal ambition, the desire for glory which 'burnt in his stomach', hinted that Gray had much secret information about Mary which he was prepared to impart: 'he can speak and tell tales if he list...'[11]

In vain Mary underlined to Gray what those around her were in danger of overlooking but she herself would never forget, that her imprisonment was illegal from the first moment, since she had not even been captured in war. Mary begged Gray to make Elizabeth realize that by liberating Mary she would be meriting the approval of James.[12] But even as Mary wrote, it was being made clear to Elizabeth that in fact this was the very last thing that would merit James's approval. While Mary pleaded pathetically with Gray to pay her a personal visit in her prison, such contacts being most suitable to make mother and son better acquainted, Gray was busy in London betraying the cause of the mother at the instigation of the son. On 28th November Nau drew up twenty-eight heads of proposals on the subject of the Association at Mary's request:[13] Mary announced herself ready to stay in England if necessary, prepared to allow an amnesty to be declared over all the wrongs she had suffered at the hands of the English, renounce the Pope's bull of excommunication, and abandon forever her own pretensions to the English crown over those of Elizabeth. Although confident of French agreement to these proposals, she also offered to join an offensive league against France, so long as an English dowry was assured to her, equivalent to that she would have to abandon in France, in the event of the French not subscribing to the idea of the Association. In Scotland she was also prepared to allow an amnesty, to agree that there should be no upset in the present state of the religion of the country; the only condition she made was that James should marry with Elizabeth's know-ledge and 'good counsel', and the only demand the immediate softening of her present harsh conditions of captivity. Such sweeping concessions on the part of Mary made it clear that sixteen years after her first English imprisonment she had one aim in view, and one aim only, to which she was prepared to sacrifice all other considerations – her freedom, by any means at all.

On 8th December, her forty-second birthday, Mary wrote to Elizabeth still wistfully hoping for two hours' personal talk with her, the talk which she still felt after all these years would settle everything between them; and with her birthday uppermost in her mind, she took the opportunity to hope that Elizabeth would live to enjoy in the future as many happy years as Mary had endured unhappy ones in the past. On 14th December Mary reminded Gray by letter that James was not the sole king of Scotland, and that Gray must at all costs prevent mother and son being driven apart by 'evil counsellors' since it was so important to Mary's cause that James should show himself a 'natural and obedient son'.[14] As late as January Mary was still hoping that liberty for her on these new terms was just round the corner, and desired the French king and queen to write separately to James acknowledging the Association in order to bring her son into accord with her.[15] Yet all the while Gray had successfully concluded his mission in London on James's behalf: he had indicated to Elizabeth that the release of Mary was not necessary to win James's friendship, and he had learnt from Elizabeth also that her friendship could be won for James by a direct channel, without taking into account the claims, rights and certainly not the desires of the imprisoned Queen of Scots. The Association was now doomed; it became stamped merely as the unrealistic scheme of a tiresome middle-aged woman in prison, to whom no further attention need be paid in this context.

It was in March 1585 that the full horrifying truth could no longer be kept from Mary: James in Scotland assembled his whole Council as Gray gleefully wrote to Elizabeth; at which point it was formally concluded that the 'Association desired by his mother should neither be granted nor spoken of hereafter'.[16] At first Mary, in her pathetic desire to protect the image of her son in her own mind, even tried to persuade herself that the betrayal could be blamed on Gray. On being informed that James could not negotiate with her while she was a prisoner, she inquired miserably with childlike logic why Elizabeth could not then free her, so that she would at least be able to negotiate with her own son. A passionate postscript to this letter, in her own hand, revealed the depth of her agitation: 'I am so grievously offended at my heart,' she scrawled, 'at the impiety and ingratitude that my child has been constrained to commit against me, by this letter which Gray made him write.' Wildly she threatened to disinherit James and give the crown to the greatest enemy he had, rather than allow this sort of treatment. In her letter to Elizabeth the same day, Gray is '*ce petit broullon*' (troublemaker) and James this badly brought up child ('*mal gouverné enfant*'). In her next letter to Elizabeth she bewailed the mischief which had been made recently between herself and James by sinister counsels[17] – unaware of the grisly truth still more unbearable to a mother's heart. That it was not a few months' trouble-making by Gray but nearly twenty years of total separation which had led to the breach between mother and son. James's welcome of the Association in July 1584 had been apparently unrestrained: his repudiation of it the following March was total. He had betrayed Mary, and so had Gray. But in the delicate game of Anglo-Scottish relations, James had discovered that whereas he held some of the cards and Elizabeth held some of the others, Mary held none at all. There was nothing Mary, still firmly within the four walls of her prison, could do except rage and weep alternately at the perfidy of her son, and the betrayal of her child.

In 1584, the year of Mary's repudiation by James, her own domestic circumstances underwent an unpleasant change. Mary had been able in the last years in prison to enjoy a pleasant quasi-maternal relationship with her own niece, little Arbella Stuart, the pretty pudgy dimpled child of Darnley's younger brother, Charles Stuart, and Bess of Hardwicke's own daughter, Elizabeth Cavendish. The marriage of Arbella's parents had been brought about under romantic circumstances within the orbit of Mary herself. In 1574 Charles's mother, countess of Lennox, now reconciled to Mary over the subject of James, had asked permission from Elizabeth to visit her ex-daughter-in-law at Chatsworth on her way to Scotland to see her grandson. To Elizabeth the possible combination of these two formidable matrons, Margaret Lennox and Bess of Hardwicke, seemed lethal; permission was refused. However, while the countess of Lennox was lodging at a neighbouring house on her way north, her son Charles fell ill; Bess of Hardwicke had already ridden over to visit the countess, bringing her daughter by the hand. As ten years before the timely illness of Darnley had led to his romance with Mary, so now once more the sick-room played its part in the fortunes of the Lennox Stuarts. Before the boy recovered, the young couple had fallen in love, and whether the circumstances of the romance were quite as fortuitous as they seemed, certainly both the grand ladies involved were pleased by it. Margaret Lennox was poor, but her son stood in line to two kingdoms as his brother Darnley had once done; furthermore she was the grandmother of a little king of Scotland. Bess of Hardwicke, on the other hand, was of low birth but had made herself rich and powerful. Once more, as with Mary's marriage to Darnley, Elizabeth flew into a violent rage at hearing of this pretty romance which was supposed to have flared up so innocently in the Midlands. Both countesses were summoned back to London, and both clapped into prison.

The terms of imprisonment were in both cases relatively short. Out of this ill-starred marriage, some time during the autumn of 1575 the little Arbella Stuart was born: her sex must have been a sad disappointment to both grandmothers, but as with Mary Stuart herself, Arbella was not destined to be replaced by the birth of a brother. Her sickly young father died of consumption in the spring of the next year; although her mother lived on till 1582, when she too died in her early twenties, from then on the child was brought up much of the time with her maternal grandmother Bess. In vain both grandmothers tried to secure the earldom of Lennox for the little girl after her father's death: the regent of Scotland admitted that the earldom had originally been granted to Charles Stuart, instead of to James, who as direct male heir and son of the elder son Darnley should rightfully have inherited it from his grandfather, Matthew, earl of Lennox; but he stated that the patent could be revoked as James had been a minor at the time, especially as Charles's child was a female. In spite of being known as the *comitessa* and having the formal title grandly painted on her portrait as a two-year-old child, little Arbella never did secure her earldom; and when Esmé Stuart rose to favour in Scotland, it was this earldom which James used to bestow honour upon him.

Only Mary Queen of Scots continued to acknowledge the baby as the claimant: her will of February 1577 referred to 'Arbelle, *ma nièce*' as earl of Lennox and commanded James to respect Arbella's right if she, Mary, died.[18] Mary also tried to get Queen Elizabeth to hand over Margaret, countess of Lennox's jewels to Arbella after the countess's death. She played with the idea of marrying Arbella to her first cousin James. In addition to these practical efforts on behalf of 'my precious jewel, Arbell', as her grandmother Bess called her, Mary also enjoyed the innocent and touching companionship of the little girl, who with her royal blood and claims to two thrones, so incongruous with the simple routines of infancy, may have reminded Mary of the child she had once been. Mary had another favourite – Elisabeth Pierrepoint, also one of Bess's grand-daughters, who was her own god-daughter, whom she loved to spoil and pet;

she called her her '*mignonne*', and 'little bedfellow' (since they sometimes shared a bed, according to the domestic custom of the time). Mary even took pains to make her little favourite a special black dress.[19] Marguerite de Valois in her memoirs condescendingly observed that it was natural for old people to love little children whereas those who were in their prime were apt to look down upon them and dislike 'their unfortunate simplicity'. In Mary's case, she had never looked down upon the unfortunate simplicity of children, showing fondness for the young such as her godson Francis Stewart even when she was barely twenty, not yet a mother herself and in the midst of the full excitement of reigning in Scotland; yet certainly once she was a prisoner, her maternal feelings increased, and the little Shrewsbury grandchildren who pattered about the many Shrewsbury palaces – or prisons – provided much solace for her affectionate nature, just as she in turn must have constituted a glamorous feature of their childhood.

Close contact between Arbella* and Mary was, however, put to an end by the reverberating row which now broke out between Mary and Bess of Hardwicke, an altercation in which Bess was entirely the aggressor since Mary was only involved as the innocent victim of the scandals surrounding the break-up of the Shrewsbury *ménage*. The Shrewsbury marriage troubles seem to have started some time after the death of Shrewsbury's son, Gilbert Talbot, in 1582; property was at the root of their quarrels. Now in her efforts to get the best of the dispute, Bess cast about her in her well-filled mental armoury and decided to accuse her husband of scandalous relations with his prisoner Mary Queen of Scots. It was a sharp-edged weapon indeed; it was typical of Bess's clever but unscrupulous tactics that she

---

* Despite her royal lineage, and the glorious plans laid for her future, Arbella Stuart never lived to enjoy the splendid destiny which might have been expected for one who combined the genes of the Stuarts with those of Bess of Hardwicke. At the age of thirty, no suitable bridegroom having been found for her, she eloped with William Seymour, grandson of Lady Catherine Grey. For this presumption, she was imprisoned in the Tower by her cousin, King James, where she died in 1615.

picked the accusation most likely to embarrass and wound her husband where it hurt – in his area of public service. Such charges horrified Shrewsbury, for they would surely confirm all the old rumours that he was as a jailer too favourably disposed towards the queen of Scots. Blown up by rumours, the scandal ballooned outwards. A certain John Palmer went on record as saying at St James's Palace that the queen of Scots had borne two bastard children to Lord Shrewsbury, and had to make a public submission in consequence.[20] One Babsthorpe wrote a book full of lewd speeches on the subject, and Shrewsbury was eventually allowed to sue him, although Elizabeth attempted to stop the case under the statute of *scandalum magnatum*.

Mary herself was indignant and furious. Her honour was outraged and she persistently demanded that she should be allowed to come to court to clear herself: it was like the conference of Westminster all over again to her sensitive spirit – there was Bess at liberty in London spreading malicious stories, and yet Mary was not even allowed the opportunity to appear and contradict them. In a long letter to Elizabeth in October 1584 she demanded that Bess and her son Charles Cavendish should be publicly examined and their servants examined also and then punished for spreading such slanders; to Walsingham, Mary threatened to make known the evil-doing of *'la bonne Comptesse'*, as she sarcastically termed Bess, to all the princes of Christianity.[21] In the end Bess's calumnies proved too much for Mary's self-control; in November she wrote a long and burning letter to Elizabeth not only rebutting Bess's charges against her, but, more to the point, detailing all the many salacious stories which Bess had spread about Elizabeth in the past. Mary described how Bess had been wont to regale the household at Chatsworth and elsewhere in days gone by with cruel stories of Elizabeth's vanity, and shocking stories of her immorality. Elizabeth believed herself to be so beautiful that she resembled a goddess of the skies – how Bess and the countess of Lennox had laughed at her behind her back! Mary had often heard Elizabeth treated as *'une comédie'* even in the presence of her own waiting-women. This ridiculous monster of vanity had also been described as lying in bed with Leicester many times and, among other scandals, taking the wretched Christopher Hatton by force. Bess was supposed to have joined disloyalty to ridicule and scandal-making: Mary also retailed how delightful Bess had been when Elizabeth fell ill because this fulfilled an astrological prediction that Elizabeth would soon be dead and Mary reigning in her place, after which James and Arbella would succeed as king and queen.[22] It is easy to believe that most of this unsavoury scandal had indeed tripped off Bess's tongue in the course of those female conversations in Bess's chamber; private conversation of a gossiping nature never looks particularly pretty set down much later and Bess's tales were no exception. As for Mary's part in passing on all this stale and unprofitable abuse, it seems that even despite provocation she had second thoughts after she had written the letter. There is no evidence that Elizabeth, to whom it was addressed, ever read this bombshell: it was found later among the Cecil papers, and although it is possible that Cecil himself intercepted it before it reached the queen, the most likely explanation seems to be that Mary herself, like so many writers, reconsidered the letter after she had exhausted her venom with her pen, and kept it among her own papers without ever sending it. From here it would have been seized with the rest of her correspondence at Chartley in 1586.

There was certainly no grain of truth in all these rumours as Lady Shrewsbury and her daughter subsequently admitted to the English Council. Mary had by now a sufficient reputation as a *femme fatale* to be the natural target for such fabricated arrows. John Palmer's stories of bastard children by Shrewsbury may be seen as being the last of a long progression of such philo-progenitive rumours throughout Mary Stuart's life, which if all had been true would have made her instead of the lioness with her one whelp the mother of a sizeable family.* Shrewsbury was not immune to Mary's charm any more than had been

* Even Elizabeth, the virgin queen, was not left free of this sort of imaginative calumny. In November 1575 the Venetian ambassador in Spain reported that Elizabeth had a natural daughter of thirteen in existence, who was about to marry Cecil's son, and thus cement their relations.[23]

Knollys, White or even Cecil himself; he had known her over a long period of time in circumstances of great intimacy. One can understand that such propinquity, coupled with the kindness Shrewsbury generally showed to Mary, may have led to moments of gentleness between them, even tenderness, especially as the femininity of Mary must have contrasted forcibly with the masculinity of Bess, who was in any case the elder of the two by twenty years. But for Shrewsbury to seek to give this tenderness such as it was any sort of external expression beyond relaxation of the conditions of captivity would have been quite out of keeping with his character. The queen of Scots might present a charming picture to him as she sat there plying her needle, but when it came to the prospect of physical relations with her she was terrifying to him as the Giant Hop O'Thumb's daughter in the fairy story, with the shadow of Elizabeth hanging over them in the role of the vengeful Giant. Mendoza was probably nearer summing up Shrewsbury's true feelings when he said that the earl was only too grateful to Elizabeth for delivering him from two demons – his wife and the queen of Scots.[24]

For reasons other than the seedy domestic wrangles of the Shrewsburys, Mary was being conducted remorselessly down the path which led to closer conditions of imprisonment. She herself at one point hesitated to complain too forcibly about the Shrewsbury scandal, lest she should be removed from his charge altogether and placed in the hands of a far more severe jailer. It was a valid fear. But even without the malice of Bess, Mary's days with Shrewsbury were numbered, due to external conditions in England over which she once more had no control. The effects of the papal bull of excommunication against Elizabeth, promulgated in 1570, only began to be properly felt towards the end of the decade when the reconversion of England was attempted once more from abroad; a trickle and then a faster flow of Jesuit missionaries, many of them Englishmen returning after training abroad, made this cause their own.* There were differences of temperament among the missionaries themselves, who ranged from men of incandescent faith and sanctity, such as Edmund Campion, to the more diplomatic-minded missionaries, such as Robert Persons, who had contacts in every European capital. Both men arrived in England in 1580, although Persons subsequently went on to Spain from where, from knowledge gained during his visit, he suggested Catholicism should be restored in England by force rather than pure missionary fervour.

The appearance of these rekindlers of Catholic flames in English hearts had a two-fold effect: in the first place the English Catholics themselves became more sanguine and therefore more zealous; secondly the English government tightened up the laws against the recusants (those who refused to attend the official Protestant services once a week), increased the fines, which became heavy from 1577 onwards, and using the double-edge weapon of the papal excommunication, began to blur the distinction between recusant and rebel. The English Catholics themselves were divided by many gradations of feeling, apart from the Faith which united them. There were many English Catholics who, although they declined to abandon the faith of their fathers at the orders of Parliament, yet equally declined to forfeit their loyalty to their Queen Elizabeth at the instigation of the hope. It was just these Catholics whom it was now possible for the English government to brand as rebels, using the papal bull as proof. As one of their number, the eloquent Jesuit missionary Father William Weston himself, wrote, these were now bitter days, filled with immeasurable suffering for the English Catholic community: 'Catholics now saw their own country, the country of their birth, turned into a ruthless and unloving land.'[26]

In view of the delicate situation of England, perpetually facing

* By 1582 the Jesuits had reached Staffordshire, close to where Mary lay; in the same year the Staffordshire county records show the first really large-scale prosecution of the recusants at the Easter sessions of the peace.[25]

the prospect of a Spanish invasion, it was a natural act of public relations on the part of the government to seek to present the Catholics from 1580 onwards as dangerous aliens within the state. The Act of Persuasions, by which it was made high treason to reconcile or be reconciled to the Catholic faith, was passed in 1581. In 1585 it was further made high treason for a Jesuit to set foot in England. Just as the dangers to England from the Catholics were constantly emphasized, so too the personal danger of Queen Elizabeth was underlined in order to boost her popularity with her subjects, as a symbol of national solidarity. Both moves – early exercises in the subtle art of propaganda – augured of course extremely ill for the future of the queen of Scots, who was both a Catholic and a rival queen to Elizabeth. To the forefront of this calculated campaign was the leading secretary of state, Sir Francis Walsingham. Walsingham was a prominent Puritan; but he drew, as he said himself, a sharp and effective distinction between private and public morality, and had no intention of bringing the strict tenets of the Puritan faith into the latter sphere. He was an experienced diplomatist, with a useful knowledge of Europe, having been employed by Elizabeth on missions to both the Low Countries and France; and in 1583 he was sent on a mission to James in Scotland. Walsingham also combined to a remarkable degree the political abilities of an Italian Renaissance statesman with a very modern conception of the uses of a spy system within the state.*

Walsingham understood to perfection the art not only of forgery but also of permeating his enemies' organizations with his own men – an art which often led to such confusion of plotting at the time that the truth is impossible to disentangle at four hundred years' distance. Walsingham now managed to

* Walsingham had already showed his enterprising attitude to the production of compromising evidence at the time of the conferences of Westminster: he offered to Cecil 'that if for the discovery of the Queen of Scots, consent to the murder of her husband, there lack sufficient proofs, he is able (if it shall please you to use him) to discover certain that should have been employed in the said murder' in London.'[7]

place at least one and probably more spies in the heart of Mary's councils in Paris. In view of this fact, it was not surprising that Mary's reputation became increasingly besmirched in the English mind and in that of Elizabeth, as a result of each of the three plots against her which were uncovered in the 1580s before the final crisis of the Babington plot. The first of these plots, the Throckmorton plot, was apparently Guise-inspired, although right at the centre of it lay one of Walsingham's most successful agents, Charles Paget. Paget came of a noble family, one of whose houses, Beaudesert, was in Staffordshire. His elder brother Thomas, Lord Paget, was a devout Catholic who refused to take the Oath of Conformity, and was eventually obliged to flee to France in 1583, although up till this time he had been kindly treated by his friends at court who had attempted to persuade him into wiser courses: indeed much of his desire to leave England seems to have arisen not only from his professed religion, but from his troubles with his vociferous wife Nazareth, Lady Paget.[28] Charles Paget was, on the other hand, an outright spy, who entered Walsingham's service secretly in 1581 when he reached Paris, at roughly the same moment that he entered the little Marian embassy of Archbishop Beaton.

The Throckmorton plot, uncovered by Walsingham's agents, led in November 1583 to the arrest of Francis Throckmorton, a Catholic cousin of Sir Nicholas, on suspicion of carrying letters to and from Mary; the earl of Northumberland was also placed in the Tower for being implicated. The details of the Throckmorton plot involved once more the invasion of England by Spain, and the release of Mary; Throckmorton, who had acted as messenger throughout, made a very full confession before his execution in which he thoroughly implicated the queen. She was said to have known every detail of the invasion plans. Mary had certainly written encouraging letters to the Spanish ambassador, who was banished for his part in it all; but the true details of this invasion scheme are still obscure, since it seems that Charles Paget in the course of a short visit to England secretly poured cold water on the scheme to Northumberland, having first of all tried in vain to dissuade the duke of Guise from asking for Spanish help.[29] In view of the troubles which Paget was also brewing up in France, it is doubtful whether such a scheme penetrated by a double-agent could ever have come to very much; nevertheless, the discovery of the plot gave Walsingham an excellent opportunity to excite a wave of popular indignation against the Catholics, and their figurehead, Mary.

Despite Throckmorton's revelations, and despite the fact that Mary had clearly the details of the intended plot, Mary herself was in fact at this point no longer in complete sympathy with her Guise relations or indeed with her ambassador of so many years, James Beaton. One of the cruellest aspects of Mary's last years from her own point of view was that while Walsingham was engaged in building up her image as this dangerous conspirator, the spider at the centre of a network of plans with agents at every foreign Catholic court, Mary herself was actually becoming increasingly alienated from her own organization abroad. She was accused increasingly in the popular imagination of crimes in which she was decreasingly involved. From 1583 onwards her relations with her ambassador Beaton were distinctly cool, and by the autumn of 1584 she actually accused him openly of mishandling her finances, regretting that such an old servant should choose this opportunity to treat her so shabbily.[30] She believed that in France Beaton's wishes rather than hers were being considered and that her other servants were being mistreated.

Such complaints were not merely the querulous imaginings of a middle-aged woman who had been too long in captivity. It was true that the handling of Mary's organization in France, and her finances in particular, left much to be desired. Much of the muddle and maladministration was due to the earlier actions of Mary's uncle, the cardinal of Lorraine, who appears to have had little grasp of finance. This dowry, so vital to Mary's existence, since it represented her only income, was further impaired by the actions of the king of France, who obliged her to exchange the profitable estates in Touraine, granted to her under her marriage settlement, for others much less profitable, in favour of his brother, the duke of Anjou. The income itself of 2000 crowns which she took yearly for personal expenses in England does not always seem to have been paid regularly: at Mary's death the king of France still owed her money. French officials battened upon the estates, an easy enough action to perform without speedy retribution, since their owner was both abroad and in prison. In 1580 the foolish or knavish Dolin was replaced as Mary's treasurer by Chérelles's brother, but even so by this time the French estates had a mortgage of 33,000 crowns upon them. Although it was believed that if Mary put her dowry out to farm she would be able to get 30,000 crowns yearly, the encumbrance of the mortgage was a fatal obstacle to this scheme. Mary was compelled to raise loans in London to pay for her necessities in captivity: she borrowed money from de Mauvissière on credit, and another loan was later arranged from Arundel, which was only repaid after Mary's death by the king of Spain, out of respect for her memory. Financial shortages, the humiliation of not being able to pay for small luxuries to be brought to her from London as well as not being able to grant *baillages* from her French estates to repay creditors freely, owing to the interference of the French court, were naturally all exacerbating to Mary, who could do little in prison except fire off anguished letters. But although she came to blame Beaton, he seems to have been the least of the offenders in this respect. Furthermore, the evidence points to the fact that there was a distinct campaign to create trouble between Mary and Beaton, a campaign once more all the more dangerous because it was directed from within rather than without her organization.

Into Beaton's service had come in the late 1570s a certain Thomas Morgan, who had once been Shrewsbury's secretary in the early days of Mary's imprisonment: he was a friend of Walsingham's chief agent Phelippes and his Catholicism was doubtful; most of the English Catholic exiles seem to have regarded him as a spy and the fact that it was he who introduced the arch spy Gilbert Gifford into Mary's service certainly tells against him.[31] Nevertheless, he managed to capitalize on the friendliness he had once shown to Mary – perhaps he convinced her he had been dismissed from Shrewsbury's service for helping her – to enlist her sympathy, and she regarded him as 'poor Morgan'. Although she did not recommend him to Beaton personally, she endorsed his application and, at different times, with her habitual sympathy for the financial plight of her servants, made him grants of money. Morgan became Beaton's chief cipher clerk, a position of enormous trust, since it put him in virtual control of the French correspondence with Mary. But Morgan, although trusted by Mary, was soon regarded as suspect in France. According to the later testimony of Father Robert Persons, neither Morgan nor Paget was fully trusted with the invasion plans of 1583, 'fearing lest they might hold secret correspondence with some of the Council in England, although the said Queen trusted in them contrary to the wish and opinion of the said Duke of [Guise] and Archbishop ambassadors'.*[32]

It was tragic that Mary's service should thus be permeated with spies and trouble-makers at this critical moment in her fortunes. From the tone of her own letters, certainly her relations with Beaton seem to have been temporarily impaired, at the very moment when she had most need to be in complete accord with him. Such discord would have been only too easy for Morgan as cipher clerk to whip up. For example Mary's outspoken complaint that Beaton had not written to her for six months may easily have been due not to Beaton's neglect – which was unlike him – but to the suppression of his letters by his clerk. This trouble-making had two effects: as Samerie, the Jesuit chaplain who visited her secretly three times in prison and was devoted to her cause, warned Mary in October 1584, there were dangers in trusting such men as Morgan and Paget: 'You wish to have too many manners of proceeding,' he wrote, 'which clearly they know', and he advised her to abandon all private ways of dealing and treat of all her affairs through her

* At this point quite a separate dispute, originating at Rome in 1578, between English Jesuits and the English secular priests (called the Welsh faction after their leader Dr Owen Lewis) was also spreading through the English Catholic community abroad and affecting the trust of Jesuits and seculars. See Leo Hicks, *An Elizabethan Problem*, for a detailed examination of the subject, in relation to Morgan and Mary.

ambassadors.[33] It was excellent advice, based on sound knowledge of Mary's predilection for intrigue. Unfortunately this
advice did not stick. In March 1585 Ragazzini, the nuncio, told
the cardinal of Como: 'This Morgan is considered by many here
and particularly the Jesuits, to be a knave; yet the Queen of
Scots relies upon him more than on her own ambassador
[Beaton] as the ambassador himself has told me many times.'[34]

The second result of such disputes within Mary's organization
was that her own feelings towards the Guises and Spain became
permeated with distrust: she began to be convinced that the
Guises were only intending to seize England in order to hand
it over to Spain and had no interest in her release. The prospect
of losing touch with reality over the years is one which every
long-term prisoner has to face. In Mary's case, at the exact
moment when her struggles to free herself through the Association were crumbling about her, and the need to concentrate
on the aid of Spain and the Guises grew more acute, she became
the prey of false notions on the subject and grew to rely more
on private schemes than on Beaton.

By January 1585, when the Association was virtually dead as
a practical scheme, Mary was murmuring against Spain. She was
indeed profoundly shocked by the new plot now uncovered in
which a Dr Parry apparently intended to assassinate Elizabeth.
Her horror was probably genuine, for she expressed it in a letter
not only to Elizabeth herself, but also to her ally, the French
ambassador in London.[35] When Parry proved to be implicated
with her own agent in Paris, the wily Thomas Morgan, Mary
could scarcely believe the news. Mary was quite right to be
horrified by the news of the Parry plot, for it seems that Parry
began his career as an *agent provocateur* for the Elizabethan
government, and was only now sacrificed by his employers for
propaganda reasons. Even without this inner knowledge, Mary
was quite clever enough to see the dangers of such involvements:
the plots of Parry against Elizabeth would always point indirectly
at Mary, but the involvement of Parry with Morgan enabled the
plot to be laid squarely at her door. In France, Morgan was put
in prison for his part in the Parry plot. It was no wonder that

Mary hastened to express her indignation. She was sympathetic towards the Jesuit Father Creighton who was captured aboard ship with a whole pile of incriminating letters and documents: she asked the French ambassador to see what could be done for the wretched man, to save him from destruction.[36] Parry on the other hand clearly brought her own neck into danger.

The point was all the more easy for Mary to appreciate since from June 1584 onwards there had been murmurings in Parliament for a new type of Association – not to be confused with Mary's Association with James – in this case a bond or pledge of allegiance. But this was a pledge with a difference. It was not enough for the signatories of this new bond to swear to bring about the death of all those who might plot against Elizabeth. In addition they also swore – and the inspiration was Walsingham's – to bring about the death of all those in whose favour such plots might be instigated, whether they had personally connived at them or not. In short, if it could be proved that a particular conspiracy had been aimed at the elimination of Elizabeth and the placing of Mary on the throne, Mary herself was as much eligible for execution as any of the plotters, even if she had been in complete ignorance of what was afoot. This bond was formally enacted into a statute by the English Parliament in the spring of 1585 when the murder of the prince of Orange brought home still further to the English the constant dangers of assassination to their own queen; in the meantime signatures poured in from loyal subjects, and were presented to Elizabeth in an endless series of documents, from the autumn onwards. Mary, ever conscious of the delicate path she was treading, and the need for Elizabeth's favour, actually offered to sign the bond herself.[37] But her pathetic offer could not gloss over the fact that the enactment of the bond into English law amounted to the drawing up of her own death warrant: it was hardly likely that many years would pass before some conspiracy or other in Mary's favour, to the detriment of Elizabeth, would be brought to book by Walsingham, and once such a charge should be proved, it was now legal in England to try and execute the Scottish queen. No one was more conscious of the dangers of the bond to Mary than Elizabeth herself, and the possibility of the trial of a crowned queen was one Elizabeth preferred not to contemplate too closely in advance:[38] she therefore chose to regard the bond of Association as a spontaneous act of loyalty on the part of her people in the first place, of whose genesis she had been quite ignorant. In the parliamentary proceedings which followed, she began by showing considerable reluctance that the statute for her safety should be enacted at all and went on to take care that James VI should be excepted from the clause which barred even the descendants of the nameless beneficiary of her murder from the succession. Parliament itself, understandably less worried by the problem of regicide, showed no such scruples. To them the bond seemed only too natural, as well as essential. In 1572, when Mary's life had been in danger, the whys and wherefores of her captivity, her original illegal detention, had seemed already remote; but thirteen years later they appeared positively prehistoric. The 'monstrous dragon' was now considered to be part of the English policy – and a singularly unpleasant part.

By the spring of 1585 there was very little that was encouraging to be discerned in the situation of the queen of Scots. Her son had repudiated and betrayed her; her French organization was in administrative chaos, and penetrated by Walsingham's spies; the English Catholics were quarrelling among themselves abroad and increasingly persecuted at home; Mary herself no longer felt complete trust for her erstwhile allies abroad and at times suspected the good faith of the Guises and Spain; in the meantime her position in England may be compared to that of someone tied down unwillingly over a powder keg, which may at any moment be exploded by a match held by an over-enthusiastic friend. To add to Mary's distress her prison was changed for the worse. In September 1584 she had been taken out of the custody of Shrewsbury and handed into that of the upright and elderly Sir Ralph Sadler. The real reason for the change was presumably to free Mary from the imbroglio of the Shrewsbury scandals; but according to Camden, in order not to offend Shrewsbury it was explained to him that Catholic plots now made it essential for Mary to be put in the charge of the Puritans.[39] Sadler was a fair and considerate jailer. But in the autumn of 1584 the edict went forth that Mary was to be taken back to the hated Tutbury for greater security. She was once more incarcerated in this loathsome if impregnable fortress in early January 1585. Not only that but at the same time the care of her person was handed over to a new and infinitely more severe jailer, Sir Amyas Paulet, who became in time as odious to her as the masonry of Tutbury itself. Under these doleful circumstances, with very little to cheer her as she surveyed her prospects for the future, Mary Stuart entered on the last and most burdensome phase of her captivity.

CHAPTER TWENTY-FOUR

The Babington Plot

~

The spring is past and yet it is not sprung;
The fruit is dead, and yet the leaves be green;
My youth is gone, and yet I am but young;
I saw the world and yet I was not seen;
My thread is cut, and yet it is not spun;
And now I live and now my life is done.

Chidiock Tichborne, one of the Babington conspirators;
written while in the Tower of London, awaiting death

The harsh character of Sir Amyas Paulet, Mary's new jailer, was apparent from his very first action. This was to take down from above her head and chair that royal cloth of state by which she set such store, since it constituted a proof of her queenship. Paulet's reasoning was that as the cloth of state had never been officially allowed, it must be removed, however long it had been there. Mary first wept and protested vigorously, then retired to her chamber in a mood of great offence; finally she secured the return of the cloth. The incident was typical of the man, who believed profoundly in the letter of the law: 'There is no other way to do good to this people than to begin roundly with them ... whatsoever liberty or anything else is once granted unto them cannot be drawn back again without great exclamation,' he wrote to London.[1] Paulet came of a West Country family, and his father had been the governor of Jersey. He himself had been English ambassador to the French court for three years, but had otherwise not enjoyed a particularly distinguished career; he was certainly not of the high rank of a Shrewsbury, or a diplomat of great age and experience such as Sir Ralph Sadler, whom he replaced. But he had been specially selected by Walsingham for the task in hand, because, as all his contemporaries agreed, he was not only a prominent Puritan but also a mortal enemy of the queen of Scots and all she stood for. Walsingham understood his man; Paulet was quite immune to the charms of the queen of Scots and, unlike Knollys and even Cecil, found her irritating and even tiresome as a character. Since honour and loyalty were his gods, and these Mary Stuart seemed to offend with every action, Paulet's Puritan conscience allowed him to hate her in advance. When they actually met, Paulet was able to transform charms into wiles in his own mind; like Knox so many years before, he disliked his captive all the more for her possible attractions.

Paulet's instructions from London were clear: Mary's imprisonment was to be transformed into the strictest possible confinement. She was not even to be allowed to take the air, that terrible deprivation which she dreaded so much, 'for that heretofore under colour of giving alms and other extraordinary courses used by her, she hath won the hearts of the people that habit about those places where she hath heretofore lain ...'.[2] In particular her sources of untapped private letters and messages were to be stopped once and for all; the only letters she was to be allowed to receive were those from the French ambassador in London – and these Paulet read in any case and stopped at will, as he thought proper. At no point in her captivity so far had Mary been cut off so completely. Her correspondence with Beaton, her ambassador in Paris, Morgan, Paget and her other foreign agents, had depended on a secret pipeline of letters, without which no foreign plotting could have taken place. During the whole of 1585, under the orders of the Elizabethan government, this pipeline was shut off, and Mary was totally deprived of the news she wanted so much.

Paulet achieved this isolation – which had a calculated position in Walsingham's scheme for Mary Stuart's downfall – by the most rigorous supervision of the Scottish queen's domestic arrangements. There were naturally to be no more pleasant sojourns at Buxton; on her last visit in the summer of 1584, still under the aegis of Shrewsbury, Mary had some premonition of this, for she wrote with a diamond on a window-pane at the springs:

> Buxtona, quae calida celebriris nomine Lymphae
> Forte mihi post hac non adeunda, Vale*

Mary complained furiously to Elizabeth of Paulet's demeanour: she described him as being more fit to act as the jailer of a common criminal than of a crowned queen. But Elizabeth merely replied smoothly that Mary had often professed herself ready to accept whatever served Elizabeth best; in which case she would surely accept Paulet.[3] In the meantime conditions under Paulet were very different from the easy days under Shrewsbury. Not only was Mary herself not allowed to ride abroad but Mary's coachman Sharp was not allowed to ride out without permission, and then he had to be accompanied. He was also deprived of the privilege of dining with Paulet's servants, as he had done with Sadler's. Paulet also went at great lengths into the difficult and, to him, vexatious subject of the royal laundresses. These elusive maidens, under the pretext of carrying out their work, had carried on a merry trade of message-bearing; what was more, two of them turned out to be the coachman Sharp's sister and sister-in-law. Paulet's puritanical brow furrowed over the subject of the laundresses, and at one point, despairing of finding co-operation in their midst, thought of importing some more malleable creatures from Somerset. It was an easier matter to prohibit all Mary's servants from walking on the thick walls of Tutbury (where they could wave, it was thought, in an enlightening manner, to passers-by). Another domestic change – of significance for the future – was that the brewer of beer and ale for the castle was installed at nearby Burton, with his family.†

---

* Buxton, whose warm waters have made thy name famous, perchance I shall visit thee no more – Farewell.

† The obtaining of beer for domestic consumption was an important item in Elizabethan housekeeping. It has been estimated that a population of four million consumed eighteen million barrels of beer annually, three quarters of it brewed privately.[4]

Mary's little private charities in which she had delighted, and by which she endeared herself to the local people, were sternly quelled by Paulet. His crushing comment – more applicable perhaps to the modern welfare state than to the Elizabethan policy – was that the laws of the realm had provided so carefully for the relief of the poor that no one could want for anything except through their own 'lewdness' or the negligence of the officers of several parishes. Mary said plaintively that she was ill in body or in mind, that she depended on the prayers of the poor to support her, and that it was barbarous to restrain her, but she did not get her way. Mary had a habit of presenting cloth to the poor on Maundy Thursday – in 1585 forty-two girls received 1¼ yards of woollen cloth and eighteen little boys, specified to be out of respect for her own son, were similarly endowed. Money was also given to the poor at Tutbury town. Paulet was furious to learn of such goings-on and demanded that they should cease; he said that such unpleasant practices might not be new to Mary, but they were certainly new to him.

In June there was further trouble over the arrangements for feeding Mary's horses and Paulet grumbled that it was all due to the fact that the Cavendishes had all become far too friendly with the queen over the years. Paulet also tried to prevent Mary from making any personal payments to the Tutbury servants, since this would give her an opportunity of secretly bribing them. As a result, his own accounts underwent a financial crisis, augmented by the rocketing food prices in England at the time. 'This Queen's servants are always craving, and have no pity at all on English purses,' wrote Paulet angrily.[5] There was indeed apparently no end to the lack of consideration Mary's servants were prepared to show: when Bastian's wife Christina gave birth to a child, Paulet had to deal with the problem of a midwife, who might so easily try to slip secret messages in or out. Furthermore, the queen's waiting-woman, Barbara Mowbray,*

---

* Barbara Mowbray was one of the two daughters of the laird of Barnbogle who served Mary Queen of Scots. She had joined her service by the beginning of 1584. About the time of her marriage, her sister Gillis Mowbray applied to join her in the royal service and was duly given a passport.

who had married Gilbert Curle in October 1585 (Paulet suspected they had been married by a priest disguised as one of Mary's French 'readers'), showed every sign of being about to produce a child herself.

Such domestic worries harried Paulet. But he stuck manfully to his duties, and executed them with as much if not more strictness than the government requested. How hopelessly optimistic then was Thomas Morgan's suggestion from the safety of Paris that Mary should try to bribe Paulet to accord her further liberty, by hinting that on her liberation he would be given virtual autonomy in Jersey where he was hereditary governor; this was not at all the stuff of which Paulet was made. This renewed sojourn at damp and draughty Tutbury thoroughly broke down Queen Mary's system, and her pleas for a change of air grew pitiful, as she wrote of the wind which whistled through the thin wooden walls into every corner of her chamber. Yet it is clear from Paulet's letter-books that he felt no sympathy with her ill-health, and seems to have regarded it as just retribution for her sins. In his attitude to her religious beliefs, he showed, to put it at its kindest, the total incomprehension of the bigot, who can see nothing fine or even sincere in the convictions of those with whom they do not agree; and some of his actions or attempted actions on the subject even verged on the sadistic, as when he tried to burn a packet sent to Mary from Chérelles in London because it was full of 'abominable trash' – including rosaries, pictures in silk marked with the words *Agnus Dei* and other comparatively harmless by-products of the Catholic religion. All in all, Paulet may be said to have justified Mary's own description of him as 'one of the strangest and most *farouche* men she had ever known'.[6]

However, in the autumn of 1585 it was the protests of the French court to Elizabeth, rather than the compassion of Paulet, which led to the search for a new prison for Mary Stuart. Not only was Mary's health itself weakened, but the famous middens of Tutbury were stinking to high heaven. Various Staffordshire residences were proposed, including Tixall, the home of Sir Walter Aston. But Sir Walter was a magistrate, and as it was by no means considered an honour to have a house chosen as a royal prison – rather the reverse – Paulet recommended against it, on the grounds that Aston was one of the few loyal men in 'this infected shire' and it would be a pity to forfeit his affections.[7] Chillington, home of the Gifford family, was well furnished but lacked brewhouses; on the other hand Beaudesert, the Paget home, lacked furniture. Burton was too near a river, and Sir Thomas Gerard's house (which Mary favoured) too small. In the end the lot fell upon Chartley Hall, an Elizabethan manor-house belonging to the young earl of Essex, with a large moat round it, which made it suitable for security reasons. However, at this point the young Essex protested violently against his mansion being used for this dishonourable purpose. Chartley had certainly been the scene of more chivalresque occasions: Queen Elizabeth herself had visited it during a round of summer visits with Leicester, and coming on from the famous festival of Kenilworth, had been entertained there by Lettice, Lady Essex. Chartley had romantic associations also, for it was there that Philip Sidney had first glimpsed Essex's sister, the thirteen-year-old Penelope Devereux, the inspiration of his muse, the Stella of his sonnets. Now Essex feared that all the trees on his estates would be cut down to warm the queen of Scots, and he also, more neurotically – if less plausibly – dreaded the damage she might do to the house deliberately, because she had hated his father (since the days when he had commanded the troops which guarded her at Tutbury), and was now said to have transferred this dislike to him.

Essex's protests managed to delay Mary's departure for Chartley throughout the autumn; but Paulet himself greatly approved of the change, especially as the amount of water round the house meant that the over-spirited laundresses would have less excuse for passing in and out of the gates as they went about their work. On Christmas Eve the journey was finally made. On arrival Mary found herself so reduced in health that she fell severely ill, and even Paulet found himself 'for charity's sake' bound to pass on her complaints about her bed which she said was 'stained and ill-flavoured'; he recommended the down bed which she herself requested.[8] On this occasion Mary was obliged to keep to her bed for more than four weeks, and it was towards the end of March, eight or nine weeks later, before she felt any real improvement from the 'painful defluxions' which plagued her. It was scarcely to be wondered at that her own servants were gravely worried for her, and feared that the move from Tutbury might have come too late to save her.

While considerations of the queen's health appeared to engross the Chartley household, deep and very different currents were swirling beneath the surface of its domestic pattern. Walsingham took the opportunity of the move from Tutbury to Chartley to mount a new stage in his campaign to incriminate the queen of Scots. His aim was of course to provide England – and Elizabeth – with sufficient evidence to prove once and for all that it was too dangerous to keep Mary alive. Already the bond of Association passed through Parliament the previous year meant that a plot had only to be made in favour of the queen of Scots – rather than by her – and she would by English law merit the death penalty. Now Walsingham, through his many and devious agents, set about enmeshing Mary in two separate conspiracies against Elizabeth, which together made up the complicated and in part bogus machinations which are known as the Babington plot.

These machinations had two separate strands. In the first place there was the plot – whether genuine or not – to assassinate the English queen. Secondly there was the plot to rescue the Scottish queen from captivity. In both cases, or in any combination of these two plans, foreign aid in the shape of a foreign invasion of England was absolutely essential for success: although Queen Elizabeth might fall a victim of the assassin's dagger, unless these assassins had sufficient resources to rescue Queen Mary immediately, they might find that by the time they reached her place of imprisonment, their candidate for the English throne had either been killed by her captors or else spirited away. In any case the English Catholics could not carry through such a revolution alone. This was a point which was thoroughly appreciated not only by all the level-headed conspirators, but also pre-eminently by Mary Queen of Scots herself, who never stopped stressing the danger to her personally of an amateur plan (as she had done many years before when Gerard and the Stanleys had thought of rescuing her). It was one of Walsingham's most subtle moves to make his agents at all points exaggerate the possibility of this foreign aid, generally supposed to be Spanish. In this way the English conspirators were led to believe that a Spanish invasion was certain, and so travelled even further along the road towards fruition of their plans. The Catholic parties abroad were on the other hand given the impression that the plans and numbers of possible English Catholic insurgents were far more stabilized and numerous than in fact they were. Although Mary, from her prison, emphasized in every letter that a Spanish invasion was a *sine qua non* of a successful rescue, these constant pleas in her letters were quite ineffective compared to the havoc wrought among the Catholic conspirators by the fact that so many of their number were actually renegades, secretly in the pay of the English government.

One false agent in a chain of correspondence can cast a completely different slant on a whole subject: the preliminaries of the Babington plot involved not only Charles Paget and Thomas Morgan, but also a new Walsingham double-agent – Gilbert Gifford – at their very heart. The assassination plot against Elizabeth, which is at first sight a dastardly conspiracy to kill the English queen, changes character as it becomes clear that much of the plot consisted of mere provocation by which Walsingham hoped to entangle Mary. The first stages of the intrigue which ended in Mary's downfall did not in fact involve Babington and his associates at all, but merely the protagonists of this earlier and dubious assassination plot. These were Gilbert Gifford, his cousin George Gifford, a failed priest of simple nature who was much under Gilbert's influence named John Savage, and a more lively ordained priest, Ballard, who was in close touch with Thomas Morgan, and who had come to believe in his own political mission to overthrow Elizabeth. The key figure in these early plottings was Gilbert Gifford. He came from an ancient, still Catholic family whose main seat was at

Chillington in Staffordshire; his cousin George came from a Hampshire branch of the same family, but in neither case was the possession of an honourable name any guarantee of integrity. Gilbert Gifford indeed seems to have had that peculiar subtle turn of mind which actually enjoys spying for spying's sake; he had gone abroad as a Catholic in 1577, had joined the English college at Rome to train as a priest, been expelled, and then roamed Europe before being innocently received back into the fold by Dr William Allen, head of the English College at Rheims. With his talents – not only was he highly intelligent but also an excellent linguist – he knew how to make a strong impression on his friends so that he easily drew over the weaker characters to his way of thinking, however tortuous. By the time he landed in England in December 1585, he had become thoroughly involved in the detailed matters of Mary's correspondence abroad, and let into the secret of all the new conspiracies to free her. On landing, however, he was apprehended and taken before Walsingham, and it was at this point that the details of their secret compact were arranged. It is not necessary to suppose that Walsingham had planned the meeting in advance; as one historian has put it, the probabilities seem to be that the opportunity suggested the expedient.[9]

The first time it was known by Mary's supporters that some change in her isolated and news-deprived condition might be expected was when this same Gifford presented himself at the French embassy. The new ambassador who had replaced Castelnau de Mauvissière was Guillaume de l'Aubespine, baron de Châteauneuf; but Gifford was actually seen by Cordaillot, a secretary at the embassy. The secret letters from Morgan which could no longer be smuggled into the Scottish queen had been piling up at the embassy for the whole year. Now Gifford offered to get packets to Mary, saying that no one in Staffordshire was likely to recognize him, not even his father or his sister, since he had been abroad for so long; as he still looked strangely young, his real identity would remain unsuspected. This story hardly matched with his earlier offer to make a perfectly legitimate visit to Staffordshire on the excuse of seeing his father, and according to Châteauneuf's later statement,[10] the French embassy themselves never totally trusted Gifford, especially when he turned out to be lodging in London with Thomas Phelippes, one of Walsingham's chief agents, and an expert decipherer. Nevertheless, whatever Châteauneuf's inner suspicions, the die was cast. Thomas Morgan's letters were entrusted to Gifford. On 16th January, 1586, to her unimaginable joy, Mary Stuart received the first secret communication she had had for over a year. Not only that, but she was informed that the same strange pipeline by which the packet had come – the local brewer – could be used to smuggle out her own notes.

The secret battle for the incrimination of the Scottish queen was now engaged. Mary was aware that Phelippes, Walsingham's arch agent, had already paid a visit to Chartley to see Paulet, for she had passed some disparaging remarks on his character and his personal appearance; unfortunately she did not realize that the object of Phelippes' visit had been to set up the exact workings of the snare in which she was to be trapped. Mary was intoxicated by the pleasure of renewed communications. As she wrote her first outward messages, to be handed to the agreeable brewer as she had been directed, she little realized that the treacherous Gifford still lurked in nearby Burton. The method by which Mary believed she contacted the outside world, but in fact merely signalled her private thoughts and schemes directly to her jailer Paulet at Chartley and her enemy Walsingham in London, was as follows:[11] Mary's secretary Nau first took down her letters, according to the queen's directions and with the help of his own notes made along the way, and then put them into code. Next he would wrap the letters securely in a leather packet and hand them privately to the Cartley brewer. The packet was then slipped through a corked tube in the bung of the cask. The merry brewer – 'the honest fellow' as Paulet sarcastically termed him – then drove away, back to Burton. Here he handed the packet to Gifford, and the same evening Gifford would bring the packet secretly back to Chartley and Paulet. If Phelippes was still at Chartley then the message was opened and deciphered on the spot, and the decipher sent forward to Walsingham in London; otherwise the original packet was sent by express riders to London and the deciphering done by Phelippes there. The code set up by the conspirators was not an especially subtle one, involving the use of a mixture of Greek letters, numbers and other symbols for the letters of the alphabet and common words. But even if it had been of a more complicated nature, the deciphering would still not have been a very arduous task: at the opening of her new communications, this particular code had been specially set up for the future between Mary and her correspondents, and passed on to them through the post; Walsingham had thus merely to note it down, and any of its variations, as and when they were established.

Once the deciphering was achieved, the packet was resealed: this was the province of Arthur Gregory, an expert in this individual art. Then Gilbert Gifford rode to London, taking the packet with him, and handed it over to the French embassy, as had been the queen's original intention. From here it went to Paris, enjoying diplomatic immunity at the ports, and was in Morgan's hands in mid-March. The journey had thus taken two months, but of course such delays were only too easy to explain, since all parties agreed on the need for extreme secrecy. Nor was the return journey any problem: the process was merely reversed. Mary received her secret post via the brewer as before, in a small packet containing a covering note from Gifford, who had brought it down from London. By the time any message from France was received by Mary, therefore, it had been deciphered, scanned and its contents well and truly noted by Walsingham.

In the spring of 1586 all those concerned in the conspiracy, from whatever angle, felt something like happiness. Mary, in blissful unconsciousness of being betrayed, revelled in the new sap flowing through her rescue schemes. Her secretary Nau even cast the 'honest fellow' in the role of Cupid: he had fallen in love with Mary's former bedfellow Bess Pierrepoint, Bess of Hardwicke's granddaughter by the marriage of her daughter Frances Cavendish to Sir Henry Pierrepoint. In this case propinquity had not led to love, or if it had, it was on Nau's side only. Nau's courtship of Bess led to an unfortunate coolness between Mary and her secretary at this critical moment. Mary's dearest '*mignonne*', so charming as a child, had grown up into a proud and rather unattractive young woman, who had inherited some of her grandmother's trouble-making nature. Despite the approval of Sir Henry, she was disdainful of the match with the voluble secretary, and enlisted Mary in her intrigues to get herself removed to court into Elizabeth's service.* Nau, however, used the secret pipeline to forward his marriage schemes.

Gifford enjoyed the luxurious god-like superiority of the spy, who can observe the whole battlefield from above. Paulet had the grim satisfaction of watching this woman he had never for a moment trusted reveal herself to be every bit as deceitful as he had suspected. As for the brewer, he was happy enough, since he was being paid twice over, once by Mary, and once by Paulet; furthermore, he thoroughly understood his own value, for what was Paulet's indignation when, despite the largesse inherent in the situation, the 'honest fellow' actually demanded a rise in his wages. Paulet's whole instinct was against employing so many people, especially people of such gross calibre – 'I had learned not to trust two where it sufficed to trust one,' he wrote.[12] But even Paulet had to admit that the harsh conditions to which Mary had previously been subjected had led her to leap joyously at any opportunity for correspondence: this, coupled with the need for secrecy which prevented Mary's side from making any effective double check on their arrangements, combined to make the operation virtually foolproof.†

It was at this point that the original and largely spurious assassination plot of the Giffords, Ballard and Savage was joined

* In the end the arrogant Bess did not marry until she was thirty-five, and then to an Erskine, created Viscount Fenton and earl of Kellie, who had been loyal to James VI during the Gowrie conspiracy and had come to England with him.
† The story of 'Barnaby' shows how ready Mary's heart was to be touched at this point. When Gifford needed to go to France, a certain 'Barnaby' was introduced to Mary by letter as being her substitute carrier; Barnaby was in fact the pseudonym for Thomas Barnes, a venal Catholic corrupted by Gifford. Mary developed such a fondness for the helpful 'Barnaby' that he was preserved as her nominal correspondent even after Gifford had in fact returned to England.

by the quite different conspiracy of a number of young English Catholic gentlemen, under the leadership of Anthony Babington. These young men showed a very different attitude to the imprisoned queen of Scots from that of the previous generation: indeed the Babington plot may perhaps be regarded as the first manifestation of that romantic approach to the beleaguered Stuart dynasty which was afterwards to play such a part in British history. After all, Mary Stuart, although always a seductive figure to those who knew her personally, had often been judged extremely harshly by those who did not know her. Her domestic policy in Scotland in the 1560s could by no stretch of the imagination be inscribed as pro-Catholic. The previous Pope, Pius V, in particular, had gone out of his way to show that he disapproved of her marriage to Bothwell – a Protestant ceremony quite apart from its scandalous genesis – and had made it clear that the promulgation of the bull *Regnans in Excelsis* was intended in origin to safeguard the spiritual welfare of English Catholics, rather than advance the cause of Mary Queen of Scots.

But by 1577 the attitude of the papacy had signally changed: Pope Gregory XIII wrote in August of that year rejoicing that calamity had taught Mary patience, approving of her new virtue, and believing that God would soon requite it with eternal glory.[13] As Pope Gregory bid his much-tried daughter to set great store by faith, hope and charity, he struck a very different note from Pope Pius. The attitude of Europe underwent an equal transformation: increasingly in the Catholic literature on the Continent, Mary came to symbolize the martyrdom of the Catholic faith in England. Gone indeed were the days when she had represented the spirit of religious compromise in Scotland. Mary's Catholic apologists were already at work long before her death. Adam Blackwood, whose dramatically pro-Marian account of her execution, *Martyre de la Royne d'Ecosse*, was later to become a classic in this field, published *De Regibus Apologia* in 1581; in this work he defended Mary against the attacks of heretics, who, he maintained, had no right to attack kings at all. Towards the end of the 1570s, lives of Catholic martyrs, brought out in answer to Foxe's Protestant martyrs, began to include the name of Mary, now considered to be a Catholic martyr in her English (Protestant) prison. Another Marian martryologist, Nicholas Sanders, was also at work in the 1570s, making such fanciful claims as that Mary had deliberately refused the English throne for the sake of the Catholic faith. The Act of Association in 1584 increased the spate. Mary, who had begun life as a beautiful young goddess of the French imagination, had progressed to become a controversial if exotic queen of Scotland, now became identified with the spirit of the Counter-Reformation.[14]

English minds were not immune to the transformation. By 1586 a whole generation had grown up in England since those far-off days at Kirk o'Field and the shameful, hasty Bothwell marriage: to these young men Mary was a Catholic princess held in an English Protestant tower.[15] To them it was Elizabeth who was the monstrous dragon who held Mary in thrall. These young men who dreamed their dreams were headed by Sir Anthony Babington: the quality of his romantic fancies can be seen in the high-flown language of his letters to the queen of Scots. Babington was a Catholic squire from Dethick, in Derbyshire: now twenty-five, he had been born about the time Mary returned to Scotland; he formed part of that Catholic Midlands society which included families like the Pagets (with whom he was on familiar visiting terms).[16] As a boy he had actually been a page to Shrewsbury, when the latter was Queen Mary's jailer, so that he had had ample opportunity to conceive a quixotic admiration for her. In 1580 he went to France and here became involved with Thomas Morgan, his schemes and his correspondence. Babington was rich – his family had benefited from two marriages to heiresses – and his income came to over £1000 a year in Elizabethan money; this put him in a position to entertain and act the host to his friends in a way which could back up any ideas he wanted to inculcate into them. Perhaps this fact was partly responsible for the influence he exercised over his immediate circle; or else Babington was one of those unlucky people who attract others to them by force of personality without possessing the other sterner attributes of leadership. In any case Babington, while admired and looked up to by his cronies, Chidiock Tichborne, Tilney and the rest, also had a strong streak of the dreamer in his nature, which made him a dangerous plotter with whom to be involved. In addition, when his character came to be tested in the crucible of an Elizabethan interrogation he lacked the necessary strength to withstand the terrible trial of pain.

Yet Babington in early 1586 was above all attractive and gay: Father William Weston gave the contemporary estimate of him – how he had 'enchanting manners and wit', he was well-read, well-travelled, good-looking with a quick intelligence, apart from his considerable wealth. Weston also commented on the appeal he exercised over his contemporaries: 'When in London he drew to himself by the force of his exceptional charm and personality many young Catholic gentlemen of his own standing, gallant, adventurous and daring in defence of the Catholic faith in its day of stress; and ready for any arduous enterprise whatsoever that might advance the common Catholic cause.'[17] It was Babington at the head of these men who concocted a second plan to rescue the queen of Scots, to be distinguished from the foreign-based plots of Ballard, the Giffords and Savage. Mendoza, the former Spanish ambassador to London, now in Paris, gave lavish promises of foreign aid; Ballard returned to England, contacted Babington and told him further wild tales of foreign armies on their way. Babington and his companions decided to rescue Mary from her prison, topple Elizabeth from her throne and place Mary on it.

These two separate plots now became entangled with each other, although the two sets of conspirators did not meet until comparatively late in the summer. In the meantime Mary received a mass of old correspondence which had been piling up in the French embassy by the secret brewer's route, throughout March, April and May. The connection with Babington did not actually arise until Mary's former emissary, Fontenay, who was Nau's brother-in-law, wrote to Mary telling her that there was a dispatch for her from Scotland which was now lodged at the house of Sir Anthony Babington in London. At the same moment Mary received from Morgan in Paris a letter which

officially approved Babington as a contact.[18] Finding Babington
independently approved from two sources, Mary now wrote off
to Babington herself on 25th June, her first letter in this
direction. It was short and to the point: 'I have understood that
upon the ceasing of our intelligence, there were addressed unto
you from France and Scotland some packets for me. I pray you,
if any have come to your hands, and be yet in place to deliver
unto the bearer thereof who will make them be safely conveyed
to me.' This communication was duly put into the beer keg with
the somewhat imprecise address of 'Master Anthony Babington,
dwelling most in Derbyshire at a house of his own within two
miles of Wingfield, as I doubt not you know for that in this
shire he hath many friends and kinsmen.'[19]

   This brief and practical letter was duly read and noted by
Walsingham and his agents. It finally reached Babington on 6th
July. In reply, spurred on by Ballard and Gifford, he composed
an extremely long letter which was neither brief nor practical,
and under no circumstances could be considered discreet;* in
short, as he himself put it, 'I writ unto her touching every
particular of this plot'.[20] The main points of the conspiracy as
outlined by Babington were as follows: first an invasion from
abroad, of sufficient strength to ensure success; secondly, the
invaders to be joined by 'a strong party at every place' of English
Catholic sympathizers; thirdly, the deliverance of Mary; fourthly,
'the dispatch of the usurping Competitor', as Babington put it,
'for the effectuating of all which it may please your Excellency
[Mary] to rely upon my service'. He supplied Mary with details
of each stage of the programme; the 'dispatch of the usurping
Competitor' (Queen Elizabeth), for example, was to be accomplished by six noble gentlemen among Babington's own friends.
Mary was to be extracted from prison by Babington himself
with ten of his other friends, at the head of a hundred followers.
Babington concluded by hoping that he might assure his con-

---

* Another example of Babington's extraordinarily foolhardy nature was the fact
that he had the whole group of conspirators sit for their portrait, with himself in
the centre and the motto painted above them: *Hi mihi sunt comites, quos ipsa pericula
dicunt.*

spirators that in the event of the plot proving successful, they would be duly rewarded by Mary's generosity and bounty.

Mary received this communication on 14th July, by which time of course it had been thoroughly scrutinized by Walsingham, and every detail of the plot was as well-known to the Elizabethan government as to Mary herself. It was Mary's reaction which was crucial: for although she was already doomed by the terms of the Act of Association, it would have been far more difficult for Walsingham to work up Elizabeth's odium against her if Mary had shown the Babingtons the cool reception she had displayed to other would-be rescuers in the past. While Mary pondered, she merely acknowledged receipt of Babington's plan. She asked for Nau's advice: Nau advised her to leave the letter unanswered as she had done before with similar offers. The English gloatingly attended her reply: 'We await her very heart in the next,' commented Phelippes. Finally on 17th July she wrote back to Babington an extremely long, full letter in principle approving his schemes.[21] Like the other letters of the secret correspondence, it was composed by Mary in French, the language which still came most naturally to her, but then drafted by Nau and Curle in English, before being translated into cipher and dispatched into the brewer's pipeline.

Babington in his letter had talked of the killing of Queen Elizabeth. There can be no doubt but that Mary in her reply took this prospect briefly into consideration, weighed it against the prospect of her own liberty, and did not gainsay it. From first to last, in this letter, she quite understandably viewed the matter from her own point of view, but when she wrote, 'Orders must be given that when their design has been carried out I can be *quant et quant* got out of here,' it was clear to the recipients of her letters – as it was to Walsingham – that the design of which she wrote and thus tacitly accepted was that same design of which they too had written, the assassination of the English queen. Throughout her own letter, Mary put all her emphasis on the practical details involved: the conspirators must have horsemen always with them to let her, Mary, know immediately that the deed had been done; otherwise, as no definite date had yet been fixed, Paulet might receive the news first and either transport her to another prison, or fortify the house successfully against her rescue; for the same reason, the conspirators must also take care to stop the progress of the ordinary posts.

Throughout the letter Mary took care to emphasize the terrible consequences to her personally should the plot explode prematurely and fail: the best that could happen to her would be that she would be buried in a dark prison for ever and ever. In this context Mary herself saw foreign help as being not so much desirable as absolutely essential. Not only did she reiterate to Babington that she would only be drawn forth from Chartley by 'a good army, or in some very good strength', but it was a point which she also tried to hammer home to Sir Francis Englefield in a letter written on 17th July, the same day as her fatal communication to Babington:[22] 'Before that they have sufficient promise and assurance, I have wished them plainly not to stir in any wise on this side, for fear they may ruin themselves in vain.' As she had told Beaton on 18th May, the action of the Spanish king must be regarded as crucial to any actions the English Catholics might take.[23]

There was no wonder that Phelippes drew a gallows mark on the outside of this letter when he passed it on to Walsingham. Mary had fallen plumb into the trap which had been laid for her. When Walsingham wrote to Leicester in the Netherlands on 9th July – a whole week, incidentally, before Mary actually penned her reply – a highly confidential communication saying that the Scottish queen would shortly be caught out in practices which would condemn her, this was exactly the sort of letter which he had in mind.[24] The schemes of Gifford, combined with the restrictions of Paulet, had worked their effect in Mary's mind. Even so, Walsingham was not totally satisfied with Mary's reply: he added a forged postscript to the end of the letter also in cipher in which she was made to ask for the names of the six gentlemen who would perform the deed. It would, he felt, represent the climax of her guilt, as well as providing the English government with some additional useful information. This forged postscript provides the final ironic touch to the setting up of the Babington plot by Walsingham and his agents:[25] 'I would be glad to know the names and qualities of the six gentlemen which are to accomplish the designment; for that it may be I shall be able, upon knowledge of the parties, to give you some further advice necessary to be followed therein. ... As also from time to time, particularly how you proceed: and as soon as you may, for the same purpose, who be already, and how far every one, privy hereunto.'

It is important to judge Mary's acceptance in principle of the Babington conspiracy against the background of her own mood in the course of the late summer of 1586 and how it developed up till July. Her mental state was by now very different from what it had once been; the old notion of establishing her on the throne of England, however much it appealed to her youthful champions, was not uppermost in the mind of the middle-aged woman, by now quite out of touch with Europe, let alone with England. Mary herself was beginning to feel weary of the prolonged battle for some sort of decent existence, in which she had now been involved for eighteen years, and the constant strain of being ever on her guard, ever plotting, ever hoping, ever planning. The period in which she was perforce cut off from her secret post contributed much to this feeling of melancholy and lassitude. She began to speak of liberty in terms of retirement rather than government. After James's betrayal of the Association, Mary told Elizabeth that her own desire had been to 'retire out of this island in some solitary and reposeful place, as much for her soul as for her body'. She described herself poignantly at the end of May 1586 as knowing not 'what line to sail, nor how to lift anchor'. This feeling of isolation and not understanding foreign matters any longer resounds through all her letters to Morgan, once the post was resumed: 'My dear friend,' she wrote to him on 20th May, 'I can found no certain judgment nor know what course in the world to take in my affairs I shall hear amply and more recently from every part.' On the same date, as if to prove her lack of contact with reality Mary also wrote to Mendoza in Paris confiding her rights to the crown of England conditionally to his master Philip II, if James had not become a Catholic by the date of her death. At the end of June, Nau told of how little Mary now felt she understood concerning the mind and intentions of other princes, thanks to her long solitude.[26]

In July this abandoned and exhausted frame of mind received a terrible fillip from the news that James and Elizabeth had actually signed a treaty of alliance. The maternal heart-break Mary had suffered in the spring of 1585 was now spiked with fearful bitterness. It was one thing to repudiate the idea of the Association but at Berwick on 6th July, only eleven days before Mary's vital answer to Babington, a proper treaty was signed between the English and Scottish sovereigns, a treaty from which Mary and her interest were totally excluded. James was now to receive an actual agreed subsidy from Elizabeth. Mary's letter of 12th July to Beaton in Paris on the subject of James was written in a tone of the utmost despair.[27] There is no doubt that the publication of the treaty sent her temporarily off her balance, and robbed her of the sustained powers of calm reason which might have led her to act far more cautiously over the Babington plot. Even the fact that her health – for so long enfeebled – was now somewhat restored by the better conditions of Chartley contributed towards her downfall. On 3rd June Paulet reported that the queen was now well enough to be carried down in her chair to the ponds near the house to watch the duck-hunting.[28] With renewed health came greater energy to escape, a prospect impossible to contemplate for an invalid endlessly confined to her chamber and her bed.

If to understand all is to forgive all, then it is certainly possible against this background to forgive Mary for tacitly acceding to – for her letter came to no more than that – a conspiracy involving the assassination of Elizabeth. Her own agreement was entirely in the context of a captive seeking to escape her guards, and may be compared to the actions of a prisoner who is prepared to escape by a certain route, even if it may involve the slaying of a jailer by another hand. If her own life in captivity could be considered to be in danger, then there was much theological doubt as to whether agreement to the slaying of Elizabeth was sinful at all. The immense theoretical problems which political assassination presented to the men of the sixteenth century caused Babington and his friends prolonged disquiet and heart-searching, but for Mary, illegally detained against her will, and not in any case concerned with the actual execution of the deed, or its instigation, the problem was considerably simpler: after so many years it was her rescue which mattered to her, not the safety of her jailer Elizabeth.* Even these same scruples of the Babington plotters do them credit in an age when many of the philosophers worked out good ethical reasons for the just death of a tyrant.

Yet in the sixteenth century the theory of resistance to one who had abused a ruler's sacred duties was given much prominence in the writings of both Jesuits, such as de Mariana, Suarez and Mola, and Calvinists, such as Hotman who wrote *Vindiciae contra Tyrannos*. The view of de Mariana in particular in *De Rege et Regis Institutione*, writing as he did in Catholic Spain, where there was religious unity, caused scandal in France and Germany where there was both religious and civil disorder: de Mariana's view that an individual might be justified in slaying a manifestly evil ruler, in accordance with the wishes of the people, was furiously condemned in countries where this imprudent advice might only too easily be put into effect.[29] Although many Jesuits rejected de Mariana openly, and later editions of his book contained modifications, the attitude of both Pius v and Gregory XIII to Elizabeth – first in the bull in 1570 and then in the ban of 1580 – was still susceptible of the interpretation by their Catholic flock that it would be a holy deed to rid England of this heretic ruler – even if they were certainly not specifically exhorted to do so. From the other side of the fence, John Knox

---

* Mary has been harshly judged for agreeing in principle to the assassination of Elizabeth, and this has been something held to justify Elizabeth's own execution of Mary. But this is to continue the propaganda of Walsingham successfully beyond the grave since there was, after all, little real danger to Elizabeth from a plot vetted throughout by Walsingham. The action of Elizabeth in suggesting that Mary, who was in her charge, should be secretly assassinated by Paulet was far more morally culpable.

had proclaimed without further ado that it was not only lawful but positively necessary to kill a king who had betrayed his people.

It says much for the innate goodness of ordinary people at the time that, although political actions like the papal bull or the bond of Association had truly wreaked havoc with the concept of public morality, nevertheless Babington and his friends were still bewildered about their moral position if they carried through Elizabeth's assassination. Babington wrote to Mary apropos 'the dispatch of the usurper, from the obedience of whom we are by excommunication of her made free', but revealed in his subsequent confession that he had been uncertain and worried as to whether this excommunication was still in force. Châteauneuf's memoir also revealed the genuine doubts which all concerned felt on the subject.[30] In an apparently violent age, when justification for the death of tyrants was openly discussed, and princes – like William of Orange – did meet their ends at the hands of the assassin, such scruples showed that it was easier for decent people to listen to the arguments in favour of such a deed than actually stifle their consciences to perform it. But such arguments, vivid as they might be throughout the sixteenth century, growing more intense after 1580, never really concerned Mary Stuart; she was never indeed at liberty in the society in which they were exploited; she continued to view the subject from the more personal standpoint of her own liberty.

The gallows letter was in Walsingham's hands by Tuesday 19th July. On 20th July Gilbert Gifford fled to the Continent; his work as an *agent provocateur* completed, he was unwilling to be involved in the holocaust of arrests and cross-examinations which he was aware was about to break in England.* On 29th July Babington himself received the gallows letter and deciphered

---

* Gifford got himself ordained priest in March 1587 in order to continue his informer's trade; he was awarded an English pension of £100 a year for his services. But the next year hubris was his undoing: he was arrested in a brothel, put in the archbishop's prison at Rheims and died there in 1590. However, all efforts to bring a case against him for his treachery to the Catholic cause in England failed, as Thomas Morgan would not testify against him.

it the next day with the help of Tichborne. On 3rd August he
wrote back to the Scottish queen acknowledging the fatal letter.[31]
By this date, however, as Mary's hope of release began to rise,
one of Walsingham's agents, William Wade, had already secretly
visited Chartley to work out with Paulet the best manner of
securing her arrest. The gossamer plot began to fall apart. On
4th August Ballard was arrested and at the news Babington fled
north through London to the leafy lanes of St John's Wood;
here he lay in safety for some time, until on 14th August he too
was seized, and brought in hideous triumph to the Tower.
William Weston, the Jesuit, lying in his own dark captivity, heard
the unusual and ominous sound of the bells pealing at midnight:
his guard told him that the city was celebrating the capture of
certain papists – 'traitors who had made a dastardly plot to
assassinate the sovereign and declare the Queen of Scots her
rightful heir'.[32] Finally on 18th August Babington made the first
of his confessions, in the course of which every detail of the
conspiracy was placed in the hands of Walsingham: the queen
of Scots, as well as all his fellow-conspirators, was fatally
incriminated. Although Babington had destroyed Mary's letters to
him, he now compliantly reconstructed their text for Walsingham
during his interrogations; and should his memory fail, Walsingham could always call on Phelippes, his decipherer, to help
with the official reconstruction document – after all, Phelippes
and Walsingham, through the medium of the secret pipeline,
had read these letters long before they ever reached Babington
himself.[33]

In the meantime Mary herself, cut off at Chartley, had absolutely
no inkling of the dramatic turn which events had taken. Her
commitment to the plot had been limited to letters; because of
the time lag between the writing and delivery of messages by
the secret post she knew very little of the various meetings
which the conspirators had held up and down the country. Her
spirits were high at the beginning of August: she felt she might
even hope again. On 11th August, when the dour Paulet
suggested that she might like to ride out of Chartley in the

direction of Tixall in order to enjoy a buck hunt, this seemed yet another favourable omen of future happiness, since such manifestations of goodwill from her jailer were rare indeed. Mary took particular trouble with her costume under the impression that she might be meeting some of the local gentry at the hunt. The ebullient Nau was also smartly arrayed as usual. Also in the party were Curle, the queen's other secretary, and Bourgoing, her personal physician (on whose journal we depend for so many of the details of the last months of Mary's life). It was a fine August day. The queen's mood was so gay and so gentle that when she noticed Paulet lagging behind, she remembered that he had recently been ill, and stopped her horse to let him catch her up.[34]

As the little procession wound its way across the moors, the queen suddenly spied some horsemen coming fast towards her. They were strangers. For one wild moment her heart leapt up and she actually believed that these apocalyptic horsemen were the Babington plotters, their plans more advanced than she supposed, coming to rescue her. The first words of their leader speedily undeceived her: this was none other than Sir Thomas Gorges, Queen Elizabeth's emissary, dressed for this momentous occasion in green serge, luxuriously embroidered. As Paulet introduced him Gorges dismounted from his horse and strode over towards Mary. 'Madame,' said Gorges in a ringing voice, 'the Queen my mistress finds it very strange that you, contrary to the pact and engagement made between you, should have conspired against her and her State, a thing which she could not have believed had she not seen proofs of it with her own eyes and known it for certain.' As Mary, taken off her guard and flustered, protested, turned this way and that, explained that she had always shown herself a good sister and friend to Elizabeth, Gorges told her that her own servants were immediately to be taken away from her, since it was known that they too were guilty.

From Gorges's tone, Mary even imagined that she might be now taken summarily to execution. She turned to Nau and Curle and begged them not to allow her to be snatched away without some defence. But there was little the wretched secretaries could do: they were now dragged from her side – in fact she never saw either of them again – and taken up to prison in London. Mary herself, with her physician, was conducted directly to Tixall, in the pretty riding clothes she had donned to impress the 'pleasant company' she expected to find there. She was so utterly unprepared for her fate that she did not even have the crucifix she habitually carried – when the inventory of her belongings was made at Chartley during her absence, it included the touching item: 'the gold cross Her Majesty generally wore'.[35] Mary tried at first to resist: at one point she actually sat on the ground and refused to proceed further. Paulet then threatened to bring her own coach and take her to Tixall by force if she would not ride on. Under duress Mary then consented to proceed; but first of all she knelt down underneath a tree and prayed out loud, asking God to remember David whom he had once delivered from his enemies, and imploring his pity. In vain Bourgoing tried to comfort her by saying that Elizabeth was dead, and that these strange proceedings were intended to ensure her safety. Mary cried out loud that she knew well she was no longer of any use to anyone in this world, and she personally desired nothing left on earth 'neither goods, honours, power nor worldly sovereignty, but only the honour of His Holy Name and His Glory and the liberty of His Church and of the Christian people'.

Tixall, to which Mary was now taken without further protest on her part, was an Elizabethan house built about thirty years earlier; it included an imaginative novelty in the shape of an exquisite four-square gatehouse, the building of which had only been begun about 1580 and can therefore have only been very shortly completed – if completed it was – at the time of the Scottish queen's incarceration there. But the beauties, or its detail, like those of the house itself – including the nearby River Trent 'by lovely Tixall graced, of Aston the ancient seat' as the Warwickshire poet Michael Drayton wrote lovingly later – must have been fairly lost on the distraught and anguished woman who was now imprisoned there. Mary did not leave her chambers for the entire fortnight which she spent at Tixall. She begged to be allowed to write to Queen Elizabeth, but Paulet refused to bring her paper. Bourgoing was sent back by Paulet to Chartley the next day. But Paulet subsequently allowed two of Mary's ladies and Martin, an equerry, to join her, who presumably brought over at least some of her luggage, since the queen was otherwise without any clothes except that hopefully gay riding-habit.

Meanwhile Mary's apartments and belongings at Chartley were thoroughly searched: her letters and ciphers were taken away to London. Paulet also took the opportunity to draw up a complete list of her household, with suggestions as to how it could be cut down 'if this lady be restrained of her liberty'.[36] The household of thirty-eight, counting the servants' servants, could easily be reduced to nineteen in Paulet's opinion, if outdoor categories like the coachmen were eliminated. Curle's wife Barbara could be dispensed with, as could Christina Pages – which removal, Paulet hoped, would result also in the departure of her husband Bastian, who had never seemed able to win the hearts of the English since that first merry masque at Holyrood. Paulet now called him 'cunning in his kind, full of sleights to corrupt young men'. The inventories of the queen's belongings showed how her prized possessions, once rich jewels like the Great Harry, now merely comprised miniatures or pictures: there were lists of these little portraits, one of her son James, one of Elizabeth, one of her first husband, one even of the dead countess of Lennox, and that other Catholic Queen Mary Tudor, as well as pictures of Henry II and many other members of the French royal family, and Mary's forebears the former kings of Scotland. It was as though she lived in the past, and sustained strength from the idea of the great many-branched family tree from which she had sprung.

After a fortnight at Tixall, in which anguish for the past mingled with apprehension for the future, Mary was conducted back to Chartley by Paulet. Outside Tixall's gatehouse a touching sight met her eyes: she found the beggars of Staffordshire had gathered to greet her, knowing the famous reputation of her charity. As the beggars cried out for alms, Mary replied sadly: 'Alas, good people, I have now nothing to give you. For I am as much a beggar as you are yourselves.' The whole incident was reported to London by Paulet in terms of the utmost indignation.[37] Back at Chartley, Mary found that her words to the beggars were only too true: her belongings had been rifled, her cupboards broken open; it was left for her to embrace her weeping servants 'as one who had returned home'. The only domestic incident which had taken place had also its sad aspects: Barbara Curle had given birth to her child in the absence both of her husband, now in prison in London, and of her mistress. Paulet had refused to baptize it, and as there was now no Catholic priest left even in disguise to perform the ceremony the queen did it herself. She named the baby 'Mary, in the name of the Father, the Son and the Holy Ghost'.*

The only thing which had not been taken from Mary was her actual money, on which she depended for paying her servants and for her own necessities; this she found still in the cupboard where she had left it. But later directives came from London that this too was to be seized; in order to effect the rapine, Paulet and Richard Bagot, a Staffordshire magistrate, forcibly entered the queen's apartments when she was lying ill in bed. Armed men were left in the ante-room and Paulet and Bagot went forward alone, sending Mary's servants out of the room, although Bourgoing managed to linger by the door, 'very sad and thoughtful'. At first Mary absolutely refused to surrender what was in fact undeniably her own property. When she saw that there was no gainsaying Paulet, she instructed Elizabeth Curle to open up the cabinet; even then, she forced herself to step out of bed, limped across the room on her crippled leg, barefoot without any slippers or shoes, and beseeched Paulet one last time to leave her the money. She had put the sum aside, she told him, as a last resort for her funeral expenses, and to enable her servants to return each to their own country after

---

* Paulet professed himself to be scandalized by the procedure, but it was well within the regulations of the Catholic Church.

her death. But Paulet was unmoved by this pleading, and the money was taken away. Mary was now left with the two things which could never be taken from her – as she told Paulet proudly on her return to Chartley – her royal blood and her Catholic religion.[38]

In the meantime the revelations which Walsingham was able to make to Elizabeth concerning the abominable perfidy of her good friend and sister Mary were eminently satisfactory from his own point of view. Elizabeth was plunged into a panic of acute physical fear, unaware how much of the assassination plot had in fact been elaborated by Walsingham's own agents. The English queen's letter to Paulet on the subject of the discovery of the Babington plot was ecstatic with relief: 'Amyas, my most faithful and careful servant,' she wrote, 'God reward thee treble fold in three double for the most troublesome charge so well discharged.' Mary was now 'your wicked murderess' and any future fate, however rigorous, no more than 'her vile deserts'.[39] It was understandable that Elizabeth should feel a mixture of keen fear at the danger to her personal safety and righteous horror at Mary's ingratitude: the confessions of the Babington conspirators, arrested and examined in turn, did nothing to reassure her. In mid-September they were tried and condemned, having pleaded guilty to the indictment of wanting to kill the queen; Mary Stuart's name was not introduced at any point into the trial, however, lest the assassination of Elizabeth would be further encouraged. The conspirators were then executed in two batches.

The manner of their ending was extremely savage, according to the general principle of the Elizabethan government that fierce penalties performed in public encouraged the people to believe the natural corollary that fierce crimes had been committed in private. As Camden put it: 'They were all cut down, their privities were cut off, bowelled alive and seeing, and quartered.' Babington murmured '*Parce mihi, domine Jesu*'; Chidiock Tichborne, whose poem written in the Tower is one of the most moving of all Elizabethan apologia, made a noble final speech, which aroused the pity of the spectators. Savage actually

broke the rope and fell before being disembowelled. Those privy
councillors present felt impelled to point out to the queen that
such blood-thirsty vengeance would do more harm than good.
The next day Salisbury, Dunn, Jones, Charnock, Travers, Gate
and Bellamy were dragged to the scaffold on hurdles as before,
but were only cut down when they were actually dead. This act
of mercy was attributed officially to Queen Elizabeth – although
she was not at this point in a particularly merciful mood.

The next desiderata to be secured by Walsingham and Cecil,
to complete their case against the queen of Scots, were the
revelations of her secretaries, Nau and Curle. The all-important
point was that they should testify to the authenticity of Mary's
'gallows' letter to Babington. At first the unhappy secretaries
denied everything: Nau said afterwards that Walsingham shook
his fist in his face, and had to be calmed down by Cecil. But
the situation was a critical one, and neither of them was a man
of steel. They were alone, helpless, and terrified out of their
wits; they were quite cut off from any possible consultation with
their mistress, and to Nau England was a dangerous foreign
country. Not only that, but their antagonists were apparently
able to produce in front of them the texts of all the secret
letters they had written, in a way which must have seemed like
some terrible witchcraft. As Curle himself said in his subsequent
apologia:[40] 'They did show me the Majesty's letters to my lord
Paget, Mr Charles Paget, Sir Frances Englefield and the Spanish
Ambassador, all penned in my own hand which I could not
deny. ... Moreover they showed me the two very letters written
by me in cipher and received by Babington. ... Upon which so
manifest and unrefusable evidence I could not deny'. In fact the
documents which Nau and Curle were shown, which they finally
attested, were not 'the two very letters' as Curle believed, since
Babington had destroyed these. They were copies, in which the
master-forger Phelippes probably had a hand, but in view of
the exact reconstruction of the text, and the fact that Babington
himself had by now vouched for the letters, it is easy to
understand how the wretched secretaries fell victim to the
deception. As for Mary's long detailed letter to Babington on

17th July, in which she ran through his plans at length, Nau and Curle were only asked to attest to the body of the letter itself; the forged postscript, added by Walsingham, in which he asked for the names of the six men destined to act as assassins, was deliberately left off the reconstructed letters. Babington specifically mentioned this postscript in his first confession; but when he was shown the reconstructed letter, he carelessly or compliantly passed it, without pointing out its absence. Had he insisted on its introduction, Nau and Curle would certainly have noticed such an obvious interpolation. Nor was the critical passage at the end of Babington's first confession, alluding to the postscript, ever read out later in court – so that the forgery should not be uncovered.[41]

Mary afterwards both believed and said publicly that she had been betrayed by Nau. Cecil also took a cynical view of the secretaries' moral stamina, when he wrote to Hatton on 4th September: 'Nau and Curle will yield somewhat to confirm their Mistress' crimes. But if they were persuaded that they themselves might escape, and the blow fall upon their Mistress betwixt her head and shoulders, surely we should have the whole from them.'[42] But in retrospect, it is difficult to blame the secretaries too harshly for attesting a text whose validity they believed they could hardly in honesty refute. In the critical and terrifying atmosphere of the interrogation, under circumstances of fear and hopelessness, the impossibility of saving their mistress in face of such evidence jostled with their very human fears for their own safety. Nau's betrayal of his mistress at the end does not necessarily mean that he was engaged in a long-term policy of villainy. It was true that Nau had fallen out with Mary over his use of the secret pipeline to forward his matrimonial plans with Bess Pierrepoint. According to his enemies, Nau was bribed with £7000 to betray Mary; he was certainly housed with Walsingham in London, and later sent back to his native France in a boat of his own after a few months, whereas the unfortunate Curle remained in close imprisonment for a year.[43] Such signs of English favour, while they may point to the fact that Nau exposed the truth about Mary's intrigues to save his own skin, does not prove any further degree of treachery. Paulet always hated Nau in the old days at Tutbury and Chartley, and wished that he could get rid of him, and Paulet's dislike was an excellent indication of Nau's loyalty towards Mary. Nau also managed to straighten out Mary's finances to an admirable extent during the period in which he served her. Nau's surrender should be equated with the outburst of Leslie in the Tower over the Norfolk conspiracy; they were both the unfortunate but explicable lapses of servants who were enmeshed in webs which were altogether too strong for men of their calibre. In the event, the betrayal of Nau and Curle can hardly be said to have much historical significance; if they had persisted in their denials, it is not likely that Walsingham would have allowed such petty obstacles to stand in his way. He would have found other ways of getting the letters vouched for.*

By now, with the Babington conspirators dead or dying, Nau and Curle under lock and key and the Act of Association, by which she was already guilty, hanging over her head, there was little left for Mary to hope for. But there was one terrible thing left for her to dread: the secret death, the slow drip of poison, the assassin's knife, all the fates by which she would be deprived of the public martyrdom by which she now hoped to proclaim the Catholic faith at her death. During her fortnight at Tixall she seems to have thought coolly and courageously towards this end: from now on, she deliberately played every scene with this climax in view. Her hope was to triumph at the moment of her death; her fear was to be extinguished meaninglessly without an opportunity of bearing witness to the truths in which she believed. In September, while describing how wretchedly she was treated, she managed to write to this effect to her cousin the duke of Guise: 'For myself, I am resolute to die for my religion. ... With God's help, I shall die in the Catholic faith and to maintain it constantly ... without doing dishonour to the

---

* When Nau reached France, the Guises accepted his story that he had merely bowed to *force majeure*. In 1605 Nau went further and actually applied to James I and VI to have his good character established.

race of Lorraine, who are accustomed to die for the sustenance of the faith.'[44] Mary was by now so convinced that death was at hand that she begged him to look after her poor servants, and gave the most detailed instructions for the disposal of her body, which she wished to have buried at Rheims, with that of her mother. Her hand was now so stricken with pain that she could hardly hold the pen to write the letter, the terror of the unknown death haunted her, and yet Mary ended proudly: 'My heart does not fail me. .... *Adieu, mon bon cousin.*' It was in this heroic frame of mind that Queen Mary allowed herself to be taken without protest out of Chartley on 21st September and set on her last journey towards Fotheringhay. It was Mary's triumph that by her deliberate behaviour in the last months of her existence, she managed to convert a life story which had hitherto shown all the elements of a Greek tragedy – disaster leading ineluctably to disaster – into something which ended instead in the classic Christian manner of martyrdom and triumph through death. This transfiguration in the last months of her life, which has the effect of altering the whole balance of her story, was no fortunate accident. The design was hers.

Trial

$\sim$

'As a sinner, I am truly conscious of having often offended my Creator, and I beg Him to forgive me, but as Queen and Sovereign, I am aware of no fault or offence for which I have to render account to anyone here below.'

Mary Queen of Scots to Sir Amyas Paulet, October 1586

On 21st September Mary Queen of Scots was taken out of Chartley Hall and away to an unknown destination. It was a sinister and frightening scene. The men who came to fetch her, Gorges and Stallenge, arrived with pistols at their belts. Her own servants were locked in their rooms and their windows guarded, so that they should not witness her departure or signal their sympathy to her. The most that Paulet had imparted to Mary officially on the subject of her new prison was the mere fact that she was going to be moved. From hints gleaned secretly through the servants, Mary actually believed she was going to a royal castle about thirty miles from London!*[1] Under these doleful conditions Mary was conducted out of Chartley and Staffordshire by a body of Protestant gentlemen of the country, including Walter Aston and Richard Bagot. The first night was spent at Hill Hall, near Abbot's Bromley, where the queen's stay was commemorated by her name and the date scratched on a pane of glass by a Paget sympathizer at the end of the century: *Maria regina Scotia quondam transibat istam villam,*

---

* The Privy Council wanted to bring the Scottish queen to the Tower of London, but Elizabeth refused to hear of it.

21st Septembris, 1586 usque Burton Fortheringhay.* The next morning Gorges, on instructions from Elizabeth, attacked the queen on the dual subject of her culpability and her ingratitude, although Mary firmly and steadfastly refused to admit either guilt or guilty intentions. The next two nights were spent at Leicester, in the house of the earl of Huntingdon in Lord's Place: here the ordinary people showed signs of favouring the prisoner rather than her jailer, Paulet, and his coach had to be guarded against demonstrations. Finally, on 25th September, the queen reached the castle of Fotheringhay in Northamptonshire, about twenty miles south-west of Peterborough.

Mary Stuart first sighted its ancient towers from a path called since the days of the Domesday Book, Perryho Lane – which according to tradition enabled her to make a melancholy little play on the name as she exclaimed aloud, 'Perio! I perish.' Quite apart from its heavy, brooding appearance, Fotheringhay had a stark history. Ironically Mary might have been able to claim it for her own, since at one point it had been made the dowry of Maud de Senlis, the English bride of King David of Scotland. It had been built in the time of the Conqueror and rebuilt in the reign of Edward III. It subsequently became a Yorkist castle and here in 1452, Richard III, that sad and twisted king, had been born. It was now used entirely as a state prison, but was considered of sufficiently bleak reputation for the wretched Catherine of Aragon to refuse to go there unless, as she said, she were to be bound with cart ropes and dragged thither. The front of the castle and the enormous gateway faced north, the mighty keep rose to the north-west; a large courtyard filled the interior of the building, which included a chapel and a great hall; there was a double moat system along three sides, and the River Nene winding along the very edge of the castle made up the fourth side of the defences. Around its grim tower stretched the level Northamptonshire countryside; this had more of the flatness of eastern England, and plains stretching onwards to

---

* The signature is not actually that of Mary herself, lacking the characteristic level letters. The pane of glass is still to be seen in the William Salt Library, Stafford.

the Fens themselves, than the mountainous midland landscape which Mary had been accustomed to in Derbyshire and Staffordshire.

Despite the size of Fotheringhay, Mary found herself incarcerated in comparatively mean apartments: this brought back all her phobia of a secret killing, the sort of barbarous death that stained the history of English medieval castles. But when her servants reported that many of the state rooms had been left empty, Mary drew the correct conclusion that she was about to be tried, and the rooms were awaiting the arrival of dignitaries from London. At this evidence that she was about to undergo the public martyrdom she sought, as Bourgoing reported: 'Her heart beat faster and she was more cheerful and she was in better health than ever before.'[2] When Paulet came to inform her on 1st October that her misdeeds were now to be punished by the interrogation of certain lords, and advised her in her own interests to beg pardon and confess her faults, before she would officially be declared culpable by law, Mary was able to meet him in an extraordinarily calm and even detached mood; she even made a little joke saying Paulet was behaving like a grown-up with a small child, asking her to own up to what she had done. Then she went on more seriously: 'As a sinner, I am truly conscious of having often offended my Creator, and I beg Him to forgive me, but as Queen and Sovereign, I am aware of no fault or offence for which I have to render account to anyone here below. ...' And she concluded loftily: 'As therefore I could not offend, I do not wish for pardon; I do not seek, nor would I accept it from anyone living.' Disgruntled, since he laid great emphasis on the fact that this sinner should personally confess her misdeeds, Paulet reported carefully back to London all that had happened.[3] A few days later Mary was cheered by the arrival of her steward Melville and his daughter, and Bastian Pages also with his daughter Mary, who was the Queen's god-daughter. However, she rightly interpreted the dismissal of her coachmen – Paulet had at last succeeded in effecting this domestic economy – as an ominous sign that her days of driving abroad were over.

In London the commissioners appointed to judge the Scottish

queen assembled at Westminster on 8th October. They were read copies of the letters sent by Babington to Mary, her answers and the evidence of Nau and Curle. It was then agreed that Mary should be brought to trial under the Act of Association enacted in 1585: this provided means whereby a commission of twenty-four peers and privy councillors might be appointed to investigate any conspiracy or attempt to hurt Elizabeth 'by any person or with the privity of any person that shall or may pretend to the title to the Crown of this realm'.[4] The punishments for anyone found guilty under this act were to be two-fold: firstly they were to be deprived of their title to the English crown forever, and secondly they could be lawfully put to death under the provisions of the Act. It had been quite clear at the time that this Act had been especially framed in order to be able to try and execute the queen of Scots: now it was coming into its own. It was under this Act that the commissioners and peers were now summoned to meet in a few days' time at Fotheringhay – including Mary's former jailer, Shrewsbury. In vain he tried to duck this unpleasant task on grounds of health. Shrewsbury was smartly reminded by Cecil that his failure to appear might be interpreted by the malicious as confirmation of all those old rumours that he had been too lenient towards his prisoner; the Lord Chancellor Bromley also wrote meaningfully to Shrewsbury: 'I would advise you not to be absent.'

The provisions of the Act of Association were so heavily weighted against Mary that she stood absolutely no chance of acquittal even if it had not been quite clear to all and sundry that her case had been pre-judged. Indeed Cecil mentioned calmly to Shrewsbury that if his health really did prevent him from attending, he ought to authorize Cecil in advance to deliver his (Shrewsbury's) opinion of Mary's guilt.[5] It was of no avail for Châteauneuf, the French ambassador, to plead with Elizabeth for Mary at least to have counsel to defend her on what was a capital charge: Elizabeth told him sharply that she did not need advice from strangers on how to manage her own business. At the forthcoming trial, therefore, Mary was to be allowed neither counsel nor witnesses in her defence; she was not even to be allowed a secretary or amanuensis to help her prepare her own case – her own secretaries being of course still in prison in London. She was to be left quite alone, a sick woman and a foreigner, who knew nothing of England, its laws, or customs, and had only begun to learn its language comparatively late in life, to conduct and manage her own defence against the best legal brains in the country. These eminent lawyers on the other hand were not even to be put to the simple task of bringing witnesses for the prosecution for none was to be called.

Yet, curiously enough, by the standards of the sixteenth century the innate injustice of the trial of Mary Queen of Scots lay not so much in its arrangements – the accused was never allowed counsel at an English treason trial at this date, and the barbarity of the Scottish treason trials has been sufficiently commented upon* – as in the fact that the trial took place at all. How, indeed, could it ever be legal for Mary as sovereign, the queen of a foreign country, to be tried for treason, when she was in no sense one of Elizabeth's subjects? In 1586 the sovereignty of a ruler was taken extremely seriously with regard to his own subjects – how much more difficult then was it to try and execute one who was actually or had been the sovereign of another country? Elizabeth herself was the first to perceive the dangers for the future of pulling down any monarch to the rank where he or she could be punished like any other subject – let alone the monarch of another country. If Mary had partaken in treasonable activities in England where in any case she was a prisoner, held against her will, the correct remedy (although of course it was never considered) was surely to expel her from the country. The mere judicial proceedings for trying a sovereign presented enormous difficulties by English common law. In England it was the foundation-stone of justice that every man had a right to be tried by his peers; Mary being a queen had

---

* The practice of allowing no counsel to the defendant at a treason trial persisted: in 1746 at the trial in London of Simon, Lord Lovat for his part in the '45, Horace Walpole described how pathetic it was to see the old man (he was over eighty) struggling with his defence without any counsel in what to him was a foreign country.

no peers in England except Elizabeth herself. Neither privy councillors nor earls nor barons gathered together in no matter what profusion could be said to be the equals of one who was an anointed queen.

As the English lawyers pondered these questions, it was even suggested that the old claims of England to feudal suzerainty over Scotland (last used by Henry VIII to justify his depredations) might be brought out again, dusted over and employed to prove that Mary was Elizabeth's subject and as such capable of both treason against her, and of trial by English law. In the end the line of proceedings taken consisted of a long narration of circumstances ranging down from ancient times – some of them very ancient indeed – when it had been considered suitable for one sovereign to try another for treason done within their state. The most recent case cited was that of Conradin, last of the Hohenstaufen, who, four centuries earlier, had been beheaded by the papal nominee for his father's thrones, Charles, duke of Anjou, after being captured in battle and subjected to a form of treason trial. But the two cases were hardly comparable, as Mary had certainly not been captured in battle, and in any case was utterly ignorant of the laws of England, a country in which she had never been permitted to live at liberty.*6

In truth, the only possible justification for what was in fact unjustifiable was the Act of Association itself which, by defining the commission which was to try anyone found coming within the terms of the Act, disposed of such knotty problems as sovereignty and a queen's peers by merely cutting through them and all the laws, both national and international, of the time. In the case of the trial of Mary Queen of Scots the traditional blindfold across the eyes of Justice was ruthlessly torn aside by the English commissioners so that the desired verdict might be reached. In order to strengthen a weak case, Cecil took trouble

---

* In his history, Froude attempted to justify the trial by pointing out that Mary had a place within the English succession which gave Elizabeth rights over her; this would be a more effective argument if Mary had not been persistently denied these rights by Elizabeth all her life despite her many attempts to secure their acknowledgment.

to recall Parliament: it so happened that the English Parliament had been prorogued until November, and the existing Commons could not be brought back before then. Therefore the old Parliament was dissolved and writs of commission for the new one sent out on 14th September, in order that the Commons might be already sitting at the time of the trial. This would help to gloss over the illegality of the proceedings in France and elsewhere or, as Cecil put it, 'to make the burden better borne, and the world abroad better satisfied'. The hatred of the Commons for the queen of Scots had in no way abated over the years, but rather increased in violence: she was now regarded, in the words of one of its members, her former keeper, Sir Ralph Sadler, as 'this most wicked and filthy woman'; Cecil knew that he could rely on the faithful Commons to present this point of view forcibly after the trial to Elizabeth, herself more likely to be haunted by the spectacle of a crowned head rolled in the dust.

On Saturday, 11th October, the commissioners began to arrive at Fotheringhay, the most important lodging in the castle, the others in the village and neighbouring farms. Mary was given a copy of the commission which had summoned them. The next day a deputation of lords waited on her – Sir Walter Mildmay, Stallenge, the usher of Parliament, Barker, Elizabeth's notary, and Paulet himself. The object of this mission was to get Mary to consent to appear in person at the trial and thus acknowledge its legality. They handed the Scottish queen an epistle from Elizabeth in which she announced to her that she had sent some peers and legal counsellors to examine Mary and judge her case since Mary persistently denied her participation in a plot against Elizabeth, despite the cogent proofs of her part in it which Elizabeth possessed. As for the legality of such proceedings – since Mary was in England, concluded Elizabeth boldly, she was subject to the laws of the country.

To this Mary replied in fine style, and without in any way conceding their right to try her: 'I am myself a Queen, the daughter of a King, a stranger, and the true kinswoman of the Queen of England. I came to England on my cousin's promise of assistance against my enemies and rebel subjects and was at once imprisoned.'* She stressed her oft expressed, never gratified, wish to speak to Elizabeth and ended: 'As an absolute Queen, I cannot submit to orders, nor can I submit to the laws of the land without injury to myself, the King my son and all other sovereign princes. ... For myself I do not recognize the laws of England nor do I know or understand them as I have often asserted. I am alone, without counsel, or anyone to speak on my behalf. My papers and notes have been taken from me, so that I am destitute of all aid, taken at a disadvantage.'⁸ On the subject of her actual guilt, whereas Mary admitted that she had thrown herself under the protection of Catholic kings and princes, she denied any knowledge of an actual attempt against Elizabeth. Mary's views were duly written down, to be communicated to the English queen.

The next morning Mary received another less courteous deputation, as she was sitting at her early dinner (ten o'clock in the morning). The Lord Chancellor Sir Thomas Bromley told her that whatever she might protest, she was subject to the laws of England, whether as a sovereign or as a captive, and that if she did not appear in person at her trial she would merely be condemned *in absentia*. Mary shed a few tears at such brusqueness and exclaimed that she was no subject, and she would rather die a thousand deaths than acknowledge herself one, since she would both betray the majesty of kings, and virtually admit that she was bound to submit to the laws of England even over religion. Once more, as she had done before, Mary offered to appear before a free Parliament and answer questions, rather than submit to the commissioners who she suspected had already condemned her unheard. But even in her distress Mary managed to produce another dramatic watchword or rallying-cry for her supporters, if the news of it should ever leak out, as she cried:

* On the subject of Mary's conviction that Elizabeth had promised her assistance if she came to England, it may be recalled that Cecil in his memorandum of summer 1568 concerning the *pros* and *contras* of the imprisonment of the queen of Scots cited, as one argument *contra*, the fact that the queen of England had made Mary promises of assistance 'frequently expressed'.⁷

'Look to your consciences and remember that the theatre of the world is wider than the realm of England.'[9]

Cecil now interrupted the conversation with considerable passion: his vehemence probably had a private cause, for there had been some embarrassing rumours that Cecil himself was favourably disposed towards Mary, based on the fact that his grandson William Cecil had visited Rome and had there been converted to the Catholic faith. Mary herself seems to have been under the illusion that the grandson had persuaded the grandfather into a more clement frame of mind.* Now Cecil was disposed to put an end publicly to such idle notions, and the process 'made him it is thought more earnest against her', for he now broke out quite rudely to the queen: 'Will you therefore hear us or not? If you refuse, the assembled Council will continue to act according to the Commission.'

The matter of Mary's personal appearance at the trial – by which she would acknowledge in some measure at least to the public eye their jurisdiction over her – was now the subject of prolonged discussion between Mary and her would-be judges. Mary continually reiterated her sovereign status: it was not until 14th October that she finally succumbed, and agreed to appear in order to answer the single charge that she had plotted the assassination of Elizabeth. During the discussions, Mary received a letter from Elizabeth in London, in which reproach and anger were mixed: 'You have planned in divers ways and manners to take my life and to ruin my kingdom by the shedding of blood,' Elizabeth wrote. 'I never proceeded so harshly against you; on the contrary, I have maintained you and preserved your life with the same care which I use for myself.' Now Elizabeth commanded Mary to reply to the peers of her kingdom as if she herself were present. The only possible note of friendliness was in the last phrase of the letter: 'But answer fully, and you may receive greater favour from us.'[10]

---

* Throughout her captivity she seems to have been under the impression that Cecil was more generously inclined towards her than his private papers actually show him to have been. This suggests that Cecil, wise in his own generation, did

Did Mary detect in these ambiguous words some hint that, if she appeared before the judges, she would in the end receive pardon, whatever her crimes, and was this then the motive that determined her to accede to their pressing demands, thus jeopardizing her sovereign position? But by this stage in her life, and in the frame of mind in which she had found herself since August, and that grim meditative fortnight at Tixall, it does not seem that Mary Stuart was animated by any hope of being shown further mercy. The strange serenity which now possessed her, on which both Paulet and Bourgoing commented from different viewpoints, was the calm of a woman who perfectly well realized that she was about to die. The heroism of her sentiments was carefully and brilliantly angled towards the martyr's death which would bear witness to the cause of the Catholic Church: as Mary herself had said, she was playing her last role towards the theatre of the world, rather than the realm of England.

Mary has been criticized for rescinding her determination never to appear before this illegal court; but there can be no doubt that her noble bearing at this trial, and the magnificent speeches she made there, all directed towards showing her in the light of the martyr queen, did much to enhance this picture when they gradually became known after her death. Furthermore the full publicity she was able to give at it to her wrongs also distracted attention from points on which she might be held considerably more vulnerable (although the court was still not competent to judge it) such as the letter she had written to Babington. Although on the one hand Mary sacrificed her royal position by appearing before a tribunal which had no right to try her, on the other she greatly improved her position in the eyes of history. The queen of Scots was clever to see this when she agreed to appear before the judges – intuition in this case being more potent than legal knowledge. Even so, the stress of making this critical decision reduced Mary to faintness, and she

not allow himself to forget altogether Mary's prominent position in the table of the English succession.

had to be revived with wine before her resolve could be committed to writing.

The trial of Mary Queen of Scots began on the next day, Wednesday, 15th October, in a room directly above the great hall of Fotheringhay Castle. Even Bourgoing considered this chamber spacious and convenient: it was nearly seventy feet long including the window, and twenty-one feet wide. The most detailed plans were made for the trial, and the position of every participant was carefully mapped out in Cecil's chart. At the upper end of the room there was a throne and a royal canopy with the arms of England over it; opposite the throne for the benefit of the prisoner was placed one of Mary's own crimson velvet chairs, and a crimson velvet cushion for her feet. The room was divided in two by a wooden barrier with a door through it. Above the barrier two parallel benches were positioned on each side of the room: on the right sat the Lord Chancellor Bromley, Cecil as Lord Treasurer, and the earls including Shrewsbury. In front of them sat the two chief justices and the high Baron of the Exchequer. On the left sat the barons and knights of the Privy Council including Walsingham, Christopher Hatton and Sir Ralph Sadler, with four other judges and two doctors of civil law in front of them. A large table in front of the canopy was for the use of the crown representatives including the Attorney-General and Solicitor-General and Barker, the notary, and on it were placed the documents to be used in the case. Below the barrier, the remaining twenty-four feet of the room was for the use of the spectators – the ordinary people of the village, and the servants of the commissioners.

Queen Mary entered the great hall at nine o'clock, with an escort of soldiers. She wore her chosen garb of the sad years of captivity – a dress and mantle of flowing black velvet, her traditional white head-dress with its widow's peak, and a long white gauzy veil. Her maid Renee de Beauregard bore her train, but Queen Mary was now so lame with rheumatism, and her muscles had lacked exercise for so long, that she could scarcely walk or even limp along, and had to be supported by Melville and Bourgoing. She was followed by her surgeon Jacques Gervais, her apothecary Pierre Gorion and three of her women, Jane Kennedy, Elizabeth Curle and Gillis Mowbray. The commissioners respectfully uncovered their heads as the queen passed, but there was still one delicate moment when the prisoner appeared to be about to jib at her treatment: this was when she realized that she was not to sit on the throne as she had imagined, but on the crimson velvet chair. Mary exclaimed spontaneously: 'I am a Queen by right of birth and my place should be there under the dais!' But after this first instinctive reaction, she recovered her composure, as though she had in advance decided to go through with the ordeal, no matter what the humiliation, and this cry had merely been wrung from her by surprise. The queen sat down quietly in the chair allotted to her and merely observed to Melville as she scanned the faces of the English peers: 'Ah! here are many counsellors, but not one for me.'[11]

The trial was opened by a speech from the Lord Chancellor in which he explained the motives which had impelled Queen Elizabeth to institute these proceedings – how she had been informed that the queen of Scots had planned her fall and was therefore bound to convoke a public assembly to examine the accusation – and ended by stating that Queen Mary would have every opportunity of declaring her own innocence. To all this Mary replied in terms very much as before, not only denying the jurisdiction of the court over a queen, but also laying great stress on the conditions under which she had first arrived in England: 'I came into this kingdom under promise of assistance, and aid, against my enemies and not as a subject, as I could prove to you had I my papers; instead of which I have been detained and imprisoned.' Queen Mary emphasized that the only reason she had condescended to appear before the commission was in order to show that she was not guilty of the particular crime of conspiring against Elizabeth's life. In answer the Lord Chancellor utterly denied that Mary had arrived in England under promise of assistance from Elizabeth, as also he declared futile her protests against the jurisdiction of the court itself over her. The commission to try the Scottish queen was then read aloud in Latin, at which Mary now made a further protest against the laws on which it was based, which she said had been expressly framed to destroy her.

Gawdy, the royal sergeant, now rose in his blue robe, with a red hood lying flatly on the shoulders. He detailed the events leading up to the Scottish queen's arrest, including the seizure of Babington, and the listing of six men who were intended to assassinate Elizabeth. To this Mary replied that she had never met Babington, had never 'trafficked' with him and knew nothing of the six men. Letters said to have been dictated by Babington before his death were then read aloud, and copies of the correspondence between Mary and Babington passed round, together with the signed depositions of Curle and Nau, and the confessions of the other conspirators. Mary strongly protested against this second-hand evidence and very sensibly continued to demand to see the originals of her so-called correspondence with Babington. She refused to admit anything at all on such indirect proofs, and suggested that her own ciphers could all too easily have been tampered with. Despite her lonely position without counsel, Mary never for a moment lost her head: she continued to draw a sharp distinction between the actions which she as a prisoner had inevitably taken to try and secure her own rescue ('I do not deny that I have earnestly wished for liberty and done my utmost to procure it for myself. In this I acted from a very natural wish') and actual connivance at the death of Elizabeth, which she strongly denied. As for the letters, once more she rejected them *in toto*. 'Can I be responsible,' she demanded passionately, 'for the criminal projects of a few desperate men, which they planned without my knowledge or participation?'

The depositions and letters of Babington were now read aloud. The mention of the name Arundel and his brothers, who had been involved in conspiracies in her favour, drew from Mary the exclamation: 'Alas, why should this noble house of Howard have suffered so much for me. ...' After the midday meal further letters were read aloud including the depositions and confessions of Nau and Curle. Throughout the trial, the speeches were addressed to the lords rather than to Mary, so that in order to make a point about a passage in a letter she had to interrupt them; she also complained that the evidence was produced in no particular order, on purpose to confuse her in her answers for she had after all no previous warning of what was going to be produced against her, no opportunity to study the letters privately, and of course no counsel to assist her in making her case. The strain of keeping sufficiently mentally alert was considerable. Nevertheless Mary continued calmly to emphasize the wrongfulness of her imprisonment and call to witness her own ill-health – 'I cannot walk without assistance nor use my arms, and I spend most of my time confined to bed by sickness'. She also said that much of her memory had faded with age, captivity and ill-health, and she hardly knew any longer how to act the queen, since it had been so long – nearly twenty years – since she had actually reigned. Although Mary vehemently contradicted the ludicrous notion that the English might have the right to try her because they had in ancient times claimed suzerainty over Scotland, which she claimed would dishonour the memory of her own ancestors, yet she freely admitted that she no longer wished to rule: 'My advancing age and bodily weakness both prevent me from wishing to resume the reins of government. I have perhaps only two or three years to live in this world, and I do not aspire to any public position, especially when I consider the pain and desperance which meet those who wish to do right, and act with justice and dignity in the midst of so perverse a generation, and when a whole world is full of crimes and troubles' – this was indeed the cry of sad, disillusioned middle-age.[12]

At this Cecil, either determined to make an impressive showing of his disapproval of the queen of Scots, or with his memory of those far-off days of the abortive Treaty of Edinburgh nearly thirty years before, in which he had been much involved, still burning in his mind, reproached Queen Mary with having assumed the English royal arms at the time of her French marriage and having thus attempted to usurp Elizabeth's throne.

Mary gave in reply her stock answer to this accusation: that being then very young, she had merely acted in obedience to the commands of her father-in-law, Henry II. To this Cecil retorted that she had later aggravated the offence by refusing to ratify the Treaty of Edinburgh in which her pretensions to the English throne were formally abandoned, and the argument then proceeded as often before on well-worn lines, except that Mary took care to reiterate at every turn the significance of her status as a queen, which meant that she could never be expected to cede her rights without receiving any concessions about the succession in return. Cecil now accused her of having personally coveted Elizabeth's throne, and Mary responded with a long and closely argued speech on the subject of the English royal succession, which she had evidently prepared carefully in advance, and may be regarded as incorporating her ultimate views on the subject. She made two main points: firstly, she had never at any time wished to usurp the English throne while Elizabeth lived; secondly, and in no way contradicting her previous point, she had 'no scruple of conscience in desiring the second rank as being the legitimate and nearest heir'. It was the right to inherit at the proper time rather than the right to reign immediately which Mary was not prepared to surrender.

The queen now went on to declare that although she knew that her enemies wished to compass her death by unlawful means, yet with God's help she would still manage to meet her end publicly, as a witness to the faith in which she believed. In a moving passage, which marked her out as far more tolerant than the age in which she lived, and contrasted with the sly venom of Cecil and the cold vindictiveness of Paulet, Mary gave her own philosophy of life, in which there was no place for revenge: 'I do not desire vengeance. I leave it to Him who is the just Avenger of the innocent and of those who suffer for His Name under whose power I will take shelter. I would rather pray with Esther than take the sword with Judith.' And she reminded the judges once more that she had come to England seeking Elizabeth's protection. Mary now attempted valiantly to combat the charges based on the cipher letters. She accused

Walsingham of inventing the ciphers and manufacturing the whole plot, and said that she had been warned long before from France to be on her guard against Ballard since he had 'great intelligence' with Walsingham. She repudiated her own letter to Babington in its entirety. She battled with Cecil in a game of wits in which Cecil denied that any Catholic had been put to death in England for religion merely, but only for treason against the queen. Walsingham, stung by Queen Mary's charges, made his own apologia, as vivid as Mary's own on the subject of vengeance, in which he drew a sharp distinction between public and private morality. 'God is my witness,' he declared, 'that as a private person I have done nothing unworthy of an honest man, and as a Secretary of State, nothing unbefitted of my duty.' Another topic discussed in this first day of the trial was that of Thomas Morgan, Mary's agent in France, now in prison there for his involvement in the Parry plot to assassinate Elizabeth. Cecil tried to make out that the fact that Morgan was her pensioner contaminated Mary with his guilt. Mary answered with some asperity that Morgan was not her pensioner, but merely someone to whom she had given money from time to time, much as England had subsidized the master of Gray, and many other Scots, including the king, James himself. It was a pertinent point.

The evidence of Nau and Curle was now examined in much detail; in vain the queen inquired angrily why the two secretaries themselves were not produced in court as witnesses, since their absence cast a sinister light on the truth of their depositions. Mary pointed out that as it was admitted that Nau had actually written the text of the letters in cipher, it would have been easy enough for him to have incorporated some extra matter without her knowledge, more especially since over the past year he had taken to doing the correspondence apart in his own little cabinet, giving the excuse that it was thus easier to compose and concentrate. 'Nau had many peculiarities, likings and intentions that I cannot mention in public,' added Mary darkly.[13] Despite this outburst, at heart Mary realized the truth about her secretaries, and even in this extremity was prepared to show the human understanding for which she was rightly famous; for she went on: 'For my part, I do not wish to accuse my secretaries, but I see plainly that what they have said is from fear of torture and death. Under promise of their lives and in order to save themselves, they have excused themselves at my expense, fancying that I could thereby more easily save myself, at the same time, not knowing where I was, and not suspecting the manner in which I am treated.' She also distinguished the betrayal of Nau from that of Curle, knowing the characters of both men, saying that if Curle had done anything wrong, he must have been forced into it by Nau. Mary and Cecil now argued about who had employed Nau – whether the fact that he was paid by the king of France might explain his disloyalty to Mary. Having made this point, however, Mary returned to her main thesis on the subject of the secretaries, that they themselves in person rather than their evidence should have been produced against her: 'If they were in my presence now they would clear me on the spot of all blame and would have put me out of case. ...' Mary was right in the importance she attached to the secretaries' evidence: Walsingham smugly reported to Leicester the next day that the fact that her own secretaries had testified against Mary was proof of her guilt, in the minds of even her friends on the commission.[14]

According to the physician Bourgoing's account, the whole trial now broke down into a bedlam of accusations on the part of Mary's judges: these *chicaneurs* (as he persistently termed them – pettifogging lawyers) attacked her like furies, sometimes one by one, sometimes all together, all shouting that she was guilty. When Mary returned to her own apartments, she was so exhausted that she told her own servants, without wishing to carry the comparison too far, that the whole scene had reminded her of the Passion of Christ: for the judges had treated her as the Jews treated Jesus, shouting at him *'Tolle, Tolle, Crucifige'*. And so ended the first day of the trial. The queen passed an anxious and sleepless night, and began the next day early praying in her private oratory.

As she entered the great hall on the second morning of her

ordeal, it was noticed that the queen was extremely pale. But her first action was to make it known that she wished to address the assembly personally. Curiosity to hear her was enormous, for over the years the legend of the imprisoned Scottish queen, whether a dragon or a captive princess, had grown quite sufficiently to arouse the keen interest of the spectators. Mary's first point was to protest strongly and movingly against the manner in which she had been treated on the previous day, being attacked on every issue, although she had only consented to answer accusations specifically related to the assassination plot against Elizabeth. Weak and ill as she was, she was alone among them, a sick woman, with no paper, no notes and no secretary, taken by surprise by a commission which had long been preparing such charges against her: under such circumstances she concluded 'there is not one, I think, among you, let him be the cleverest man you will, but would be incapable of resisting or defending himself were he in my place'.[15]

Strangely enough this speech met with a moderate reply from Cecil, in contrast to the roughness of the previous day. Bourgoing noted that the whole behaviour of the judges was now more courteous and that Cecil on several occasions gave them hints on how to proceed. Not only that, but servants, with the quick observation of those long imprisoned, noticed that many of the nobles had come to the assembly in riding-dress and boots, from which they deduced that the proceedings were already designed, willy-nilly, to end that day. The morning was spent in going over most of the main points again – the pretended overthrow of Elizabeth, Mary's correspondence with foreign princes and her attempts to be delivered from prison. Cecil took particular care to try and persuade Mary that she was being well treated, and that although she was only being examined on the subject of the assassination, all the other evidence had to be taken into account. Cecil concluded by saying that Mary had behaved particularly badly in seeking to escape at the exact moment when the last treaty for her freedom had been about to be concluded (he was referring to the Association with James) and sending Parry to kill Elizabeth. At this corruption of the truth, Mary burst out, 'Ah! You are indeed my adversary!' 'I am the adversary to the adversaries of Queen Elizabeth,' replied Cecil smoothly.[16]

The second stage of the trial concerned Mary's transference of the inheritance rights of the Scottish crown to Philip II. In a tone not unlike that of her cousin Elizabeth when her Commons grew too presumptuous, Mary sharply repudiated the right of the court even to consider this matter. It was true that as an English prisoner she hardly had much of a crown to offer, but in any case 'It is not your affair to speak of matters concerning princes, and to inquire whether they have secret intelligences with each other'. When Cecil questioned her as to how she would have acted if the Spanish army had arrived, Mary stuck to the answer that she was not answerable for the Spanish, and again and again declared: 'I desired nothing but my own deliverance.' Accusations were now piled on her head from the intended murder of the queen to the prayers said at Rome for Mary as the true queen of England. Throughout all these speeches, Mary adhered steadfastly to the statement that she had neither planned nor known of any lethal enterprise. She appealed to her own reputation for mercy and how in Scotland she had always been blamed for being so tolerant to the Protestants: 'It has been the cause of my ruin,' she reflected sadly, 'for my subjects became sad and haughty and abused my clemency; indeed they now complain that they were never so well off as under my government.'[17]

In short Mary took her stand on the two things which she had always desired, and freely admitted to having done so – her own deliverance and the support of the Catholic cause in England. Beyond these aims, she no longer wished for anything, neither honours nor kingdoms; and in defence of this last aim she was prepared to die. If the Pope in Rome had chosen to give her the title of queen of England, it was not for her to correct him. As for the famous bull, she herself had offered to prevent its execution. Yet she felt herself more than ever as one with the whole Catholic community in England, whose prayers were sustaining her, and against whose cruel persecution she once more vigorously protested. The queen's last demand was to be granted a full hearing in front of Parliament, instead of being limited to this unjust trial, and to be permitted to confer personally with Queen Elizabeth. Mary then rose. As she proceeded from her chair, she regarded the whole assembly, and most regally declared that she pardoned them for what they had done. Mary then had a few private words with Walsingham, which seemed to displease him, for she once more turned and addressed the assembly as a whole: 'My lords and gentlemen, I place my cause in the hands of God.' As the queen passed the table full of lawyers she permitted herself a last little pleasantry: she called on God to pardon them for the way they had treated her – 'somewhat rudely', as she put it – and she added with a smile: 'May God keep me from having to do with you all again.' At this the lawyers also exchanged smiles.[18]

In answer to the express wish of Elizabeth who wanted no sentence pronounced before she herself had considered the proceedings, the court was now prorogued, to meet in ten days' time at the Star Chamber at Westminster. The noblemen, booted and spurred in advance, rode away from Fotheringhay. Mary was left to go back once more to the little round of captivity. Her tranquillity was not in the slightest disturbed by the harrowing ordeal through which she had just passed. It was as though she had predicted long ago in her own mind the course which events were likely to take and had even found in the working out of her prophecies, melancholy as they were, a source of strength. Just as the populace had been curious to see the baleful queen of Scots, Mary herself had derived some minor enjoyment from this brief glimpse of English society – the only true sight of it she ever had. Throughout the trial she questioned Paulet concerning the faces of various English gentlemen among the judges, many of whose names had been long familiar to her. After so many years of virtual solitude the crowded court scene brought at least the compensation of satisfying her curiosity about England.

Paulet of course found her conduct at the trial utterly distasteful: to his way of thinking, the queen of Scots was never more odious than when displaying the full counterfeit charm of her character. He wrote to London that her intention had been by 'long and artificial speeches' to excite the pity of the judges, and throw all the blame on Elizabeth, or rather, upon her Council. Whereas Mary told her servants she had discerned expressions of compassion among the crowd, Paulet cheered himself with the reflection that they had all been 'of one consent and mind to hear her cause with indifference'.[19] But to those less prejudiced than the queen's jailer, and to those who would come after him and attempt to pass the judgement of history upon the Scottish queen, Mary would elicit not so much pity as profound admiration for the cool and clever manner in which she had single-handedly conducted her defence against all the odds. In her *Essay on Adversity* she had referred to the 'disagreeable and ugly slough of pusillanimity', the one pitfall into which those called by God to wield the sceptre should never fall.[20] It was not a trap into which Mary had fallen herself. Throughout her trial she had shown herself unwaveringly regal, and not all the petty spite of Paulet could take this triumph from her.

The next few weeks represented a strangely serene interlude in Mary's life, the Indian summer of her captivity, when she was able to add to the self-discipline of the long-held prisoner the peace of mind of one who knew her confinement was rapidly moving towards its finish. Mary now read much concerning English history, a habit she had already begun to develop at Chartley, since the inventory of her belongings in June 1586 mentions a number of books on the subject as well as a map. She embroidered. She made arrangements in her own mind for the final journey she was now convinced lay ahead. Bourgoing found her so far from being troubled by what had passed that 'I had not seen her so joyous, nor so constantly at her ease for the last seven years. She spoke only on pleasant subjects, and often in particular, gave her opinion on some points of the history of England, in the study of which she passed a good portion of the day, afterwards discoursing on the subject of her reading with her household, quite familiarly and joyously, showing no signs of sadness, but with even a more cheerful countenance than previous to her troubles.'²¹ It was clear that Mary's words at her trial were no hypocrisy – she truly did not fear to die in a good cause. Mary, like many other philosopher-prisoners, took comfort in the perusal of the past, from whose study one lesson can always be learnt: that the single action of a human being, be it a heroic life or a noble death, can have incalculable effects upon the course of history.

On 25th October the commissioners met again in the Star Chamber in London. On this occasion Nau and Curle were actually produced, raising once more the question why in all decency they could not have appeared at Fotheringhay. Both reaffirmed their evidence on oath and stated that they had given it 'frankly and voluntarily'. The commission accordingly found Mary guilty of 'compassing and imagining since June 1st matters tending to the death and destruction of the Queen of England'. Only Lord Zouch, a youngish peer, who had lived through a somewhat wild youth in which he spent his patrimony, had the courage to express himself not altogether satisfied. The commission took particular trouble to except King James from his mother's guilt since, by the terms of the Act of Association, her disablement from the succession would have applied also to her son. The two Houses of Parliament now presented an address to Queen Elizabeth in which they prayed fervently for the execution of the Scottish queen for the sake of Elizabeth's own safety which would be in peril 'so long as the said Scottish Queen shall be suffered to continue and shall not receive that due punishment, which by justice and the laws of this your realm she hath so often and for so many ways for her most detestable and wicked offences deserved'. Elizabeth replied in a long and ambivalent speech in which she showed how much she personally was aware, even if her Commons were not, that 'we princes are set as it were upon stages, in the sight and view of all the world' and that the execution of Mary was one thing for the Commons to demand, quite another for Elizabeth, a fellow-queen, to confirm.²² Twelve days later, Elizabeth, having indicated that it would be highly desirable in any case to secure a full confession from the queen of Scots, asked her two Houses with further ambiguity whether they could not devise some better remedy whereby the queen of Scots' life might be spared and her own security provided for.

Mary herself was not immediately informed that the sentence of death had been passed against her in London. In the meantime Paulet endeavoured to carry out his instructions from London and secure that full confession, that humiliating pleading for pardon from the Scottish queen, for which the English queen so passionately wished. On 1st November, the Feast of All Saints, which Mary spent in prayer and reading the lives of the saints since she was still deprived of her chaplain, de Préau, she received a visit from Paulet after dinner. Paulet showed unexpected courtesy in actually waiting until her prayers were over. They argued a little on the subject of history. Mary observed how blood never ceased to flow in the course of English history, and Paulet commented that this was the same in many countries, especially in time of national peril. Mary then inquired after one or two people at her trial whom she had imagined to be sympathetic to her, and asked their names that she might remember them. 'Not one of them was favourable to your cause,' said Paulet crossly. 'And everyone else is astonished to see you so calm under the circumstances in which you find yourself. No living person has ever been accused of crimes so frightful and odious as yours.' But Mary was not disposed to admit in any way to these frightful and odious crimes. Instead she reiterated her claim that she stood witness for the truths of the Catholic religion, and argued with Paulet about whether or not Elizabeth claimed to be supreme head of the Church. Paulet maintained that Elizabeth was on the contrary 'head and governor under God of things ecclesiastical and temporal in England', but Mary dismissed the difference between the two titles in an expressive French phrase: '*C'était manteau blanc ou blanc manteau*,' she remarked. Paulet was obliged to report back to London his disappointment: 'I see no change in her, from her former quietness and serenity, certified in my letters,' he

wrote. In the meantime Paulet greatly disliked these battles of
wits, in which he could scarcely hold himself to be the winner.
He told Walsingham: 'I pray you let me hear from you whether
it is expected that I should see my charge often, which as I do
not desire to do, so I do not see that any good can come of
it.'²³

On the evening of 19th November, Lord Buckhurst, who
had arrived at Fotheringhay with Beale, the clerk of the Council,
delivered his message to Mary. Buckhurst now warned Mary
that it was considered impossible that both she and Elizabeth
should continue to live. Although Elizabeth had not given her
consent to the execution, Buckhurst solemnly called on Mary to
repent; to that end he offered her the services of a Protestant
clergyman, the bishop or dean of Peterborough. Mary described
the whole interview in her letter to Beaton in Paris at the end
of November. 'I thanked God and them,' she wrote proudly,
'for the honour they did me in considering me to be such a
necessary instrument for the re-establishing of religion in this
island. ... In confirmation of all this as I had before protested,
I offered willingly to shed my blood in the quarrel of the
Catholic Church.' This was of course the very last answer which
Paulet and Buckhurst were prepared to receive: they told Mary
roughly that as she was to die for the intended murder of
Elizabeth, she would certainly not be regarded as either a saint
or a martyr. But Mary was quite intelligent enough to see that
despite Paulet's protests matters were going in the direction she
hoped. It was no wonder Camden heard that her face was now
illumined with extraordinary joy at the thought that God had
thus chosen her to be a martyr. It was left to Paulet to castigate
her speeches angrily in his report to London as 'superfluous
and idle', and tell Walsingham that he had no doubt Buckhurst
too had found the queen of Scots' endless speech-making
extremely tedious.²⁴

Such pieces of oratory might be superfluous and idle to Paulet
but to Mary they were essential planks in the platform from
which she intended to undergo her martyrdom for the Catholic
faith: Paulet's opinion was a matter of indifference to her, so

long as her words would one day echo forth in the theatre of the world. But Paulet's next action – the removal of the royal cloth of state over Mary's chair, by which she set such store – offended her in the vital matter of her queenship. The reasons which Paulet gave hardly added to the grace of the occasion: 'You are now only a dead woman,' he said, 'without the dignity or honours of a Queen.' Mary responded with a spirited defence of her station, in which her studies in English history prompted her to compare herself to King Richard II in the hands of his enemies. Her own attendants refused to obey Paulet's command to remove the canopy, so that it had to be thrown down by his own men. Paulet now added insult to injury by sitting in the queen's presence with his head covered, and furthermore ordering the removal of the royal billiard table, on the grounds that it was now no time for the queen to be indulging in amusement. However, it would seem from Paulet's own account of the scene that he had exceeded his instructions to a certain extent; the removal of the canopy was due to his own excess of zeal, prompted rather by a rumour from London that Elizabeth disliked the idea of the canopy, than by the specific instructions of the English queen. The next day Paulet went to Mary and offered to write to London for official leave to restore the canopy, saying it had been removed on the Council's orders. This merely gave Mary opportunity to point sublimely to the symbol which she had already hung in the place of the vanished cloth of state – a crucifix. In her own words to Henry of Guise, 'I showed them the Cross of my Saviour in the place where my canopy had been'.⁵

It was now the end of November. Mary imagined that her days were truly numbered. She spent two days writing her farewell letters, with a hand crippled by rheumatism.* She wrote to the Pope at length, professing the truth of the Catholic faith by which she had always lived, and towards which she had ever

---

* These letters, which Mary handed to her servants to deliver, did not reach their destinations until the following autumn, owing to the long imprisonment of these servants after their mistress's death.

done her duty in the past, so far as the dour conditions of captivity and illness had enabled her. Now, however, she was to be granted a supreme opportunity, as the one remaining Catholic member of the royal house of England and Scotland, to testify on behalf of her religion by her death 'for my sins and those of this unfortunate island'.[26] Religious rather than dynastic interests were now paramount in her mind, and it was the Catholic faith, rather than maternal feelings, which now swayed Mary in the dispositions she laid down for the English throne after her death: she begged the Pope to let the Catholic king of Spain secure her rights to the crown of England, in place of James, if he remained obstinately outside the Catholic Church.

Another letter went to Mendoza, that companion of her intrigues, now in Paris, assuring him that she had all the courage necessary to receive her sentence for the honour of God.[27] To Mendoza, Mary repeated solemnly her bestowal of the rights of the English throne upon the Spanish king if James did not embrace the Catholic religion. She recommended to him her poor destitute servants, including Leslie, the bishop of Ross, whom she had heard was in dire straits, and bequeathed to Mendoza, who had cared so prolongedly and so passionately for the cause of her deliverance, the diamond which Norfolk had given her so long ago. Lastly Mary wrote to her cousin, Henry of Guise, whom she now held to be her closest blood relation since the betrayal of James and addressing him 'as you whom I hold as dearest to me in the world'. To him once more she stressed the nobility of the end which awaited her: 'Although no executioner has ever before dipped his hand in our (Guise) blood, be not ashamed of it, my dear friend, for the condemnation of heretics and enemies of the Church (and who have no jurisdiction over me, a free Queen) is profitable before God for the children of His Church.' As for the Faith: 'I esteem myself born, both on the paternal and the maternal side to offer my blood for it. ...'[28] Yet lest the full details of her martyrdom should be concealed by the English, and because not everything could be trusted to letters, Mary begged Henry of Guise and

Mendoza to listen carefully to the eye-witness accounts of her own servants after her death, when they should manage to deliver them.

As she wrote, Queen Mary could hear the banging of the workmen in the great hall of the Council. She imagined quite genuinely that she was listening to the sound of her own scaffold being erected. She mentioned the subject to Mendoza as she wrote: 'I think they are making a scaffold to make me play the last scene of the Tragedy. ...' In fact it was to be over two months before this final scene was actually played. The reason of course was that Elizabeth obstinately hesitated to confirm the sentence. The most the Parliament could secure from her was the public proclamation of the sentence of death on 4th December, on the understanding of which Parliament was prorogued till the spring. The English people might rejoice and ring their bells at the news, but their queen was still very far from resolving her own dilemma. Quite apart from the fact that Mary was an anointed queen and her own cousin, there were the problems of foreign relations to consider. How would France, where Mary had once been queen, react to the news of her death – and still more Scotland, where Mary had once actually reigned, and her own son now ruled. As the prospect of war with Spain loomed nearer, the goodwill of France and the continuance of the alliance with Scotland became more important than mere diplomatic friendship. Were such vital benevolences really worth sacrificing for the death of one old and sick woman, who had been a prisoner for nearly twenty years? It was Mary the prisoner at Fotheringhay who was calm and tranquil, who wrote her letters, considered how she could best dispose her affairs for her servants, contemplated her crucifix, and showed herself more joyous than she had been for years. It was Elizabeth the jailer, in London, muttering to herself *Aut fer aut feri, ne feriare, feri* – suffer or strike, strike or be struck – who suffered the torments of indecision.

CHAPTER TWENTY-SIX
The Dolorous Stroke

Rue not my death, rejoice at my repose
It was no death to me but to my woe;
The bud was opened to let out the rose,
The chain was loosed to let the captive go.
From Decease, release, *ode by Robert Southwell, SJ,*
on the death of Mary Queen of Scots

When King James first heard the news of his mother's arrest at Chartley, he contented himself with observing that she should 'drink the ale she had brewed' and in future be allowed to meddle with nothing except prayer and the service of God.[1] Not only did he ostentatiously ignore the possibility that his mother might now be in danger of her life, but he also chose this moment to sound out Elizabeth on the question of a marriage between them, through the medium of Archibald Douglas. Elizabeth was now over fifty, thirty years senior to James, and, although James was evidently prepared to pardon the disparity in their ages most magnanimously if he could thus strengthen his claim to the English throne, Elizabeth herself showed no inclination towards this bizarre union.[2] Nevertheless throughout the autumn James continued to maintain in public that he had no objections to his mother being imprisoned in the most rigorous manner in the world – let her be put in the Tower or some other 'firm Manse' – so long as her actual life was not forfeited. It was not until after the trial and death sentence that it was made clear to James by Archibald Douglas from London that he might shortly have to choose between his mother's life and the continuation of the newly formed Anglo-

Scottish alliance, which in turn involved his hopes of inheriting the English throne.

James's dilemma in Scotland did not cause him the human anguish which Elizabeth in her reluctance to confirm the death sentence was undergoing in England. She told the French ambassador at the beginning of December that she had never shed so many tears over anything, not even at the deaths of her father, her brother Edward or her sister Mary, as at what she termed this 'unfortunate affair', and whether her grief was at her own indecision or at the prospect of shedding Mary's blood, there is no reason to doubt the genuineness of her emotion.[3] James, on the other hand, felt considerable perplexity as to what course to take, but no purely personal feelings; the chief concern of the Scottish mission to Elizabeth in November was to ensure that nothing would be done against Mary 'to the prejudice of any title of the King's'. In the meantime it was widely rumoured in Scotland that James feared to request any sort of favour from Elizabeth as regards Mary, lest he should lose the goodwill of the English queen, although Scottish public opinion was reacting most strongly to the idea that their former sovereign should be executed by a foreign country. As Gray wrote to Douglas on 23rd November, James would find it hard to keep the peace if her life were touched. 'I never saw all the people so willing to concur in anything as in this. They that hated most her prosperity regret her adversity.' James himself pointed out his invidious position to Elizabeth in language which made clear that it was fear of a national outcry which animated him, rather than some more personal emotion: 'Guess ye in what strait my honour will be, this disaster being perfected,' he wrote, 'since before God I already scarce dare go abroad, for crying out of the whole people.'[4]

Despite these fears, the one sanction which James had it in his power to invoke to save his mother's life – and which in the opinion of at least one historian would have effectively preserved her from execution at English hands[5] – was never made. James hovered over the subject of the death sentence with a series of dire but meaningless threats. At no point did he say that he would break the Anglo-Scottish league if his mother's death was brought about by England, although Elizabeth anxiously inquired of his ambassadors whether that was in fact his intention. His fulminations and his embassy were both intended to save his face in Scotland; they were not intended to save his mother's life in England. Nor did all his emissaries agree with Gray in expressing their disgust at the idea of the execution: Sir Alexander Stewart expressed the damaging view that James would somehow manage to digest his mother's death.* Once it became apparent to the English that despite all James's protests the league was to be considered inviolable whatever action they took against Mary, the date of the Scottish queen's death drew appreciably nearer.

The protests made by the French were more authentically passionate, but proved in the end equally ineffective: a special ambassador, de Bellievre, was sent by King Henry III to plead with Elizabeth who was answered, in Cecil's words, 'that if the French King understood her Majesty's peril, if he loveth her as he pretendeth, he would not press her Majesty to hazard her life'. The resident French ambassador, Châteauneuf, continued to make valiant efforts to save Mary, but in January his attempts were sharply curtailed by the fortunate discovery by Walsingham of yet another plot against Elizabeth's life. This providential coincidence led to Châteauneuf's house arrest, and rendered him impotent to help Mary further during the crucial weeks in the new year; it also aroused a wave of anti-French feeling in England – although the plot itself was highly dubious in origins, and seems to have been largely concocted by Walsingham to produce these precise effects.[7] In December Cecil had drawn up in his own handwriting a list of reasons against the execution of the queen of Scots. Among the reasons cited was the cogent argument *Sanguis sanguinem procreat* – blood breeds blood – the supposition that Mary's health was in any case so afflicted that

---

* Dr D. H. Willson, in his biography of James I, thinks it not impossible that Stewart had secret instructions over Gray's head on the subject; in spite of James's publicly expressed anger at Stewart's statements, Stewart was allowed to return to Scotland with impunity.[6]

she might die naturally at any moment, and the fact that the king of France had promised to go surety in the future for the end of the attempts on Elizabeth's life.[8] By January, it appeared that as Mary's foreign champions had either retired or were being swept from the lists, the fact that blood might breed blood was no longer so important.

There was certainly to be no question of the captive eluding her fate: at Paulet's request the garrison at Fotheringhay was strengthened by seventy foot-soldiers and fifty bowmen. In November Paulet had been joined in his charge by Sir Drue Drury. In mid-December Mary sent for both her custodians, and asked them to dispatch on her behalf a farewell letter to Elizabeth. Dramatically, Mary wiped her cheeks with both sheets, in order to show that the leaves were not poisoned. She then sealed the letter with Spanish wax and closed it with white silk.[9] Mary's main points to Elizabeth concerned firstly the disposal of her body after death – she was anxious that her servants should be allowed to convey it to France, rather than Scotland, where the Protestant burial rites would constitute a profanation by her standards; secondly she expressed her fears of the 'secret tyrannies' of those whom Elizabeth had placed around her, which she dreaded would result in her secret assassination; thirdly Mary asked to be allowed to send a jewel and last farewell to her son James; finally Mary raised once more the vexed question of the royal dais. She concluded on a magisterial note of warning to Elizabeth: 'Do not accuse me of presumption if, on the eve of leaving this world and preparing myself for a better one, I remind you that one day you will have to answer for your charge, as well as those that are sent before. ...' Mary signed the letter: 'Your sister and cousin, wrongfully imprisoned.'[10]

Despite the innocuous character of Mary's last requests, Paulet and Drury did not immediately dispatch this missive, not so much out of fear of Elizabeth's anger, as out of dread that its mildness might move the English queen to clemency, and further delay the execution of justice. Paulet confided to Davison, the secretary of the Council, that as they were strongly hoping the sentence would be carried out before Christmas, it was planned that the letter should arrive a few days afterwards, when the queen of Scots would be already dead and it would be too late for Elizabeth to exercise mercy. In Paulet's opinion, there were many pressing reasons why the sentence should be carried out as fast as possible, not the least among them being the return of Mary's priest (or almoner as she always termed him) de Préau.[11]

On de Préau's arrival, Paulet took the precaution of searching his papers, and was rewarded by finding two leaves of paper in the form of a diary inserted among his philosophical exercises; luckily he decided de Préau was of no particular account – being 'of weak and slender judgment'. All the same, for what he chose to describe as Christian reasons, Paulet wished that de Préau had been restricted to a single visit to the queen on the eve of her death: the spiritual perils of his continual association with his mistress seemed yet another reason for bringing Mary's life to a speedy close. After all, expostulated Paulet, Mary showed no signs of repentance, no signs even of wishing to live, and an ignorant papist priest would surely only confirm her in such reprobate tendencies. The return of the little store of money which had been seized from Mary at Chartley, although performed by Paulet with some reluctance, seemed a minor evil compared to this quite unnecessary display of tolerance on behalf of the central government.

Around Christmas Paulet either fell ill or pleaded a diplomatic illness to avoid those argumentative interviews with Mary which he so greatly disliked. Paulet's withdrawal affected Mary herself depressively: Paulet might dread the interviews, but to Mary they were her solitary contact with the outside world, and represented her only source of stimulus, to rehearse her arguments, and in arguing to keep up her spirits. The weeks now passed slowly and heavily; without Paulet to joust with verbally, for the first time Mary began to feel the suspense of her situation. By 8th January Mary was begging Paulet to pay her another visit, for although both were within the confines of the same castle, she had not seen him since before Christmas, and as to his illness she had heard he had been out of doors the previous day. Part of Mary's anxiety arose through having heard nothing from Elizabeth in answer to her farewell requests. On 12th January she wrote another long letter, in which she pleaded with Elizabeth to end the miserable uncertainty of the situation, not so much for herself as for her poor servants, on whom the strain was telling. In her last paragraph she even tried to tempt Elizabeth's curiosity once more by inquiring to whom she might confide her death-bed's secrets; it was as though the notion of the unfulfilled meeting still haunted her after all these years, and she had some wild hope that Elizabeth might still pay her a personal visit at the end. The bait, however, was never extended where Elizabeth might see it for Paulet refused to dispatch this second letter at all, on the grounds that he was lying in bed with his arms bandaged, and that Mary must content herself with awaiting the answer to her first missive. Later he explained that he would not send the letter at all, because he had no orders to do so.[12]

Slowly the winter days passed by. It was now over three months since those booted and spurred judges had galloped away from Fotheringhay and there was still no news from London that the end was even near. It was inevitable that the hopes of those faithful partisans and observers, Mary's servants, should begin to rise. Although Mary had no doubts herself that sooner or later she would die, when Christmas had passed, the long delay encouraged her retainers to begin to hope on her behalf. On 20th January Melville interpreted a remark of Paulet's on the subject of the royal servants' wages as meaning that the period of their service to Mary was likely to be extended indefinitely into the future. This made the blow which fell upon them the next day all the more painful to bear: brusquely Paulet informed Melville and the chaplain de Préau that although they were to continue in residence at Fotheringhay, henceforth they were to be parted from their mistress. Only the physician Bourgoing was to be allowed to continue in attendance. The removal of these loyal servants lowered Mary's spirits further: her old fears of a secret death were revivified. But when Mary expressed these anxieties to Paulet through the medium of Bourgoing, she succeeded in causing him considerable offence: he fell into a rage at her taunts, and told Bourgoing that 'he was a man of honour and a gentleman, and he would not wish so to dishonour himself as to wish to exercise such cruelty or to conduct himself like a Turk'.[13] Man of honour as he professed himself – and time was to prove the truth of his claim – Paulet had no objections to imposing a series of further petty humiliations on his prisoner. On the following Monday Mary's butler was forbidden to carry the rod before her meat dishes, a service he was performing in the absence of the steward Melville. Once again Mary jumped to the conclusion that this regal dignity was being stripped from her in order to kill her secretly. In answer to her protest she received the chilling reply from Paulet that her priest, her steward, her canopy and her rod had all been taken from her for the same reason: because she was no longer a queen but 'an attainted, convicted and condemned woman'. It was left for Mary to derive what consolation she could from the reflection that King Richard II also had been treated in this opprobrious manner.

Attainted, convicted and condemned Mary might be, yet there was still no official word concerning her execution. But it was said afterwards that on the Sunday, 29th January, between midnight and one o'clock in the morning, the heavens gave their own portent that the end was not far off, for a great flame of fire illuminated the windows of the queen's room three times. The light was bright enough to read by, and blinded the guards stationed beneath her chamber, already made nervous and apprehensive by the phenomenon, which was seen nowhere else in the castle.[14] This supernatural warning,* if warning it was, was certainly borne out by events. Three days later, at her court at Greenwich, Queen Elizabeth at last sent for Davison to bring the warrant for the execution, which for so long had lacked her

---

* A more rational explanation might be that the mysterious fire was produced by a comet. In Elizabethan England, comets were traditionally associated with the deaths of famous people, or as Shakespeare put it in *Julius Caesar:* 'When beggars die, there are no comets seen; the heavens themselves blaze forth the deaths of princes.'[1]

own signature. Davison discreetly placed the warrant in the middle of a pile of other papers which the queen was due to sign. The ruse – for Elizabeth had made it increasingly clear to her anxious ministers that she must be the subject of a ruse – was successful. It was thus, in the midst of an innocuous conversation on the subject of the weather, that Elizabeth finally signed the warrant, with all her other papers, and having done so, threw them idly down on the table. But the queen could not quite bear to let this vexatious yet momentous subject, on which she had expended so much emotion, pass so easily. She asked Davison teasingly if he felt distressed to see her give the famous signature after so long. Davison replied tactfully that he preferred to see the death of a guilty person to that of an innocent one. Elizabeth now instructed Davison to get the Great Seal of England attached to the warrant by the Lord Chancellor and then take it to Walsingham. Her vein of humour was not exhausted: 'I fear the grief thereof will go near to kill him outright,' said Elizabeth happily. She then concluded the subject with a practical direction – the execution was under no circumstances to be held in public, but in the great hall of the castle. Elizabeth then laid it down that she personally was to be told no more on the subject until the execution was successfully completed.[16]

Despite this Pilate-like observation, Elizabeth still did not totally wash her hands of the matter. Mary's fears of a secret death were not altogether groundless. Even before Elizabeth had affixed her signature to the warrant, she had been heard muttering in the hearing of her ministers that the provisions of the Act of Association might make it a positive duty for a loyal subject to kill the queen of Scots ... thus ridding the English queen of the responsibility. Her ministers, understanding her intentions only too well, pretended not to grasp her meaning. On 1st February, however, Elizabeth was more explicit. Having signed the warrant she murmured wistfully to Davison that if a loyal subject were to save her from embarrassment by dealing the blow, the resentment of France and Scotland might be disarmed. The obvious loyal subjects to assume this helpful role were Paulet and Drury at Fotheringhay. Davison's first reaction was to fear yet another excuse for delaying the execution itself. But against his advice, the queen insisted on the point being made to Paulet: a letter was duly sent to the custodians regretting that they had not 'found out some way to shorten the life of that Queen [Mary] considering the great peril she [Elizabeth] is subject unto hourly, so long as the said Queen shall live'.[17]

Now the issue which Mary had so long dreaded was squarely placed before her jailer; and it is one of the ironies of history that Paulet, the man whom Mary had for so long both disliked and feared, hesitated for an instant, but seized his pen and wrote back to his royal mistress in the most trenchant language refusing the odious commission: 'I am so unhappy to have lived to see this unhappy day,' he replied, 'in which I am required by direction from my most gracious sovereign to do an act which God and the law forbiddeth. ... God forbid that I should make so foul a shipwreck of my conscience, or leave so great a blot on my poor posterity, to shed blood without law or warrant.'[18] Paradoxically Mary was saved from the private extinction which she dreaded by the action of the Puritan who had done so much to make her last months uncomfortable and humiliating. Elizabeth, on the other hand, by a course of action which did neither her courage, her character nor her reputation any credit, gave Paulet a chance to redeem himself at the bar of history – unimaginative, bigoted, petty tyrant be might be, he was still no assassin. It was left to Elizabeth when his answer was conveyed to her to exclaim furiously over his 'daintiness', the 'niceness' of 'those precise fellows' such as Paulet, who professed great zeal for her safety, but would perform nothing.[19]

Elizabeth's Council, experienced in the ways of their mistress, did not wait for Paulet's answer before acting. With the warrant in their possession, it was unanimously decided to set proceedings in hand immediately. Elizabeth's ability to continue to toy with the subject despite her signature was confirmed on 5th February when she told Davison roguishly that she had dreamt the night before she was running him through with a sword for causing the death of Mary. Her interest in assassination was also not exhausted: she appeared to play with the idea of having Mary smothered by Robert Wingfield, pretending that this had been the advice of Archibald Douglas. The Council did not wait to see through the full comedy of such behaviour before acting. The warrant was handed to Beale, the clerk of the Council, who was instructed to set forth immediately for Fotheringhay, accompanied by Shrewsbury and the earl of Kent, with a covering commission to go into Hertfordshire and Bedfordshire to hear 'hues and cries', in order to cloak his mission in the utmost secrecy.* The greatest thought was given to the details of the execution in Walsingham's memorial on the subject – down to the speeches which the two earls were to make at the ceremony. Cecil added his own comment on the subject in the margin of the memorial: the speeches should be used 'To express her many attempts both for destruction of the Queen's person, and the invasion of this realm'.[20]

More practical aspects of the affair were not neglected. Walsingham made himself responsible for contacting the actual executioner. In the greatest secrecy, his servant Anthony Hall acquired the services of one Bull, £10 being the agreed fee for 'his labour'. Another of Walsingham's servants, Digby, conducted Bull down to Fotheringhay, disguised as a serving-man with 'his instrument' – the axe – hidden in a trunk. Such efficiency resulted in the smooth working of all the preliminary arrangements, except that Sir Walter Mildmay, whether out of fear of public opinion, apprehension regarding Elizabeth's reactions, or genuine fastidiousness, refused to house the executioner at his own house of Apethorpe, so that he had to be lodged secretly in an inn at Fotheringhay. On arrival, in order to give every appearance of legality to the proceedings, Beale

---

* Afterward Beale believed that this mission had fatally blighted his career: in 1599 he attributed his failure to find advancement 'for that my name was made odious to the whole world for conveying down the Commission for the execution of the Scottish Queen'.

took care to inform the local justices of the peace and officials, both of Northamptonshire and Huntingdon, including the sheriff of Northampton who was to be responsible for providing the surgeons for the occasion.[21]

Still the sadly depleted royal household at Fotheringhay had no inkling of what was afoot. On the Saturday, 4th February, Bourgoing went to Paulet and asked if he could go visit the neighbouring villages and search for certain herbal remedies which might help the queen against her rheumatism for the rest of the winter season. Paulet was evasive, and said he could take no decision until the Monday. On Sunday, however, Mary learnt that Beale had arrived at Fotheringhay and, interpreting the significance of his arrival correctly, told Bourgoing he might cease searching for a cure since she would now have no need of it. But no authoritative intimation was given to the queen concerning her fate, which left her servants free to continue to hope for the next few days. It was not until the Tuesday, 7th February, that the arrival of several more people at the castle, including Shrewsbury and Kent who had been lodging at Orton nearby, 'threw the household into a terrible state of apprehension. Having for the last three months imagined many coming evils for Her Majesty,' as Bourgoing put it,[22] there could now be no doubt that the blow so long anticipated was about to fall.

The official time given to the queen to prepare for death was of the minimum. It was not until after dinner that the two custodians and the two earls asked to see Mary. She had retired to bed, but on being told that the matter was urgent, asked for a little time in which to dress, and then received them in her room, seated in a chair at the foot of her bed. Of the deputation, including Beale, it was Shrewsbury who told Mary that she had been found guilty and condemned to death. Beale now read aloud from the warrant, from which the yellow wax Great Seal of England dangled, in order to emphasize once more that Mary's judges were acting legally, in accordance with the Act of Association. Mary received the news with absolute calm. When

Beale had done, she replied with great dignity and no show of emotion: 'I thank you for such welcome news. You will do me great good in withdrawing me from this world out of which I am very glad to go.' She touched on her queenly position and royal blood, adding that in spite of this 'all my life I have had only sorrow', and saying that she was now overjoyed to have the opportunity at the end to shed her blood for the Catholic Church. Mary then placed her hand on the New Testament and solemnly protested herself to be innocent of all the crimes imputed to her. When Kent objected that it was a Catholic version of the Bible, Mary answered: 'If I swear on the book which I believe to be the true version, will your lordship not believe my oath more than if I were to swear on a translation in which I do not believe?'

But Mary's captors were not prepared to concede either the sincerity of her religious convictions or the need to display a certain tolerance towards a woman *in extremis*. They now offered her the services of the Protestant dean of Peterborough to help her make ready for her end, and eliminate from her mind at the last 'the follies and abominations of popery'. Mary crossed herself, and utterly refused even to consider the suggestion, saying that when she had first arrived in England she had listened to both sides of the question, but now all that was passed, and the hour of her death was the very moment to show constancy. The result of this interchange, in which as Paulet reported afterwards 'we prevailed nothing', was that when Mary proceeded to ask for her own chaplain to be readmitted to her presence, in order to make ready her soul, in Paulet's words 'we utterly denied that unto her'. This was a serious blow to Mary, who had not anticipated this final inhumanity. However, when Kent exclaimed: 'Your life would be the death of our religion, your death would be its life,' her face lit up.[23] At least his words revealed that already in the opinion of the world her death was linked with the survival of the Catholic Church in England.

When the queen asked at what hour she was to die, Shrewsbury replied in a faltering voice: 'Tomorrow morning at eight

o'clock.'* Mary remarked that the time was very short since it
was already late. She then made a series of requests, all of which
were denied to her: she applied for her papers and account
books, which were refused on the grounds that they were still
in London in the hands of Wade; once more she begged vainly
for her chaplain; thirdly she asked that her body might be
interred in France at either St Denis or Rheims, only to be told
that Elizabeth had ruled against it. Her last questions were on
the subjects of Nau and Curle, and whether they were already
dead; on hearing that Curle was in prison, and that Nau had
gone to France, Mary exclaimed sadly that she was about to die
for him who had borne false witness against her. Mary's servants,
in a state of hysteria, tried to get some sort of reprieve or at
least a stay of execution, weeping and crying and protesting that
the time was too short. Bourgoing pleaded with Shrewsbury,
recalling not only how he had cured him of his illness, but also
all the mercies which Shrewsbury himself had shown to Mary
in the past. Shrewsbury either was not or dared not be moved.
He said there was to be no delay.[24]

The queen of Scots was left alone to spend the last evening
of her life with her servants, some of whom like Jane Kennedy
had spent a whole generation in her service. She tried to rally
them. 'Well, Jane Kennedy,' said the queen. 'Did I not tell you
this would happen? ... I knew they would never allow me to
live, I was too great an obstacle to their religion.' Mary then
asked for her supper to be served as speedily as possible, in
order that she might have time to put her affairs in order. It
was a heart-breaking meal, the servants outdoing themselves in
the assiduousness of their service, as though there was some
comfort to be had in making each little gesture as perfect as
possible: Bourgoing, acting as steward in Melville's absence,
presented the dishes to his mistress and, as he did so, he could
not control the tears from pouring down his cheeks. The queen
herself ate little. She sat in a sort of dream, from time to time

* In fact, so far as can be made out from divergent accounts, the queen did not
die at 8 a.m., but later.

referring to Kent's outburst on the subject of her death and her religion: 'Oh how happy these words make me,' she murmured. 'Here at last is the truth.' When the meal was over, the queen asked her servants to drink to her, and as they did so, kneeling before her, their tears mingled with the wine.

Mary now seated herself and went through the contents of her wardrobe in detail. Her remaining money she sorted personally into little portions, and placed in packets, on which she wrote in her own hand the name of the servant for whom they were destined. From belongings she divided off certain mementoes for royalties and her relations abroad, such as the king and queen of France, Queen Catherine, and the Guises; from the rest she bestowed numerous little personal objects on all her servants:* Bourgoing received rings, silver boxes, her musicbook bound in velvet to remind him of the many musical evenings of the captivity, as well as the red hangings of Mary's bed; Elizabeth Curle received miniatures set in gold and enamelled tablets of Mary, Francis II and James; Melville received a little tablet of gold set with another portrait of James. Having thus disposed of those actual physical possessions which remained within her sphere, the queen drew up an elaborate testament[25] of which Henry, Duke of Guise, Beaton, the bishop of Ross, and du Ruisseau, her chancellor in France, were to be executors. She asked for Requiem Masses to be held in France, and made elaborate financial arrangements for the benefit of her servants, whether of her household or superior rank such as Beaton in France: Curle, for example, was to receive the marriage portion which had been promised him but never paid, and even the graceless Nau was to be allowed his pension, if he should manage to prove his innocence. Beyond that, there were charitable bequests for the poor children and friars of Rheims,

* These objects did not appear in the later inventories as Paulet reported: 'They have nothing to show for these things from their mistress in writing ... all the smaller things were delivered by her own hands.' It seems, from the subsequent history of some of these mementoes, that in certain instances they were entrusted to servants still in attendance at Fotheringhay to be handed on to others who had left, or been debarred from the queen's service, at the end.

and instructions that her coach was to be used to convey her women to London, when the horses were to be sold to defray their expenses, and her furniture likewise, that they might be able to afford to return to their countries of origin.*

Having completed these detailed dispositions for the welfare of those she would leave behind, Mary considered her own spiritual welfare in the shape of a farewell letter to be handed to the chaplain de Préau. Deprived of his physical presence, she used the medium of the letter as a general confession of her sins, in which she asked him to spend the night in prayer for her.[26] Mary's last letter of all was to her brother-in-law, King Henry of France: she related the abrupt circumstances in which her sentence had been broken to her, and her conviction that it was her religion, coupled with her place in the English succession, which was the true cause of her death, as it had been with Francis of Guise; she begged him to listen to the personal testimony concerning her execution which her physician should give to him so soon as he could reach France, and not trust to her letter alone; her last thoughts were the faithful servants who had served her for so long – she asked that their pensions and wages might be paid throughout their lives, and in particular that de Préau her chaplain might be awarded some little benefice in France from which he could spend the rest of his days in prayer for his dead mistress.[27] When these elaborate dispositions were finally completed, it was already two o'clock in the morning. Mary's letter to the king of France was thus dated Wednesday, 8th February, 1587, the day of her execution.

The traveller was now ready for her last journey on earth. The queen lay down on her bed without undressing. She did not try to sleep. Her women gathered round her already wearing their black garments of mourning, and Mary asked Jane Kennedy to read aloud the life of some great sinner. The life of the good thief was chosen, and as the story reached its climax on the

---

* It is notable that in his extremely detailed account of the queen's last hours, Bourgoing does not mention that she paused to compose or extemporize the Latin prayer *O Domine Deus! speravi in te* traditionally attributed to her, on the eve of her execution.

cross, Mary observed aloud: 'In truth he was a great sinner, but not so great as I have been.' She then closed her eyes, and said nothing further. Throughout the night the sound of hammering came from the great hall where the scaffold was being erected. The boots of the soldiers could be heard ceaselessly tramping up and down outside the queen's room, for Paulet had ordered them to watch with special vigilance in these final hours, lest their victim escape her captors at the last. The queen lay on her bed without sleeping, eyes closed and a half smile on her face.

So the short night passed. At six o'clock, long before light, the queen rose, handed over the will, distributed her purses, and gave her women a farewell embrace. Her men servants were given her hand to kiss. Then she went into her little oratory and prayed alone. She was extremely pale but quite composed. Bourgoing handed her a little bread and wine to sustain her. The day now dawned fine and sunny; it was one of those unexpected early February days when it suddenly seems possible that the spring will come. It was between eight and nine when a loud knocking was heard at the door, and a messenger shouted through it that the lords were waiting for the queen. Mary asked for a moment to finish her prayers, at which the lords outside in a moment of panic feared some sort of last-minute resistance might be planned; unable to believe in the courage of their captive, they had given credit to reports that the queen of Scots had said she would not come to the block of her own accord, but would have to be dragged thither. But when the sheriff of Northampton, Thomas Andrews, entered, he found Mary kneeling quietly in prayer in front of the crucifix which hung above her altar.

It was this crucifix which her groom Hannibal Stuart now bore before her as she was escorted towards the great hall. The queen was totally calm, and showed no signs of fear or distress. Her bearing was regal, and some of the contemporary observers afterwards even described her as cheerful and smiling.[28] The last moment of agony came in the entry chamber to the hall, when her servants were held back from following her and the queen was told that she was to die quite alone, by the orders of

Elizabeth. Melville, distracted at this unlooked-for blow, fell on his knees in tears and exclaimed: 'Oh Madam, it will be the sorrowfullest message that I ever carried when I shall report that my Queen and dear mistress is dead.' The queen dashed away her own tears and said gently: 'You ought to rejoice and not to weep for that the end of Mary Stuart's troubles is now done. Thou knowest, Melville, that all this world is but vanity and full of troubles and sorrows. Carry this message from me and tell my friends that I died a true woman to my religion, and like a true Scottish woman and a true French woman. ...' And commending Melville to go to her son, and tell him that her dearest wish had always been to see England and Scotland united, that she had never done anything to prejudice the welfare of the kingdom of Scotland, she embraced Melville and bade him farewell.

Mary now turned to Paulet and the lords and pleaded with them to allow at least her own servants to be with her at the death, so that they could later report the manner of her death in other countries. Kent replied that her wish could not well be granted, for before the execution her servants were sure to cry out and upset the queen herself, as well as disquieting the company, while afterwards they might easily attempt to dip their napkins in her blood for relics which, said Kent grimly, 'were not convenient'. 'My Lord,' replied Mary, 'I will give my word and promise for them that they shall not do any such thing as your Lordship hath named. Alas poor souls, it would do them good to bid me farewell.' As for her women she refused to believe that these were the instructions of Queen Elizabeth herself, for surely Elizabeth, herself a maiden queen, would not condemn a fellow-woman to die without any ladies about her to attend her, besides which, added Mary, 'You know that I am cousin to your Queen and descended from the blood of Henry VII, a married Queen of France, and the anointed Queen of Scotland.' She then appealed to history where she had read in chronicles that other gentlewomen had had their ladies with them at their execution. After a hurried whispered consultation, the lords decided that Mary might have after all the choice of six of her servants to accompany her. Thus Melville, Bourgoing, Gervais, and the old man Didier who had been for many years Mary's porter, were allowed to go forward, together with the two dearest of Mary's women, who shared her bed, Jane Kennedy and Elizabeth Curle. Mary then went to follow the sheriff, having first bestowed a small gift (probably a seal) on Sir William Fitzwilliam, the castellan of Fotheringhay: he, unlike Sir Amyas Paulet, had shown especial courtesy to her in the carrying-out of his office.

The queen now entered the great hall in silence.* The spectators gathered there – about 300 of them by one account – gazed with awe and apprehension at this legendary figure whose dramatic career was about to be ended before their eyes. They saw a tall and gracious woman, who at first sight seemed to be dressed entirely in black, save for the long white lace-edged veil which flowed down her back to the ground like a bride's, and the white stiffened and peaked head-dress that too was edged with lace, below which gleamed her auburn hair. Her satin dress was all in black, embroidered with black velvet, and set with black acorn buttons of jet trimmed with pearl; but through the slashed sleeves could be seen inner sleeves of purple, and although her shoes of Spanish leather were black, her stockings were clocked and edged with silver, her garters were of green silk, and her petticoat was of crimson velvet. She held a crucifix and a prayer book in her hand, and two rosaries hung down from her waist; round her neck was a pomander chain and an *Agnus Dei*. Despite the fact that Mary's shoulders were now bowed and stooping with illness, and her figure grown full with the years, she walked with immense dignity. Time and suffering had long ago rubbed away the delicate youthful charm of her

---

* An adagio piece of music marked as having been played at the execution of Mary Queen of Scots was reproduced by George Robert Gleig in his *Family History of England* (1836); he related that 'a fortunate accident' had thrown a copy of it in his way. But as the contemporary sketch of the scene within the great hall itself does not illustrate musicians, and none of the contemporary accounts mentions the fact that there was music, the piece, if authentic, must presumably have been played before the queen's appearance.[29]

face, but to many of the spectators her extraordinary composure and serenity had its own beauty. Above all, her courage was matchless, and this alone in many people's minds, whatever honours and dignities had been stripped from her by Paulet, still gave her the right to be called a queen.

In the centre of the great hall, which lay on the ground floor of the castle, directly below the room in which Mary had been tried, was set a wooden stage, all hung with black, about twelve feet square and two feet high off the ground. Within the precincts of the stage were two stools for Shrewsbury and Kent. Beside them was placed, about two feet high, also draped in black, the block, and a little cushioned stool on which it was intended that the queen should sit while she was disrobed. The great axe was already lying there – 'like those with which they cut wood', said Bourgoing later. Outside the stage were two other seats for Paulet and Drury, and a rank of soldiers enclosing it; behind them gathered the ordinary people who had been given the privilege of watching the execution, as well as some local dignitaries including Shrewsbury's eldest son Lord Talbot, Sir Edward Montagu, and his son and brother, Sir Richard Knightly, and Mr Thomas Brudenell. A huge blaze had been lit in the fireplace against the cold of the great hall.

Once led up the three steps to the stage, the queen listened patiently while the commission for her execution was read aloud. Her expression never changed. Cecil's own official observer, Robert Wise, commented later that from her detached regard, she might even have been listening to a pardon, rather than the warrant for her own death. The first sign of emotion was wrung from her when Dr Fletcher, the Protestant dean of Peterborough – he who afterwards described the fine weather as a sign that Heaven looked with favour on the execution – stepped forward, and proposed to harangue the queen according to the rites of the Protestant religion. 'Mr Dean,' said the queen firmly, 'I am settled in the ancient Catholic Roman religion, and mind to spend my blood in defence of it.' Shrewsbury and Kent both exhorted her to listen to him, and even offered to pray with the queen, but all these proposals Mary resolutely rejected.

'If you will pray with me, my lords,' she said to the two earls, 'I will thank you, but to join in prayer I will not, for that you and I are not of one religion.' And when the dean, in answer to the earls' direction, finally knelt down on the scaffold steps and started to pray out loud and at length, in a prolonged and rhetorical style as though determined to force his way into the pages of history, Mary still paid no attention but turned away, and started to pray aloud out of her own book in Latin, in the midst of these prayers sliding off her stool on to her knees. When the dean was at last finished, the queen changed her prayers, and began to pray out loud in English, for the afflicted English Catholic Church, for her son, and for Elizabeth, that she might serve God in the years to come. Kent remonstrated with her: 'Madam, settle Christ Jesus in your heart and leave those trumperies.' But the queen prayed on, asking God to avert his wrath from England, and calling on the Saints to intercede for her; and so she kissed the crucifix she held, and crossing herself, ended: 'Even as thy arms, O Jesus, were spread here upon the cross, so receive me into Thy arms of mercy, and forgive me all my sins.'

When the queen's prayers were finished, the executioners asked her, as was customary, to forgive them in advance for bringing about her death. Mary answered immediately: 'I forgive you with all my heart, for now I hope you shall make an end of all my troubles.' Then the executioners, helped by Jane Kennedy and Elizabeth Curle, assisted the Queen to undress – Robert Wise noticed that she undressed so quickly that it seemed as if she was in haste to be gone out of the world. Stripped of her black, she stood in her red petticoat and it was seen that above it she wore a red satin bodice, trimmed with lace, the neckline cut low at the back; one of her women handed her a pair of red sleeves, and it was thus wearing all red, the colour of blood, and the liturgical colour of martyrdom in the Catholic Church, that the queen of Scots died.* According to their usual

* But it was a dark red, a sort of crimson-brown, not scarlet as is sometimes suggested.[30]

practice, the executioners stretched forth their hands for the queen's ornaments which were their perquisites. When they touched the long golden rosary, Jane Kennedy protested, and the queen herself intervened and said that Bull would be compensated with money in its place, and the same promise had to be made regarding the *Agnus Dei*.* Yet all the time her belongings were being stripped from her, it was notable that the queen neither wept nor changed her calm and almost happy expression of what one observer called 'smiling cheer'; she even retained her composure sufficiently to remark wryly of the executioners that she had never before had such grooms of the chamber to make her ready. It was the queen's women who could not contain their lamentations as they wept and crossed themselves and muttered snatches of Latin prayers. Finally Mary had to turn to them and mindful of her promise to Shrewsbury that they would not weep aloud if they were admitted to the hall, she admonished them softly in French: *'Ne crie point pour moi. J'ai promis pour vous ...'* Once more she bade them not mourn but rejoice, for they were soon to see the end of all her troubles; turning to her menservants, standing on a bench close by the scaffold, who also had tears pouring down their faces and were calling out prayers in French and Scots and Latin, and crossing themselves again and again, she told them to be comforted, with a smile on her lips to reassure them. She asked the men too to pray for her unto the last hour.

The time had come for Jane Kennedy to bind the queen's eyes with the white cloth embroidered in gold which Mary had herself chosen for the purpose the night before. Jane Kennedy first kissed the cloth and then wrapped it gently round her mistress's eyes, and over her head so that her hair was covered as by a white turban and only the neck left completely bare. The two women then withdrew from the stage. The queen, without even now the faintest sign of fear, knelt down once

---

* This gold rosary was intended for Mary's friend Anne Dacres, wife of Philip, earl of Arundel, to whom it was subsequently delivered by Jane Kennedy; it is now in the possession of the earl of Arundel's descendant, the 16th duke of Norfolk.

more on the cushion in front of the block. She recited aloud in Latin the Psalm *In te Domino confido, non confundar in aeternum* – In you Lord is my trust, let me never be confounded – and then feeling for the block, she laid her head down upon it, placing her chin carefully with both her hands, so that if one of the executioners had not moved them back they too would have lain in the direct line of the axe. The queen stretched out her arms and legs and cried, '*In manus tuas, Domine, confide spiritum meum*' – 'Into your hands O Lord I commend my spirit' – three or four times. When the queen was lying there quite motionless, Bull's assistant put his hand on her body to steady it for the blow. Even so, the first blow, as it fell, missed the neck and cut into the back of the head. The queen's lips moved, and her servants thought they heard the whispered words: 'Sweet Jesus.' The second blow severed the neck, all but the smallest sinew, and this was severed by using the axe as a saw. It was about ten o'clock in the morning of Wednesday, 8th February, the queen of Scots being then aged forty-four years old, and in the nineteenth year of her English captivity.

In the great hall of Fotheringhay, before the wondering eyes of the crowd, the executioner now held aloft the dead woman's head, crying out as he did so: 'God save the Queen.' The lips still moved and continued to do so for a quarter of an hour after the death. But at this moment, weird and moving spectacle, the auburn tresses in his hand came apart from the skull and the head itself fell to the ground. It was seen that Mary Stuart's own hair had in fact been quite grey, and very short at the time of her death: for her execution she had chosen to wear a wig. The spectators were stunned by the unexpected sight and remained silent. It was left to the dean of Peterborough to call out strongly, 'So perish all the Queen's enemies', and for Kent, standing over the corpse, to echo: 'Such be the end of all the Queen's, and all the Gospel's enemies.' But Shrewsbury could not speak, and his face was wet with tears.

It was now the time for the executioners to strip the body of its remaining adornments before handing it over to the embalmers. But at this point a strange and pathetic memorial to that devotion which Mary Stuart had always aroused in those who knew her intimately was discovered: her little lag dog, a Skye terrier, who had managed to accompany her into the hall under her long skirts, where her servants had been turned away, had now crept out from beneath her petticoat, and in its distress had stationed itself piteously beneath the severed head and the shoulders of the body. Nor would it be coaxed away, but steadfastly and uncomprehendingly clung to the solitary thing it could find in the hall which still reminded it of its dead mistress. To all others save this poor animal, the sad corpse lying now so still on the floor of the stage, in its red clothes against which the blood stains scarcely showed, with its face now sunken to that of an old woman in the harsh disguise of death, bore little resemblance to her whom they had known only a short while before as Mary Queen of Scots. The spirit had fled the body. The chain was loosed to let the captive go.

At Fotheringhay now it was as if a murder had taken place. The weeping women in the hall were pushed away and locked in their rooms. The castle gates were locked, so that no one could leave and break the news to the outside world. The body was lain unceremoniously in the presence chamber, and even, so Brantôme heard from Mary's distraught women who had peeped through a crack in the door, wrapped in the coarse woollen covering of her own billiard table. The blood-stained block was burnt. Every other particle of clothing or object of devotion which might be associated with the queen of Scots was burnt, scoured or washed, so that not a trace of her blood might remain to create a holy relic to inspire devotion in years to come. The little dog was washed and washed again, although he subsequently refused to eat, and so pined away. The remaining rosary which Jane Kennedy had not managed to rescue and which the queen had worn was burnt. Even the executioners were not allowed to enjoy the benefits of the perquisites for which they had fought, since the custodians confiscated them, and replaced them with money.* At about four o'clock in the afternoon the body was further stripped and the organs including the heart were removed and handed to the sheriff, who with the fear of creating relics ever in his mind, had them buried secretly deep within the castle of Fotheringhay. The exact spot was never revealed. The physician from Stamford examined the body before he embalmed it with the help of two surgeons: he found the heart sound, and the health of the body itself, and the other organs apart from a slight quantity of water, not so much impaired as to justify Cecil's prognosis that the queen would have died anyway. The body was then wrapped in a wax winding-sheet and incarcerated in a heavy lead coffin, on Walsingham's explicit orders.

Only Shrewsbury's eldest son, Lord Talbot, was allowed to gallop forth from the castle at about one o'clock, hard towards London, to break the news of what had taken place that morning to Elizabeth. He reached the capital next morning at nine. The queen was at Greenwich and had been out riding early; on her return she held a conversation with the Portuguese pretender. When she was told the news, according to Camden, she received it at first with great indignation, and then with terrible distress: 'her countenance changed, her words faltered, and with excessive sorrow she was in a manner astonished, insomuch as she gave herself over to grief, putting herself into mourning weeds and shedding abundance of tears'.[31] In the meantime, before grief could overcome her altogether, she turned like an angry snake on the secretary Davison and had him thrown into prison for daring to use the warrant for the execution which she herself had signed. Elizabeth now maintained that she had only signed the warrant 'for safety's sake' and had merely given it to Davison to keep, not to use. Her Council were cross-examined as though they were criminals, and Davison impeached before the Star Chamber. Further ostentatious manifestations of her displeasure

---

* These rigorous precautions on the part of the English government, carried out savagely, cast a doubtful light on the many so-called relics of Mary Stuart which are said to date from her execution.

might have followed, had not Cecil himself felt obliged to remonstrate with Elizabeth. He pointed out that such theatricals even if they salved her own conscience would cut little ice with the outside world, when it was known that Davison had both her Commission and her seal at his disposal. On the other hand, the papists and the queen's enemies might all too easily be encouraged, if it was suggested that the queen of Scots had been killed unlawfully. In the end Davison, the scapegoat, underwent a token period of imprisonment and had a fine of £10,000 imposed on him; the other members of the Council went free. Unlike its queen London itself suffered from no such doubts: the bells were rung, fires were lighted in the streets and there was much merry-making and banqueting to celebrate the death of her whom they had been trained to regard as a public enemy. Some bold spirits even asked the French ambassador to give them some wood for their bonfires, and when he indignantly refused, lit an enormous blaze in the street in front of his house.

But at Fotheringhay itself nothing was changed. It was as though the castle, cut off from the rest of the world, had fallen asleep for a thousand years under an enchantment, as a result of the dolorous stroke which had there slain Mary Queen of Scots. The queen's servants were permitted to have one Requiem Mass said by de Préau the morning after her death, but otherwise everything went on as before. Her attendants were still kept in prison within the castle, in conditions which were harsher than ever; nor were any of them allowed to return to their native lands of France and Scotland as Mary had so urgently stipulated at the last. Sir Amyas Paulet, made a knight of the Garter in April for his pains, was still in charge of arrangements at Fotheringhay, and continued to complain over the excessive expenses of his prisoners' diet.[32] The queen's farewell letters to the Pope remained unposted and undelivered, lingering in the hands of her household. Spring turned to summer. The snow-drops which had scattered the green meadows round the River Nene on the day of her death gave place to purple thistles, sometimes romantically called Queen Mary's tears. Still the body of the dead queen, embalmed and wrapped in its heavy lead coffin, was given no burial, but remained walled up within the precincts of the castle where she had died.

CHAPTER TWENTY-SEVEN

Epilogue: The Theatre of the World

~~~~~

'Remember that the theatre of the world is wider than
the realm of England.'

Mary Queen of Scots before her judges, October 1586

A s the gates of Fotheringhay were locked, so were the
English ports closed immediately after the death of the
queen of Scots. It was three weeks before the French
ambassador Châteauneuf could write back to his master in Paris
with tidings of the calamity. The news of the death of Mary
Stuart, their own queen dowager, was received in France with
national and solemn mourning. On 12th March a Requiem Mass
was held in the black-draped cathedral of Notre Dame; the
whole court was present including King Henry III, the Queen
Mother Catherine, others who had known Mary well such as
her uncle René of Elboeuf, and the younger generation of
Guises. The preacher was Renaud de Beaune, archbishop of
Bourges, a man old enough to recall in poignant language that
day nearly thirty years before when Mary had been married in
that self-same cathedral to the dauphin of France:* 'Many of us
saw in the place where we are now assembled to deplore her,
this Queen on the day of her bridal, arrayed in her regal
trappings, so covered in jewels that the sun himself shone not

---

* To be compared in eloquence with the famous passage of Edmund Burke on
Marie-Antoinette as dauphiness, written over 200 years later.

more brightly, so beautiful, so charming withal as never woman was. These walls were then hung with cloth of gold and precious tapestry; every space was filled with thrones and seats, crowded with princes and princesses, who came from all parts to share in the rejoicing. The palace was overflowing with magnificence, splendid fêtes and masques; the streets with jousts and tourneys. In short it seemed as if our age had succeeded that day in surpassing the pomp of all past centuries combined. A little time has flowed on and it is all vanished like a cloud. Who would have believed that such a change could have befallen her who appeared then so triumphant, and that we should have seen her a prisoner who had restored prisoners to liberty; in poverty who was accustomed to give so liberally to others; treated with contumely by those on whom she had conferred honours; and finally, the axe of a base executioner mangling the form of her who was doubly a Queen; that form which honoured the nuptial bed of a sovereign of France, falling dishonoured on a scaffold, and that beauty which had been one of the wonders of the world, faded in a dreary prison, and at last effaced by a piteous death. This place, where she was surrounded with splendour, is now hung with black for her. Instead of nuptial torches we have funereal tapers; in the place of songs of joy, we have sighs and groans; for clarions and hautboys, the tolling of the sad and dismal bell. Oh God, what a change! Oh vanity of human greatness, shall we never be convinced of your deceitfulness...."

Despite the vivid sorrow of the French nation and in spite of Mary's own desire to be buried in France, either at St Denis or Rheims, her wishes in this respect were never met. Elizabeth could scarcely plead ignorance of her request, since it had been expressed most passionately in Mary's letter of 15th December, the letter which Paulet had finally forwarded. However, in other respects, Mary's last wishes were being met. By 7th March Mendoza, who was in Paris, was able to spread the tale of her heroic death to Spain for, despite all the English precautions, news of her bravery during the last hours had leaked out. Not only her courage but even her sanctity was discussed. Pierre l'Estoile recorded in his Journal that Paris was the scene of mass demonstrations, as well as sermons that virtually canonized Mary as a saint who had died in the cause of the Catholic faith.[2] Among those who hailed her death as a form of martyrdom in the cause of the faith was the youthful Maffeo Barberini, the future Pope Urban VIII, who wrote a lyrical elegy on the subject referring to her 'darkened sorrows turned to glorious joy'. The woman who deliberately chose the story of the good thief to be read aloud to her on the eve of her death because she considered herself in all humility to be a great sinner would have viewed this popular canonization with detachment; on the other hand Mary would undoubtedly have been pleased at the way the Catholic League and Philip II were galvanized by her death as by a Catholic rallying-cry; even the French king, who generally viewed the Guise-inspired Catholic League with suspicion, gave vent to some newly bellicose sentiments towards the Protestants, on receiving the news of Mary's death.

The grief of the French court was genuine enough in its personal aspects. That of the Scottish court was more difficult to estimate, and contemporary accounts differ radically in their reports of how James received the news of his mother's execution. According to one story, he shammed sorrow in public, but observed to his courtiers gleefully in secret: 'Now I am sole King.'[3] Archibald Douglas on the other hand was told that the 'King moved never his countenance at the rehearsal [telling] of his mother's execution, nor leaves not his pastimes more than of before.'[4] Still other reports spoke of his evident grief, how he became very sad and pensive when the intelligence reached him, and went to bed without eating. Whatever James's outward show of lamentation, it is difficult to believe that the news of his mother's death aroused at long last the filial passion of which he had shown so little evidence during her life. His conduct subsequently showed that so long as the English crown still dangled within his reach, he was prepared to swallow the insult to his family and his nation. The Scottish people as a whole showed more spirit than their king, and seemed to evince both humiliation and anger at the killing of one who had once sat on the throne of Scotland. When James ordered the Scottish court into mourning as a formal gesture, according to one tradition[5] the earl of Sinclair appeared before him dressed in steel armour in place of black. When James asked him whether he had not seen the general order for mourning, Sinclair replied sternly: 'This *is* the proper mourning for the Queen of Scotland.' Prayers were said for the defunct queen in a form specially prescribed by the Council. Some of Mary's former subjects discussed plans for reprisals. One of Cecil's spies heard that the Hamiltons had proposed to burn Newcastle with a levy of 5000 men, if only James would match their force with an equivalent army. Walsingham was also advised that there were posters in the streets against England and James, and a general clamour for war. To indicate the prevailing atmosphere, his agent in Scotland sent him a piece of hemp tied like a halter and the accompanying jingle, aimed by a patriot at Elizabeth:

> To Jezabel that English whore
> Receive this Scottish chain
> A presage of her great malheur
> For murdering our Queen.

James did make the gesture of breaking off formal communications with England. Sir Robert Carey was sent north by Elizabeth with the unenviable mission of explaining that his mistress had not authorized the execution personally and had been dumbfounded and grief-stricken when it was carried out. James refused at first to receive him. But by the end of February Gray was writing to Douglas in London, indicating that James would now be susceptible to further arguments from Elizabeth and that old Latin tag – *necesse est unum mori pro populo*; it is necessary for one person to die for the sake of the people – might perhaps be brought into play.[6] Finally James consented to listen to Carey's arguments, and accepted Elizabeth's explanation of her own 'unspotted' part in the execution. By mid-March the English were confident that James would not fight to avenge his mother's death. The Anglo-Scottish alliance remained unsevered by the axe of Fotheringhay.

It was, however, in deference to James's feelings, or the sort of appropriate feelings he might be supposed to cherish for his mother, that the subject of the burial of the queen of Scots was raised again in the summer after her death. Walsingham had specified in his instructions that the coffin should be bestowed 'by night' on an upper shelf of the local Fotheringhay church – and Cecil afterwards underlined the word *upper* in his own hand.[7] But in fact the coffin had not been accorded even this obscure resting-place, but remained quite unburied, like the corpse of Achilles, within Fotheringhay itself. Now it was planned to give the coffin an honourable burial at Peterborough Cathedral. So far as anything explained this curious ceremony the line adopted seemed to be that Mary had been a revered dowager queen of Scotland who happened to die in England of natural causes. Under the auspices of Garter King of Arms, heralds, nobles and mourners were imported from London to give the occasion the right degree of solemnity due to the mother of the king of Scotland.[8] But no Scots were present, and although the cathedral was hung with black paid for by the master of the wardrobe, and the heraldic details of the decoration worked out with care – there were the royal arms of Scotland, for example, as well as those of Mary's first two husbands Francis II and Darnley (James's father) – neither in the escutcheons nor in the service was there any reference to her third husband Bothwell, to the events leading to her imprisonment in England, let alone the manner of her death.

Although the red lion of Scotland blazed forth in the nave of Peterborough Cathedral, and Elizabeth's personal friend, the countess of Bedford, acted the role of chief mourner with due gravity, while the procession was headed with 100 poor widows also dressed for the occasion in black at the government's expense, the dichotomy at the heart of this strange, apologetic ceremony was revealed by the fact that the coffin was actually transported from Fotheringhay to Peterborough at dead of night for fear of demonstrations. On Sunday, 30th July, Queen Mary's body left the castle for the last time by the light of torches, in a coach draped in black velvet from which little pennons fluttered – 'a chariot' the state accounts called it later.[9] The accompanying heralds rode with bared heads. They reached Peterborough at two o'clock in the morning, being met by a distinguished convoy of ecclesiastics including the bishop and the egregious Dean Fletcher. The coffin was then lodged temporarily in the Bishop's Palace.

The whole ceremony was of course Protestant and thus sung in English. But the late queen's servants, who had been allowed out of their seclusion at Fotheringhay to attend the service, were all pious Catholics with the exception of Andrew Melville and Barbara Mowbray. They therefore withdrew from the body of the church once the procession was over. Even so, the fact that the chaplain de Préau walked with a heavy gold crucifix on his breast during the procession called forth angry Protestant criticism. At the head of the procession, just behind the bailiff of Peterborough with his black staves of mourning, was borne the royal standard of Scotland with the motto: *In my defence God me defend.* Among the distinguished English mourners were Cecil's elder son, and Shrewsbury's daughter and daughter in-law, Lady Mary Savill and Lady Talbot. The ladies of Mary's former household walked just ahead of the attendants of the English peeresses, in black taffeta headdresses, with veils of white lawn hanging down behind: their names recalled those last melancholy months at Fotheringhay, for they included Barbara Mowbray and her sister Gillis, Elizabeth Curle, Jane Kennedy, Christina Pages and her daughter Mary.

In one respect the ceremony deviated from the common practice at state funerals: it was not found possible to process the coffin round the cathedral owing to the great quantity of lead used on Walsingham's instructions, estimated at over nine hundredweight. Not only was the weight inordinate, but it was feared by the prudent that the casing might even rip and 'being very hot weather, might be found some annoyance'. The coffin was therefore placed immediately in its vault in the south aisle of the cathedral. Otherwise the arrangements were as was customary in such interments: a 'representation' or effigy of the queen of Scots was carried in the procession beneath a canopy supported by four knights.*[10] The five pursuivants from London, Portcullis, Rouge Dragon Clarenceaux, the Somerset and the York herald bore the emblems of state, the sword, target, crown, the crest, the helmet and the like which were later hung formally over the grave. Even the sermon given by William Chaderton, bishop of Lincoln, represented a clumsy attempt to gloss over the very different circumstances in which the woman whom they were now burying with such honour had actually died. He called on God to bless the happy dissolution of the late Scottish queen, adding 'of whose life and departure, whatsoever shall be expected, I have nothing to say, for that I was unacquainted with the one, and not present at the other'. By citing what he termed a charitable saying of Martin Luther, 'Many one liveth a Papist and dieth a Protestant', he even suggested that the queen of Scots might have undergone a last-minute conversion to the reformed faith, before adding that at any rate he had heard she took her death patiently, recommending herself at the last to Jesus Christ.

The service completed, the procession filed out of the

---

* It is thought that this effigy was modelled from a death mask taken shortly after the execution by the surgeons at Fotheringhay. The death mask from which this effigy was taken cannot, however, be identified with the Lennoxlove death mask, discovered at Holyrood Palace in the last century. This, although beautiful, is clearly the mask of a much smaller woman. It measures seven inches long and 4¾ inches across, to be compared with the Westminster Abbey monument which is nine inches by seven inches across. (Queen Elizabeth's monument, also taken from a death mask, measures eight inches by eight inches and portraits confirm that she had a much broader face than Mary.) Nor can the Lennoxlove measurements be explained by wax shrinkage: Mr Wismark of Madame Tussaud's told the author that a two-inch shrinkage would destroy portraiture altogether, ¼ inch being the maximum for which allowance could be made. In any case the Lennoxlove mask bears only a superficial resemblance to the Queen of Scots: the mouth and setting of the eyes are quite different; the nose is blunt at the end in profile, lacking any sort of aquiline finish, and in front view looks almost *retroussé*; the width of the jaw is remarkable in a small face, and quite unlike the bone structure shown in all Mary's known portraits. The Lennoxlove face is also thin, lacking the fullness upon which every observer at Mary's execution commented, and which is present, for example, in the face on the Westminster monument.

cathedral once more, and as they passed the mourning women who had once served Queen Mary, standing at the side, in order to take no part in the Protestant service, some of the grand English ladies, many of whom like Shrewsbury's family had known them well in happier days, embraced and kissed them sympathetically. The courtiers and the ecclesiastics now adjourned to the Bishop's Palace for a funeral banquet of considerable festivity: but Mary's former servitors were not so easily transferred from tears into laughter; what to the worshipful company from London was only a ritual proceeding to round off a distasteful incident in English history, was to them the last obsequies of their beloved mistress. There, while the English caroused, Mary's servants gathered in another room and wept bitter tears.

The most passionate desire left to these poor people was that they should now be released from their melancholy prison and allowed to go their several ways. Despite the completion of the interment, there was a further delay of two months before they were allowed to depart, possibly because some report of their obstinate heretical behaviour at the burial service and their unseemly grief at the banquet had come to Elizabeth's ears and displeased her. Shortly after the service, Adam Blackwood, one of Mary's most loyal partisans, who was already at work on the task of presenting her to the world as a royal heroine and a Catholic martyr, came secretly to Peterborough and put up on the wall above her tomb a long epitaph in Latin protesting against the crime of regicide which had taken place at Fotheringhay: 'A strange and unusual monument this is, wherein the living are included with the dead: for, with the Sacred Ashes of this blessed Mary, know, that the Majesty of all kings, and princes, lieth here, violated and prostrate. And because regal secrecy doth enough and more admonish Kings of their duty – traveller, I say no more.' But this loyal monument was pulled down. Nor did 'regal secrecy' admonish any kings of their duty, beyond the £321 which Queen Elizabeth spent on this funeral to placate King James, of which pantry and buttery charges accounted for one third.[11]

At last in October the ordeal of the little royal household was at an end. Bourgoing went to King Henry III, as he had been instructed, and told his tale of the uplifting last months and hours of the late queen of Scots. Gorion went to Mendoza, handed him the diamond ring which Mendoza subsequently passed to Philip II, and he too related the story of his mistress's martyrdom. The farewell letters written nearly a year before reached their destinations at last, and King Philip, moved by this reminder from beyond the grave of the woman who had once been his sister-in-law, and long his Catholic confederate, out of natural chivalry honoured Mary's last requests for the payments of her servants' wages, and her debts in France. He also pursued in correspondence with Mendoza the subject of what he believed to be Mary's last gift to him in her will – the reversion of the English crown. In the interests of his own foreign policy, Philip conveniently allowed himself to credit the story that Mary had finally disinherited James altogether on the eve of her execution, and had consequently ceded to Philip directly her own claims to the English throne.* It was now late in 1587. It was in the next year, 1588, that King Philip took the momentous decision to pursue his supposed English inheritance with the great force of the Spanish Armada. Ironically enough, therefore, the mighty Spanish fleet of rescue for which Mary had waited so long and so hopefully only sailed towards England after, and as a direct result of, her death.

Mendoza was left in France to deal with the problems of these old servants: Philip had authorized a pension of 300 crowns a year for Jane, and forty crowns a month for Gilbert Curle, and Mendoza acted with kindness and charity in the course of his administration, receiving in the course of it such tremulous confidences as the fact that it had been Jane Kennedy

---

* But Philip was allowing himself to be deluded. Although Mary had twice confided England conditionally to Philip, if James failed to become a Catholic – in her will of 1577 and in her letter to Mendoza of May 1586 – no such clause existed in the last testament which Mary made on the eve of her death at Fotheringhay, and no other will has ever been found supporting his claims.[12] In any case, it is clear from the contemporary accounts that Mary went to her death serenely, rather than in the bitter mood which might have led to a last-minute official disinheritance of her son.

not Elizabeth Curle who had tied the blindfold round the queen's eyes at the end, 'because I was of better family'.[13] Having delivered a diamond ring which Mary bequeathed to Thomas Morgan for faithful service – many of her supporters would willingly have denied it to him for his supposed treachery – Jane Kennedy returned to Scotland, where she had the melancholy privilege of describing the scene of his mother's death personally to King James. She subsequently married Mary's steward, Andrew Melville; despite the differences in their religion they were drawn to each other by memories of the past and long years together in the royal service. But Jane did not live long enough to enjoy a peaceful old age with her husband: in 1589 King James commissioned her to go to Denmark to fetch back his bride Princess Anne, as a reward for her faithful service to his mother, and she was drowned in a storm at the outset of her journey. Gillis Mowbray also went back to Scotland, where she married Sir John Smith of Barnton: her relics of her royal mistress, which she bequeathed to her granddaughter, now form the heart of the Penicuik Bequest in the National Museum of Antiquities at Edinburgh.

Elizabeth Curle, and her sister-in-law Barbara Curle, born Mowbray, ended their lives together at Antwerp. Gilbert Curle, the sad but good-hearted secretary, died in 1609; but Barbara lived to 1616, and Elizabeth to 1620, over thirty years after the death of Mary. Before her death, Elizabeth Curle had an interesting memorial to the queen carried out in the shape of a full-scale portrait of her mistress at the time of her execution, the figure presumably modelled on the miniature which Mary confided to Jane on the eve of her death. The portrait was bequeathed by Elizabeth to her nephew Hippolytus Curle, a Jesuit, and from him it was handed on to the Scots College at Douai. On either side of the standing figure of the queen are shown two vignettes of the execution scene at Fotheringhay: on the left, the queen kneels at the block, and on the right are shown Elizabeth Curle and Jane Kennedy standing together, wearing the black religious habits these good ladies appear to have adopted for the rest of their lives in perpetual and devout mourning for their mistress. At Douai the portrait even survived the depredations of the French revolutionaries, rolled up and built into a chimney; it has now come to rest at the Blairs College, Aberdeen. The pious legend that Elizabeth Curle somehow managed to carry the head of Mary Queen of Scots abroad and have it buried with her in her tomb may be dismissed in view of the extraordinary and zealous precautions which were taken at the time to prevent even a drop of the dead woman's blood being taken as a martyr's relic; the head itself was certainly replaced on the body by the surgeons, wrapped securely in the heavy lead coffin that very afternoon. But the joint memorial to Elizabeth and Barbara in St Andrew's Church, Antwerp, flanked with their respective patron saints, is today still crowned with a portrait of Mary Stuart, the woman whom Elizabeth believed to have been a martyred queen, and to whose life she dedicated her service; the Latin inscription on the memorial still proclaims proudly that it was she, Elizabeth Curle, who received the last kiss of Mary Queen of Scots.

With the departure at last of the sorrowing servants, the castle of Fotheringhay was released from its spell; soon its very masonry began to decay. Although Camden loyally but inaccurately reported that it was King James who had the stones beaten to the ground in a rage, to avenge the deed of shame which had taken place there,[14] in fact its demolition was a gradual process, increased as local builders and landowners helped themselves to its materials. The antiquarian Sir Robert Cotton, conscious of his royal Bruce ancestry, actually acquired the great hall in which the execution had taken place, and incorporated it in his own nearby manor of Connington in Huntingdonshire (although that too was pulled down in the eighteenth century). Today not even the ruins of Fotheringhay survive. The interested wayfarer finds the site of the castle, which is not in public hands, but belongs to the owners of the nearby farm, at the end of a cart track. All that can be seen of the once mighty castle of Fotheringhay is a grassy mound indicating the position of the keep, and a huge Ozymandias-like hump of masonry, encased in railings, recalling Shelley's line on the trunkless stone in the desert, 'Look on my works ye mighty and despair'. The river meanders by. Sheep peacefully graze on the meadows opposite. There is no national memorial or official commemoration of the stirring events, so much part of British history, which once took place at Fotheringhay.*

Even now with the burial at Peterborough, the earthly pere-grinations of the queen of Scots were not at an end. When James ascended the throne of England in the spring of 1603, he marked his respect for his mother's tomb the following August by dispatching a rich pall of velvet to Peterborough, with instructions to the bishop to hang it over her grave. By the time, however, that James had erected a large and handsome monument to Queen Elizabeth in Westminster Abbey, it was generally felt that something still further ought to be done for his mother's memory. Considerable influence in this respect was exerted by James's favourite Henry Howard, earl of North-ampton, brother of Mary's Norfolk, who had strongly Catholic sympathies all his life and died an outright member of the Church. In 1606 Cornelius Cure, master mason of works, was instructed to commence the carving of an imposing monument, which was later continued and finished by his son William. By September 1612 the work was sufficiently completed for the order of exhumation to be given to the clergy at Peterborough: the corpse of James's 'dearest mother' was to be taken up in 'as decent and respectful manner as is fitting'. James did not, however, lose his head over the splendour of his gesture – for although the monument in Westminster Abbey was costly and sumptuous, the sculptors alone receiving £825, and an overall

---

* In 1913 two small notices were placed privately on the railings surrounding the block of masonry; one, at the instance of the Richard III Society, recorded his birth in the castle in 1452; the other, affixed by the Stuart History Society, commemorated Mary Queen of Scots' death in 1587. More colourful were the visits of an eccentric Jacobite sympathizer, at the turn of the present century, who used to make an annual pilgrimage from Edinburgh to Northamptonshire on the anniversary of the queen's death to lay a wreath at Fotheringhay. Unfortunately, in his enthusiasm for the cause of Mary Stuart, he used such violent language about the existing British royal family that his visits had to be discouraged by the then owners of the site.

sum of £2000 being mentioned, James had not forgotten that rich pall he had sent down to Peterborough nine years earlier. This was to be employed again, and if the chapter happened to think it belonged to them, it was to be redeemed for a reasonable fee. Today the site of the original vault is covered by a marble pavement. The heraldic symbols over the grave were pulled down at the time of the Civil War, when the tomb of Queen Catherine of Aragon was also destroyed. The twenty-five-year-long sojourn of the queen of Scots' body in Peterborough Cathedral is marked by a stone tablet on an adjoining pillar, and two Scottish banners hang facing the site, placed there in 1920 by the Peterborough Caledonian Society.

In Westminster Abbey at last, the queen of Scots' body found its final resting-place. The tomb is magnificent, a monument to James's taste if not to his filial piety. By the white marble of which it is composed, Mary Stuart becomes once more '*la reine blanche*' of her first widowhood. It shows her lying full-length beneath a great ornamental canopy, her face serene and noble, her eyes closed, her long fingers stretched out in an attitude of prayer; she wears the simple peaked head-dress in which she died, but a royal cloak edged with ermine stretches around her body; at her feet rests the lion of Scotland. The face is extremely realistic and was evidently modelled on either the death mask or the effigy taken from it at Peterborough, since it shows all the features which observers noticed at the time of her death, and bears also a strong resemblance to the later portraits. The chin is full and soft although still pointed, the oval shape of the face is characteristic as is the setting of the eyes with its pronounced gap before the hairline. The nose has a Roman bridge to it, and the aquiline tendency of later years, consonant with the Sheffield-type portraits, which was probably exaggerated by the conditions of the death mask. The mouth shows the delicate almost sensual curve of the portraits, but is set in a more tranquil expression than the sad martyr of the Sheffield-type pictures. Altogether the whole impression of this awe-inspiring catafalque is of beauty – beauty which is made up of both majesty and repose.

A long Latin epitaph was composed by the earl of Northampton and is now to be seen on the tomb: it extols Queen
Mary's virtues, and deplores her misfortunes and her wrongful
English imprisonment, without going into the controversial
events which led to this imprisonment. The Cotton MSS show
that Northampton had composed other still more eulogistic
versions, in which it was suggested that, as Mary had stated
herself, she had been executed solely for her religious faith, and
lured into England by the false promises of Elizabeth. These,
however, James discarded in favour of an uncontroversial pan-
egyric – which, however, Northampton still signed 'H. N.
Gemens' – Henry Northampton mourning.[15]

So the queen of Scots found peace at last. There can be little
doubt that Mary who cared so much and so prolongedly for the
English succession would have been satisfied at the last with
her burial place in Westminster Abbey among the kings and
queens of England. Her rights as a queen, to which she attached
such importance to the end, had thus been respected. Viewing
that splendid edifice in marble, white in the darkness of the
Henry VII Chapel, the last of the royal monuments and
the most imposing of them all, she would surely have felt that
the cruelty of Elizabeth in denying her the French burial she
craved had been atoned for in an unlooked-for and glorious
manner. Nor was the significance of her tomb entirely royal: a
few years after this new interment, pious Catholics were spreading the news that holy benefits could be gained from a visit to
the tomb as to a shrine; Demster in Bologna wrote in his history
of the Scottish Church, published in 1627: 'I hear that her
bones, lately translated to the burial place of the Kings of
England at Westminster, are resplendent with miracles.'[16] As
Mary's literary supporters developed the theme of the martyr
queen, the white tomb itself became a place of pilgrimage for
the faithful.

Once more, however, the repose of the queen of Scots was
destined to be disturbed. In 1867 a search was instituted by
Dean Stanley within the royal tombs of Westminster Abbey for
the body of James I, whose position was unrecorded. It was

eventually discovered in the tomb of Henry VII, the first Tudor and the first Stuart monarch of England lying appropriately together with Elizabeth of York, the woman who had made the foundation of both dynasties possible. But in the course of the search, among the places it was thought he might have appropriately chosen for his own sepulchre was the tomb of his mother. An entry was made below the monument to Mary, and at the foot of an ample flight of steps marked WAY was found a large vault of brick, twelve feet long, six feet high and seven feet wide. A startling and harrowing sight greeted the gaze of the Victorian searchers: the queen of Scots was far from lying alone in her tomb. A vast pile of lead coffins rose upwards from the floor, some of them obviously of children, some so small as to be of mere babies, all heaped together in confusion, amid urns of many different shapes, which were scattered all through the vault.

It was discovered that Mary shared her catacomb with numbers of her descendants, including her grandson Henry, Prince of Wales, who died before his prime, her granddaughter Elizabeth of Bohemia, the Winter Queen, and her great-grandson Prince Rupert of the Rhine, among the most romantic of all the offshoots of the Stuart dynasty. Most poignant of all were the endless tiny coffins of the royal children who had died in infancy: here were found the first ten children of James II, and one James Darnley, described as his natural son, as well as the eighteen pathetic babies born dead to Queen Anne, and her sole child to survive infancy, the young duke of Gloucester.

Finally the coffin of the queen of Scots herself was found, against the north wall of the vault, lying below that of Arbella Stuart, that ill-fated scion of the royal house who had been the child-companion of Mary's captivity. The coffin itself was of remarkable size, and it was easy to see why it had been too heavy to carry in procession at Peterborough Cathedral at the first burial. But so securely had the royal body been wrapped in lead at the orders of the English government on the afternoon of the execution that the casing had not given way in the slightest, even after nearly 300 years. The searchers felt profoundly moved even by this inanimate spectacle. No attempt was made to open it now. 'The presence of the fatal coffin which had received the headless corpse at Fotheringhay,' wrote Dean Stanley, 'was sufficiently affecting without endeavouring to penetrate further into its mournful contents.'[7] The vault was thus reverently tidied, the urns rearranged, and a list made of the contents. But the queen's own coffin was left untouched, and the little children who surrounded her were not removed.

Meanwhile in the opposite chapel, underneath the monument to Queen Elizabeth I also raised by James, were found together in one grave the two daughters of Henry VIII, Mary Tudor and Elizabeth. Barren in life, they had been left to lie alone together in death. Mary, however, lies amid her Stuart posterity, her face locked in the marble of repose on the monument above, and her hands clasped in prayer, her body in the vault below which harbours so many of her descendants. She who never reigned in England, who was born a queen of Scotland, and who died at the orders of an English queen, lies now in Westminster Abbey where every sovereign of Britain since her death has been crowned; from her every sovereign of Britain since her death has been directly descended, down to the present queen, who is in the thirteenth generation. As Mary herself embroidered so long ago at Sheffield on the royal cloth of state which was destined to hang over the head of a captive queen: *In my end is my Beginning.*

The English and Scottish Versions
of the Long Casket Letter

1. The contemporary English copy of the long (second) casket letter was made by the clerk at the Westminster Conference, December 1568. Calendar of Scottish Papers, Vol. 2, Appendix 2, pp. 722ff. An ellipsis of four dots represents a gap left in the original; an ellipsis of three dots represents words torn off or worn from the original.

Being gon from the place where I had left my harte, it may be easily judged what my countenance was, consydering what the body may, without hart, which was cause that till dynner I had used lyttle talke, neyther wold any body advance him selfe therunto, thinking that it was not good so to doo. Fowre myles from thence a gentleman of the Erle of Lennox cam to made [sic] his commendacions and excuses unto me, that he cam not to meete me, because he durst not enterprise so to doo, consydering the sharp wordes that I had spoken to Conyngham, and that he desyred that I wold com to the inquisition of the facte which I did suspecte him of. This last was of his own head without commission, and I tolde him that be had no receipte against feare, and that he had no feare, if he did not feele him selfe faulty, and that I had also sharply aunsweared to the doubtes that he made in his lettres, as though ther had bene a meaning to poursue him. To be short: I have made him hold his peace; for the rest, it weare to long to tell you. Sir James Hamilton cam to meete me, who told me that at another tyme he went his waye when he hard of my comming; and that he sent unto him Houstoun, to tell him that he wold not have thought that he wold have followed and accompany him selfe with the Hamiltons. He aunsweared that he was not come but to see me, and that he wolde not follow Stuard nor Hamilton, but by my commandement. He prayed him to go speake to him: he refused it. The Lard Lus, Houson, and the sonne of Caldwell, and about xl hors came to meete me, and he told me that he was sent to one day a lau from the father, which shuld be this daye, against the signing of his own hand which he hathe; and that knowing of my comming he hath delayed it, and hath prayed to go see him; which he hatt refused, and swearith that he will suffer nothing at his handes. Not one of the towne, is come to speake with me, which makith me to think that they be his, and then he speakith well of them, at leaste his sonne. The King sent for Joachim, and asked him why I did not lodge nighe to him? and that he wold ryse sooner, and why I cam, whither it wear for any good appoynment that he cam, and whither I had not take Paris and Guilbert to write, and that I sent Joseph. I wonder who hath told him so muche, evin of the marriage of Bastian. This bearer shall tell you more upon that. I asked him of his lettres, and where he did complayne of the crueltye of som of them, he saide that he did dreme, and that he was so glad to see me that he thought he should dye. Indeede that he had found faulte with me. ... I went my waye to supper, this berer shall tell you of my arryv ... praied me to com agayne, which I did, and he told me his grefe and that he would make no testament but leave all unto me, and that I was cause of his sicknes for the sorrow he had that I was so strange unto him, 'And' (said he) 'you asked me what I ment in my lettre to speake of cruelty: it was of your cruelty who will not accepte my offres and repentance: I avowe that I have don amisse, but not that I have always disavowed: and so have many other of your subjectes don, and you have well perdonid them, I am yong. You will saye that you have also perdonid me many tymes, but that I returne to my faultes. Many not a man of my age for want of counsell, fayle twise or thrise, and mysse of promes, and at the last repent and rebuke him selfe by his experience? Yf I may obtayn this perdon, I protest I will never make faulte agayne, and I aske nothing but that we may be at bed and at table together as husband and wife. And if you will not, I will never rise from this bed. I pray you tell me your resolution heerof; God knowith that I am punished to have made my God of you, and had no other mynd but of you: and when I offende you som tyme, you are cause thereof, for if I thought whan any body doth any wrong to [me] that I might for my refuge make my mone therof unto you, I wold open it to no other. But whan I heare any thing, being not familiar with you, I must keepe it in my mynde, and that troublith my wittes for anger.' I did still answear him, but that shall be to long. In the end I asked him why he wold go in the English shipp? He doth disavow it and swearith so, but confessith to have spoken to the men. Afterward I asked him of the inquisition of Hiegate? He denyed it till I tolde him the very woordes, and then he said that Minto sent him word that it was said that som of the counsayle had brought me a lettre to signe to putt him in prison, and to kill him if he did resiste, and that he asked this of Minto him selfe, who said unto him that he thought it was true. I will talke with him tomorrowe upon that poynte: the rest as Wille Hiegate hath confessed, but it was the next daye that he cam hither. In the end he desyred much that I shuld lodge in his lodging; I have refused it. I have told him that he must be pourged, and that could not be don heere. He said unto me, 'I have hard saye that you have brought the lytter, but I would rather have gon with your self.' I told him that so I wolde myselfe bring him to Cragmillar, that the phisicians and I also might cure him without being farre from my sonne. He said that he was ready when I wolde, so as I wolde assure him of his requeste. He hath no desyre to be seene, and waxeth angry whan I speake to him of Wallcar, and sayth that he will pluck his eares from his head, and that he lyeth: for I asked before of that and what cause he had to complayne of . . . the Lordes, and to threaten them? He denyeth it and sayth that he had already prayed them to think no such matter of him. As for myself: he wold rather lose his lyfe than doo me the leaste displeasour.

And then used so many kindes of flatteryes so coldly and so wysely as you would marvayle at. I had forgotten that he sayde that he could not mistrust me for Hiegates wordes, for he could not beleve that his own flesh (which was my selfe) wold doo him any hurte (and in deede it was sayde that I refused to have him lett blud) but for the others he wold at leaste sell his lyfe deere ynoughe: but that he did suspecte no body, nor wolde, but wolde love all that I did love. He wolde not lett me go, but wold have me to watche with him. I made as though I thought all to be true, and that I would think upon it. And have excused my selfe from sytting up with him this night, for he sayth that he sleepith not. You never hard one speake better nor more humbly, and if I had not proofe of his hart to be as waxe and that myne weare not as a dyamant, no stroke but comming from your hand, could make me but to have pitie of him. But feare not, for the place shall contynue till death. Remember also in recompense therof not to suffer yours to won by that fals race that wold doo no lesse to your selfe. I think they have bene at schoole togither, he hath allwais the teare in the eye. He saluteth every man evin to the meanest, and makith much of them, that they may take pitie of him. His father hath bled this daye at the nose and at the mouth: gesse what token that is! I have not seene him, he is in his chambre. The King is so desyrous that I shuld give him meate with my own handes, but trust you no more there where you are than I doo here. This is my first journay, I will end tomorrow. I write all, how little consequence so ever it be of, to the end that yau may take of the wholle that that shall be best for *you to judge*.* I doo here a work that I hate but only by muche flattering him and pr[essing?] him to laughe, to see me so trymly make a lye, at the leaste, dissemble? and to mingle truthe therwith? He hath almost told me all on the bisshops behalfe and of Suderland, without touching any word unto him of that which you had told me, but only by muche flattering him and pre[ssing?] him to

* On margin 'your purpose'.

assure him selfe of me, and by my complayning of the r ... en the wormes out of his nose.*

You have hard the rest. We have tyed to with two false races, the goodyeere untye us from them. God forgive me, and God knytt us togither for ever, for the most faythfull couple that ever he did knytt together. This is my fayth, I will dye in it. Excuse it, yf I write yll, you must gesse the one halfe, I can not doo with all, for I am yll at ease, and glad to write unto you when other folkes be asleepe, seeing that I cannot doo as they doo, according to my desyre, that is betwene your armes, my deere lyfe, whom I besech God to preserve from all yll, and send you good rest as I go to seeke myne till tomorrow in the morning, that I will end my bible. But it greevith me that it shuld lett me from wryting unto you of newes of myselfe, so much I have to write. Send me word what you have determinid heerupon, that we may know the one the others mynde for marryng of any thing. I am weary and am asleepe, and yet I cannot forbeare scribling, as long as ther is any paper. Cursed be this pocky fellow that troublith me thus muche, for I had a pleasanter matter to discourse unto you, but for him. He is not muche the worse, but he is yll arayde. I thought I shuld have bene kylled with his breth, for it is worse than your uncles breth, and yet I was sett no neerer to him than in a chayre by his bolster, and he lyeth at the furder syd of the bed.

The message of the father by the waye:—

The talke of Sir James Hamilton of the ambassade—

That that the Lard a Luss hathe tolde me of the delaye.

The questions that he asked of Jochim of my state, of my companye, and of the cause of my coming, and of Joseph.

The talke that he and I have had, and of his desyre to please me, of his repentance, and of th'interpretation of his lettre of Will Hiegates doinges and of his departure, and of the L. of Levinston.

I had forgotten of the L. of Levinston, that at supper he sayd softly to the Lady Rivees [Reres] that he dronk to the persons

---

* Follows here on margin, 'I have disclosed all, I have known what I wold'.

that I knew [if] I wold pledge them. And after supper he said softly ... I was leaning upon him and warming myselfe – 'You may well go and see sick folkes, yet can you not be so wellcom unto them, as you have this daye left som body in payne, who shall never be meary till he have seene you agayne.' I asked him who it was? he tooke me about the body, and said 'One of his folkes that hath left you this daye.' Gesse you the rest.

This daye I have wrought till two of the clock upon this bracelet to putt the keye in the clyfte of it, which is tyed with two laces. I have had so lyttle tyme that it is very yll, but I will make a fayrer, and in the meane tyme take heed that none of those that he heere doo see it, for all the world wold know it, for I have made it in haste in theyr presence. I go to my tedious talke; you make me dissemble so muche, that I am afrayde thereof with horrour, and you make me almost to playe the parte of a traytour. Remembre that if it were not for obeyeng you, I had rather be dead; my hart bleedith for yt. To be shorte: he will not com but with condition that I shall promise to be with him as heeretofore at bed and borde, and that I shall forsake him no more, and upon my worde he will doo whatsoever I will, and will com, but he hath prayed me to tarry till after tomorrow. He hath spoken at the fyrst more stoutly, as this bearer shall tell you, upon the mater of his Englishmen, and of his departure; but in the end he commith to his gentlenes agayne. He hath told me among other tak, that he knew well that my brother had told me at Sterling that which he had said there, whereof he denyed the halfe, and specially that he was in his chambre. But now to make him trust me, I must fayne something unto him: and therfore when he desyred me to promise that when he shuld be wholle, we shuld make but one bed, I told him (fayning to beleve his faire promesses ... did not change his mynde betwene this tyme and that, I was contented, so as he wold saye nothing therof: for (to tell it betwene us two) the Lordis wisshed no yll to him, but did feare, leste (consydering the threateninges which he made in case we did agree togither) he wolde make them feele the small accompte they have maid of him, and that he wold persuade me to poursue som of them; and for this respecte shuld be in jelousy if *at one instant**** without their knowledge, I did breake a game made to the contrary in their presence. And he said unto me very pleasant and meary, 'Think you that they doo the more esteeme you therfore? but I am glad that you talke to me of the lordis. I here that you desyre now that we shall lyve a happy lyfe, for if it weare otherwise, it could not be but greater inconvenience shuld happen to us both than you think: but I will doo now whatsoever you will have me doo, and will love all those that you shall love, so as you make them to love me allso. For so as they seeke not my life, I love them all egally.' Therupon I have willed this bearer to tell you many prety thinges, far I have to muche to write, and it is late, and I trust him upon your worde. To be short, he will goe any where upon my worde; alas! and I never deceavid any body, but I remitt myself wholly to your will: and send me word what I shall doe, and whatever happen to me, I will obey you. Think also yf you will not fynde som invention more secret by phisick, for he is to take phisick at Cragmillar, and the bathes also, and shall not com fourth of long tyme. To be short, for that that I may learne, he hath greate suspicion, and yet nevertheles trustith upon my worde, but not to tell me as yet anything. Howbeit if you will that I shall *avowe* him, I will know all of him, but I shall never be willing to beguile one that puttith his trust in me. Nevertheles you may doo all, and doo not estyme me the lesse therfore, for you are the cause ther of; for, for my own revenge, I wold not doo it. He givith me certain charges (and those strong) of that that I feare evin to saye, that his faultes be published, but there be that committ some secret faultes and feare not to have them spoken of so lowdely, and that ther is speeche of great and small. And evin touching the Lady Rires, he saide, 'God graunte that she serve you to your honour,' and that men may not think nor he neyther, that myne owne powre was not in my selfe, seeing I did refuse his offres. To conclude, for a surety he mistrustith us of that that you know, and for his

* 'By and by' written above.

lyfe. But in the end, after I had spoken two or three good wordes to him, he was very meary and glad. I have not seene him this night, for ending your bracelet, but I can fynde no claspes for yt: it is ready therunto, and yet I feare least it shuld bring you yll happ, or that it shuld be knowen if you were hurte. Send me worde whither you will have it, and more·monney, and whan I shal returne, and how farre I may speake. Now as farre as I perceave, *I may do much with you:** gesse you whither I shall not be suspected. As for the rest: he is wood when he hearith of Ledinton, and of you and of your brother he sayth nothing, but of the Erle of Arguile he doth. I am afraide of him to heare him talke, at the leaste he assurith him selfe that he hath no yll opinion of him. He speakith nothing of those abrode, nether good nor yll, but avoydith speaking of them His father keepith his chamber; I have not seene him. All the Hamiltons be heere, who accompany me very honestly. All the frendes of the other doo com allwais when I goe to visitt him. He hath sent to me and prayeth me to see him ryse to morrow in the morning early. To be short, this bearer shall declare unto you the rest, and if I shall learne any thing, I will make every night a memoriall therof. He shall tell you the cause of my stay. Burne this lettre, for it is to dangerous, neyther is ther anything well said in it, for I think upon nothing but upon greefe if you be at Edinboroughe. Now if to please you my deere lyfe, I spare nether honour, conscience, nor hazard, nor greatnes, take it in good parte, and not according to the interpretacion of your false brother in lawe, to whom I pray you give no credit, against the most faythfull lover that ever you had or shall have. See not also her whose faynid teares you ought not more to regarde than the true travails which I endure to deserve her place, for obtayning of which against my own nature, I doo betraye those that could lett me. God forgive me, and give you my only friend the good luck and prosperitie that your humble and faythfull lover doth wisshe unto you; who hopith shortly to be an other thing unto you, for the reward of my paynes. I have not made

* On margin, 'Jay bien la vogue avec vois'.

one worde, and it is very late, althoughe I shuld never be weary in wryting to you, yet will I end, after kyssing of your handes. Excuse my evill wryting, and reade it over twise – excuse also that ... for I had yesternight no paper, wher I tooke the paper of a [memoriall] ... Remembre your frende and wryte unto her and often. Love me all [wais] ...

2. The Scottish translation of the long (second) casket letter was first published in George Buchanan's *Detection*, 1571. The text here is taken from Andrew Lang's *The Mystery of Mary Stuart*, London, 1901.

Being departit from the place quhair I left my hart, it is esie to be judgeit quhat was my countenance, seeing that I was evin als mekle as ane body without ane hart; quhilk was the Occasioun that quhile Denner tyme I held purpois to na body; nor zit durst ony present thameselfis unto me, judging yat it was not gude sa to do. Four myle or I came to the towne, ane gentilman of the Erle of Lennox come and maid his commendatiounis unto me; and excusit him that he came not to meit me, but ressoun he durst not interpryse the same, becaus of the rude wordis that I had spokin to Cuninghame: And he desyrit that he suld come to the inquisitioun of ye matter yat I suspectit him of. This last speiking was of his awin heid, without ony commissioun. I answerit to him that thair was na recept culd serve aganis feir; and that he wold not be affrayit, in cace he wer not culpabill; and that I answerit bot rudely to the doutis yat wer in his letteris. Summa, I maid him hald his toung. The rest wer lang to wryte. Schir ames Hammiltoun met me, quha schawit that the uther tyme quhen he hard of my cumming he departit away, and send Howstoun, to schaw him, that he wald never have belevit that he wald have persewit him, nor zit accompanyit him with the Hammiltounis. Heanswerit, that he was only cum bot to see me, and yat he wald nouther accompany Stewart nor Hammiltoun, bot be my commandement. He desyrit that he wald cum and speik with him: he refusit it. The Laird

of Lusse, Howstoun, and Caldwellis sone, with xl. hors or
thairabout, come and met me. The Laird of Lusse said, he was
chargeit to ane Day of Law be the Kingis father, quhilk suld be
this day, aganis his awin hand-writ, quhilk he hes: and zit
notwithstanding, knawing of my cumming, it is delayit. He was
inquyrit to cum to him, quhilk he refusit, and sweiris that he
will indure nathing of him. Never ane of that towne came to
speik to me, quhilk causis me think that thay ar his; and
euertheles he speikis gude, at the leist his sone. I se na uther
Gentilman bot they of my company. The King send for Joachim
zisternicht, and askit at him, quhy I ludgeit not besyde him?
And that he wald ryse the soner gif that wer; and quhairfoir I
come, gif it was for gude appointment? and gif I had maid my
estait, gif I had takin Paris [this berer will tell you sumwhat
upon this], and Gilbert to wryte to me? And yat I wald send
Joseph away. I am abaschit quha hes schawin him sa far; zea he
spak evin of ye mariage of Bastiane. I inquyrit him of his letteris,
quhairintill he plenzeit of the crueltie of sum: answerit, that he
was astonischit, and that he was sa glaid to se me, that he belevit
to die for glaidnes. He fand greit fault that I was pensive. I
departit to supper. Yis beirer wil tell yow of my arryuing. He
prayit me to returne: the quhilk I did. He declairit unto me his
seiknes, and that he wald mak no testament, bot only leif all
thing to me; and that I was the caus of his maladie, becaus of
the regrait that he had that I was sa strange unto him. And thus
he said: Ze ask me quhat I mene be the crueltie contenit in my
letter? it is of zow alone that will not accept my offeris and
repentance. I confess that I haue failit, bot not into that quhilk
I ever denyit; and siclyke hes failit to sindrie of zour subjectis,
qutiilk ze haue forgeuin. I am zoung. Ze will say, that ze have
forgevin me oft tymes, and zit yat I returne to my faultis. May
not ane man of my age, for lacke of counsell, fall twyse or
thryse, or inlacke of his promeis and at last repent himself, and
be chastisit be experience? Gif I may obtene pardoun, I protest
I sall never mak fault agane. And I crafit na uther thing, bot yat
we may be at bed and buird togidder as husband and wyfe; and
gif ze wil not consent heirunto, I sall never ryse out of yis bed.

I pray zow, tell me your resolutioun. God knawis how I am punischit for making my God of zow, and for hauing na uther thocht but on zow; and gif at ony tyme I offend zow, ze ar the caus, becaus quhen ony offendis me, gift, for my refuge, I micht playne unto zow, I walk speik it unto na uther body; bot quhen I heir ony thing, not being familiar with zow, necessitie constranis me to keip it in my breist; and yat causes me to tyne my wit for verray anger. ... I answerit ay unto him, but that wald be ovir long to wryte at lenth. I askit quhy he wald pas away in ye *Inglis* schip. He denyis it, and sweiris thairunto; bot he grantis that he spak with the men. Efter this I inquyrit him of the inquisitioun of Heigairt. He denyit the same, quhill I schew him the verray wordis was spokin. At quhilk tyme he said that Mynto had advertisit him, that it was said, that sum of the counsell had brocht an letter to me to be subscrivit to put him in Presoun, and to slay him gif he maid resistance. And he askit the at same Mynto himself; quha answerit, that he belevit ye same to be trew. The morne I wil speik to him upon this Point. As to the rest of Willie Heigait's, he confessit it, bot it was the morne efter my cumming or he did it. He wald verray fane that I suld ludge in his ludgeing. I refusit it, and said to him, that he behovit to be purgeir, and that culd not be done heir. He said to me, I heir say ze have brocht ane lytter with zow; but I had rather have passit with zow. I trow he belevit that I wald have send him away Presoner. I answerit, that I wald tak him with me to Craigmillar, quhair the mediciner and I micht help him, and not be far from my sone. He answerit, that he was reddy quhen I pleisit, sa I wald assure him of his requeist. He desyris na body to se him. He is angrie quhen I speik of Walcar, and sayis, that he sal pluk the eiris out of his heid and that he leis. For I inquyrit him upon that, and yat he was angrie with sum of the Lordis, and wald threittin thame. He dnyis that, and sayis he luifis thame all, and prayis me to give traist to nathing aganis him. As to me, he wald rather give his lyfe or he did ony displesure to me. And efter yis he schew me of sa money lytil flattereis, sa cauldly and sa wysely that ze will abasche thairat. I had almaist forzet that he said, he could not dout of me in yis purpois of Hiegaite's; for he wald never beleif yat I, quha was his proper flesche, wald do him ony evill; alsweill it was schawin that I refusit to subscrive the same; But as to ony utheris that wald persew him, at leist he suld sell his lyfe deir aneuch; but he suspectit na body, nor zit wald not; but wald lufe all yat I lufit. He wald not let me depart from him, bot desyrit yat I suld walk with him. I mak it seme that I beleive that all is trew, and takis heid thairto, and excusit my self for this nicht that I culd not walk. He sayis, that he sleipis not weil. Ze saw him never better, nor speik nair humbler. And gif I had not ane prufe of his tart of waxe, and yat myne wer not of ane dyamont, quhairintill na schot can make brek, but that quhilk cummis forth of zour hand, I wald have almaist had pietie of him. But feir not, the place sall hald unto the deith. Remember, in recompence thairof, that ye suffer not zouris to by wyn be that fals race that will travell na les with zow for the same. I beleve thay have bene at schuillis togidder. He hes ever the teir in his eye; he salutis every body, zea, unto the leist, and makis pieteous caressing unto thame, to make thame have pietie on him. This day his father bled at the mouth and nose; ges quhat presage that is. I have not zit sene him, he keipis his chalmer. The king desyris that I suld give him meit with my awin handis; bot gif na mair traist quhair ze ar, than I sall do heir. This is my first journay. I sall end ye same ye morne. I wryte all thingis, howbeit thay be of lytill wecht, to the end that ze may tak the best of all to judge upon. I am in doing of ane work heir that I hait greitly. Have ze not desyre to lauch to se me lie sa weill, at ye leist to dissembill sa weill, and to tell him treuth betwix handis? He schawit me almaist all yat is in the name of the Bischop and Sudderland, and zir I have never twitchit ane word of that ze schawit me; but allanerly be force, flattering, and to pray him to assure himself of me. And he pleinzeing on the Bischop, I have drawin it all out of him. Ye have hard the rest. ... We ar couplit with two fals races; the devil sinder us, and God knit us togidder for ever, for the maist faithful coupill that ever be unitit. This is my faith, I will die in it. Excuse I wryte evill, ye may ges ye half of it; but I cannot mend it, because I am not weil at eis;

and zit verray glaid to wryte unto zow quhen the rest are sleipand, sen I cannot sleip as thay do, and as I wald desyre, that is in zour armes, my deir lufe, quhome I pray God to preserve from all evill, and send zow repois: I am gangand to seik myne till ye morne, quhen I sall end my Bybill; but I am faschit that it stoppis me to wryte newis of myself unto zow, because it is sa lang. ... Advertise me quhat ze have deliberat to do in the mater ze knaw upon this point to ye end that we may understand utheris weill, that nathing thairthrow be spilt. I am irkit, and ganging to sleip, and zit I ceis not to scrible all this paper in sa mekle as restis thairof. Waryit mot this pokishce man be that causes me haif sa mekle pane, for without him I suld have an far plesander subject to discourse upon. He is not over mekle deformit, zit he hes ressavit verray mekle. He hes almaist slane me with his braith; it is worse than zour uncle's; and zit I cum na neirer unto him, bot in ane chyre at the bed-seit, and he being at the uther end thairof. The message of the father in the gait. The purpois of Schir James Hamilton. Of that the Laird of Lusse schawit me of the delay. Of the demandis that he askit at Joachim. Of my estait. Of my company. Of the occasion of my cumming: and of Joseph. *Item*, the purpois that he and I had togidder. Of the desyre that he hes to pleis me, and of his repentance. Of the interpretatioun of his letter. Of Willie Hiegaite's mater of his departing. Of Monsiure de Levingstoun. I had almaist forzet, that Monsiure de Levingstoun said in the Lady Reres eir at supper, that he wald drink to ye folk yat I wist of, gif I wald pledge thame. And efter supper he said to me, quhen I was lenand upon him warming me at the fyre, Ze have fair going to se seik folk, zit ze cannot be sa welcum to thame as ze left sum body this day in regrait, that will never be blyth quhill he se zow agane. I askit at him quha that was. With that he thristit my body, and said, that sum of his folkis had sene zow in fascherie; ze may ges at the rest. I wrocht this day quhill it was two houris upon this bracelet, for to put ye key of it within the lock thairof, quhilk is couplit underneth with twa courdounis. I have had sa lytill tyme that it is evill maid; bot I sall mak ane fairer in the mean tyme. Tak

heid that nane that is heir se it, for all the warld will knaw it,
becaus for haist it was maid in yair presence. I am now passand
to my fascheous purpois. Ze gar me dissemble sa far, that I haif
horring thairat; and ye caus me do almaist the office of a
traitores. Remember how gif it wer not to obey zow, I had
rather be deid or I did it; my hart bleidis at it. Summa, he will
not cum with me, except upon conditioun that I will promeis
to him, that I sall be at bed and buird with him as of befoir,
and that I sall leif him na ofter: and doing this upon my word,
he will do all thingis that I pleis, and cum with me. Bot he hes
prayit me to remane upon him quhil uther morne. He spak
verray braifly at ye beginning, as yis beirer will schaw zow, upon
the purpois of the Inglismen, and of his departing: Bot in ye
end he returnit agane to his humilitie. He schawit, amangis uther
purposis, yat he knew weill aneuch that my brother had schawin
me yat thing, quhilk he had spoken in Striviling, of the quhilk
he denyis ye ane half, and abone all, yat ever he came in his
chalmer. For to make him traist me, it behovit me to fenze in
sum thingis with him: Thairfoir, quen he requesistit me to
promeis unto him, that quhen he was haill we suld have baith
ane bed: I said to him fenzeingly, and making me to beleve his
promisis, that gif he changeit not purpois betwix yis and that
tyme, I wald be content thairwith; bot in the meane tyme I had
him heid that he leit na body wit thairof, becaus, to speik
amangis our selfis, the Lordis culd not be offendit not will evill
thairfoir: Bot thay wald feir in respect of the boisting he maid
of thame, that gif ever we aggreit togidder, he suld make thame
knaw the lytill compt thay take of him; and that he counsallit
me not to purchas sum of thame by him. Thay for this caus
wald be in jelosy, gif at anis, without thair knawledge, I suld
brek the play set up in the contrair in thair presence. He said
verray joyfully, And think zow thay will esteme zow the mair of
that? Bot I am verray glaid that ze speik to me of the Lordis;
for I beleve at this tyme ze desyre that we suld leif togidder in
quyetnes: For gif it wer utherwyse, greiter inconvenience micht
come to us baith than we are war of: bot now I will do quhatever
ze will do, and will lufe all that ze lufe; and desyris zow to make

thame lufe in lyke maner: For sen thay seik not my lyfe, I lufe
thame all equallie. Upon yis point this beirer will schaw zow
mony small thingis. Becaus I have over mekle to wryte, and it
is lait: I give traist unto him upon zour word. Summa, he will
ga upon my word to all places. ... Allace! I never dissavit
ony body: Bot I remit me altogidder to zour will. Send me
advertisement quhat I sall do, and quhatsaever thing sall cum
thairof, I sall obey zow. Advise to witts zourself, gif ze can find
out on ymair secreit invention be medicine; for he suld take
medicine and the bath at Craigmillar. He may not cum furth of
the hous this lang tyme. Summa, be all that I can leirne, he is
in greit suspicioun, and zit notwithstanding, he gevis credit to
my word; bot zit not sa far that he will schaw ony thing to me:
bot nevertheles I sall draw it out of him, gif ze will that I avow
all unto him. Bot I will never rejoyce to deceive ony body that
traistis in me: Zit notwithstanding ze may command me in all
thingis. Have na evill opinioun of me for that caus, be ressoun
ze are the occasion of it zourself; becaus, for my awin particular
revenge, I wald not do it to him. He gevis me sum chekis of
yat quhilk I feir, zea, evin in the quick. He sayis this far, yat his
faultis wer publeist; bot yair is that committis faultis, that belevis
thay will never be spokin of; and zit thay will speik of greit and
small. As towart the Lady Reres, he said, I pray God that scho
may serve zow for your honour: and said, it is thocht, and he
belevis it to be trew, that I have not the power of myself into
myself, and that becaus of the refuse I maid of his offeris.
Summa, for certainetie he suspectis of the thing ze knaw, and
of his lyfe. Bot as to the last, how sone yat I spak twa or thre
gude wordis unto him, he rejoéis, and is our of dout. I saw him
not this evening for to end your bracelet, to the quhilk I can
get na lokkis. It is reddy to thame: and zit I feir that it will bring
sum malhure, and may be sene gif ze chance to be hurt.
Advertise me gif ze will have it, and gif ze will have mair silver,
and quehen I sall returne, and how far I may speik. He inragis
when he heiris of Lethingtoun, or of zow, or of my brother. Of
your borother he speikis nathing. He spiekis of the Erle of
Argyle. I am in feir quhen I heir him speik; for he assuris

himself yat he hes not an evill opinioun of him. He speikis nathing of thame that is out, nouther gude nor evill, bot fleis that point. His father keipis his chalmer, I have not sene him. All the Hammiltounis ar heir, that accompanyis me verray honorabilly. All the freindis of the uther convoyis me quhen I gang to see him. He desyris me to come and se him ryse the morne betyme. For to mak schort, this beirer will tell zow the rest. And gif I leirne ony thing heir, I will mak zow memoriall at evin. He will tell zow the occasioun of my remaning. Burne this letter, for it is ovir dangerous, and nathing weill said in it: for I am thinkand upon nathing bot fascherie. Gif ze be in Edinburgh at the ressait of it, send me word sone. Be not offendit, for I gif not ovir greit credite. Now seing to obey zow, my deir lufe, I spair nouther honour, conscience, hasarde, nor greitnes quhat sumevir tak it, I pray zow, in gude part, and not efter the interpretatioun of zour fals gudebrother, to quhome, I pray zou, gif na credite agains the maist faithful luifer that ever ze had, or even sall have. Se not hir, quhais fenzeit teiris suld not be sa mekle praisit nor estemit, as the trew and faithful travellis quhilk I sustene for to merite hir place. For obtening of the quhilk againis my naturall, I betrayis thame that may impesche me. God forgive me, and God give zow, my only lufe, the hap and prosperitie quhilk your humble and faithful lufe desyris unto zow, quha hopis to be schortly ane uther thing to zow, for the reward of my irksum travellis. It is lait: I desyre never to ceis fra wryting unto zou; zit now, efter the kissing of zour handis, I will end my letter. Excuse my evill wrything, and reid it twyse over. Excuse that thing that is scriblit, for I had na paper zisterday quhen I wrait that of ye memoriall. Remember upon zour lufe, and wryte unto hir, and that verray oft. Lufe me as I sall do zow. Remember zow of the purpois of the Lady Reres. Of the Inglismen. Of his mother. Of the Erle of Argyle. Of the Erle Bothwell. Of the ludgeing in Edinburgh.

Reference Notes

The following abbreviations have been commonly used:

C.S.P. Foreign Calendar of State Papers, Foreign Series, Elizabeth
C.S.P. Roman Calender of State Papers relating to English affairs
                 (Rome)
C.S.P. Scot.: Calendar of State Papers relating to Scotland
C.S.P. Spanish Calendar of State Papers relating to Spain, Elizabeth
C.S.P.
  Venetian Calendar of State Papers, Venetian
D.N.B. Dictionary of National Biography
Hamilton Hamilton Papers
Hat. Cal.: Calendar of manuscripts at Hatfield House
Keith: R. Keith, *History of the Affairs of Church and State in
          Scotland*
Knox: John Knox, *History of the Reformation*, translated and
          edited by W. C. Dickinson
Labanoff: *Lettres de Marie Stuart*, edited by Prince Labanoff
R.P.C.: Register of the Privy Council of Scotland

For further details of these and other books cited (which have been
described below in the shortest convenient form) the reader is referred
to the bibliography.

CHAPTER NINETEEN: *In Foreign Bands*

1 Diurnal of Occurrents, p. 129
2 Henderson, *Mary Queen of Scots*, II, p. 494
3 Labanoff, II, p. 76
4 Argyll Papers
5 Brantôme, *Oeuvres complètes*, V, p. 99
6 Labanoff, II, p. 117
7 *Ibid.*, VI, p. 472
8 Nau, *Memorials*, p. 95
9 Labanoff, II, p. 71
10 Strickland, *Queens of Scotland*, VI, p. 103
11 C.S.P. Scot., II, p. 410
12 H.M.C., Vol. V, Appendix to 5th Report, p. 615; Ailsa Muniments folio 7
13 C.S.P. Venetian, VII, p. 416
14 C.S.P. Scot., II, p. 409
15 *Ibid.*, p. 428
16 *Ibid.*, p. 416
17 *Ibid.*, p. 420
18 *Ibid.*, p. 448
19 *Ibid.*, p. 453; Macgeorge, *Miscellaneous Papers*, p. 17
20 Arbuthnot, *Queen Mary's Book*, p. 100
21 C.S.P. Scot., II, p. 452
22 Labanoff, II, p. 91
23 C.S.P. Scot., II, p. 433
24 Conyers Read, *Cecil*, p. 402
25 Mahon, *Indictment*, p. 3
26 C.S.P. Scot., II, p. 442
27 Conyers Read, *op. cit.*, p. 401
28 C.S.P. Scot., II, p. 435
29 *Ibid.*, p. 457
30 *Ibid.*, p. 443
31 *Ibid.*, p. 509; p. 510
32 Goodall, *Casket Letters*, II, p. 360
33 C.S.P. Scot., II, p. 494
34 *Ibid.*, p. 510
35 *Ibid.*, p. 495
36 Labanoff, II, p. 182
37 *Ibid.*, p. 237
38 C.S.P. Scot., II, p. 516
39 *Ibid.*, p. 541
40 Labanoff, II, p. 181

CHAPTER TWENTY: *Her Privy Letters*

1 R.P.C., I, p. 641
2 C.S.P. Scot., II, p. 526
3 Hat. Cal., I, p. 369
4 Ailsa Muniments, folio 31; Labanoff, II, p. 225
5 Labanoff, II, p. 420
6 Hosack, *Mary Queen of Scots*, I, p. 549
7 Goodall, *Casket Letters*, II, p. 261
8 Labanoff, II, p. 254
9 *Ibid.*, p. 257
10 Goodall, *op. cit.*, p. 305
11 Macgeorge, *Miscellaneous Papers*, p. 13
12 Lady Baille-Hamilton, 'A Historical Relic'. Quoted Lang, *Mystery of Mary Stuart*, p. 368
13 Public Record Office, London, SP/52/2; Cecil

Papers 252/1–4; Cotton
M.S.S.: Caligula, 1, folio 271

14 C.S.P. Scot., II, Appendix II,
p. 722; Mahon, *Mary Queen of
Scots*, p. 111

15 *Ibid.*, Appendix II, p. 722

16 *Ibid.*, Appendix II, p. 728

17 Hat. Cal., I, p. 376

18 Gatherer, *Buchanan*, p. 173

19 C.S.P. Scot., II, Appendix II,
p. 722

20 Hat. Cal., I, p. 379

21 Henderson, *Casket Letters*, pp.
171, 172; Armstrong-
Davison, *Casket Letters*, p. 195

22 Hosack, *op. cit.*, I, Appendix
F, p. 562

23 Cotton M.S.S.: Caligula 1,
folio 271; Goodall, *op. cit.*, II,
p. 54

24 Hosack, *op. cit.*, I, p. 549

25 Goodall, *op. cit.*, II, p. 54

26 *Ibid.*, II, p. 256

27 Labanoff, II, p. 203

CHAPTER TWENTY-ONE: *My
Norfolk*

1 C.S.P. Scot., II, p. 907

2 Morris, *Letter-books of Sir
Amyas Paulet*, p. 108

3 Plot, *History of Staffordshire*;
Somerville, *Guide to Tutbury
Castle*

4 Labanoff, VI, p. 176

5 C.S.P. Scot., II, p. 616

6 Lodge, *Illustrations of British
History*, p. xvii

7 Bagot Letters, Microfilm no
11, nos. 820–821

8 C.S.P. Scot., II, p. 632

9 Girouard, *Robert Smythson and
Elizabethan Architecture*, p. 58

10 Hat. Cal., I, p. 400

11 C.S.P. Scot., II, p. 632

12 *Ibid.*, p. 649

13 Hat. Cal., I, p. 400

14 Edwards, *Dangerous Queen*, p.
30

15 Neale, *Elizabethan House of
Commons*, p. 186

16 Labanoff, II, p. 369

17 *Ibid.*, II, p. 5

18 Camden, *Annales*, p. 129

19 Labanoff, III, p. 19

20 Maidment, *Miscellany of
Abbotsford Club*, I, p. 23

21 Lee, *Moray*, p. 261

22 Harris, *Unpublished documents
relating to Town Life in Coventry*,
p. 98

23 Labanoff, III, p. 6

24 C.S.P. Scot., II, p. 574

25 Labanoff, III, p. 387

26 Hat. Cal., I, p. 505

27 *Ibid.*, p. 510

28 *Ibid.*, p. 512

29 Black, *Reign of Elizabeth*, p. 150

30 Labanoff, III, p. 188

31 *Ibid*, p. 221; C.S.P. Roman, I,
p. 401

32 Labanoff, III, p. 110; p. 117

33 *Ibid.*, p. 115

34 Lockie, *Political Career of the
Bishop of Ross*

35 Edwards, *Marvellous Chance*, p. 107
36 Hat. Cal., I, p. 564
37 *Ibid.*, p. 563
38 Labanoff, IV, p. 48

CHAPTER TWENTY-TWO: *The Uses of Adversity*

1 Argyll Papers
2 Melville, *Memoirs*, p. 224; C.S.P. Scot., III, p. 92
3 C.S.P. Scot., IV, p. 590; p. 600
4 Shrewsbury Papers (Lambeth Palace Library), M.S. 698, folio 1
5 Johnston, *Shrewsbury*
6 Hat. Cal., II, p. 428
7 Johnston, *op. cit.*, 19 September 1582
8 *Ibid.*, 15 April 1574; Lodge, *Illustrations, op. cit.*, 117
9 Paget Papers, Staffordshire County Record Office, D(W) 1734/3/3/280
10 Johnston, *op. cit.*, 5 September 1571
11 Heape, *Buxton under the Dukes of Devonshire*, p. 15
12 Johnston, *op. cit.*, 4 August 1576
13 *Ibid.*, 9 July 1580
14 *Ibid.*, 10 July 1584
15 Morris, *Letter-books of Sir Amyas Paulet*, p. 40
16 Johnston, *op. cit.*, 11 May 1570
17 Labanoff, IV, p. 183; p. 10; VI, p. 187
18 Seton, *History of the Family of Seton*
19 Shrewsbury Papers, M.S. 705, folio 33
20 C.S.P. Scot., II, p. 1014
21 C.S.P. Domestic (James I) 17 July 1613
22 Lang, *Portraits and Jewels of Mary Queen of Scots*, p. 58; Labanoff, V, p. 89
23 Pollen, *Babington Plot*, p. 56
24 MacNalty, *Mary Queen of Scots*, p. 235
25 Labanoff, IV, p. 251
26 C.S.P. Foreign, IX, p. 346; p. 372
27 Vatican Archives, Fondo Borghese 1.824, folios 49v; 50v; Labanoff, III, p. 231
28 Arbuthnot, *Queen Mary's Book*, p. 112
29 C.S.P. Roman, II, pp. 215 *et seq.*
30 *Ibid.*, p. 250
31 Gore-Browne, *Lord Bothwell*, p. 456; Herries, *Memoirs*, p. 96
32 Labanoff, IV, p. 256
33 *Ibid.*, p. 390
34 Cust, *Authentic Portraits of Mary Queen of Scots*, p. 78
35 C.S.P. Domestic 1591–4, p. 99
36 *Tudor and Jacobean Portraits* (N.P.G.), p. 221
37 Arbuthnot, *op. cit.*, p. 116
38 Burns, 'Catholicism in Defeat'
39 Labanoff, V, p. 280

40 Pollen, 'Mary Stuart's Jesuit Chaplain'
41 Arbuthnot, *op. cit.*, p. 106
42 *Ibid.*, p. 129

CHAPTER TWENTY-THREE:
Mother and Son
1 Calderwood, *History*, III, p. 207; Hat. Cal., III, p. 26
2 *Tudor and Jacobean Portraits* (N.P.G.), p. 221
3 Willson, *King James VI and I*, p. 39
4 Hat. Cal., II, p. 47
5 Register House, Edinburgh: Blairs College Correspondence, R.H. 2/7/9
6 C.S.P. Scot., III, p. 35
7 Labanoff, V, p. 264
8 Hat. Cal., III, pp. 46 *et seq.*
9 *Ibid.*, p. 47
10 Labanoff, VI, pp. 14 *et seq.*
11 Hat. Cal., III, p. 71
12 Labanoff, VI, p. 30
13 *Ibid.*, p. 58
14 *Ibid.*, p. 65; p. 70
15 *Ibid.*, p. 77
16 Hat. Cal., III, p. 95
17 Labanoff, VI, p. 125; p. 129
18 *Ibid.*, IV, p. 356
19 *Ibid.*, V, p. 370
20 Shrewsbury Papers, M.S. 698, folio 39v
21 Labanoff, VI, p. 33; p. 42
22 *Ibid.*, p. 50
23 C.S.P. Roman, II, p. 238
24 D.N.B., XIX, p. 315

25 Caraman, *William Weston*, p. 31
26 *Staffordshire Historical Collections*, Introduction, p. xxxii and pp. 35–62
27 C.S.P. Scot., II, p. 551
28 Paget Papers, VI, *passim*
29 Hicks, *Elizabethan Problem*, p. 21
30 *Ibid.*, p. 119; Labanoff, VI, p. 14
31 Hicks, *op. cit.*, pp. 80 *et seq.*
32 Persons, *Notes concerning the English mission*, quoted Hicks, *op. cit.*, p. 7
33 Hicks, *op. cit.*, p. 123
34 Knox, *Allen*, p. 434
35 Labanoff, VI, p. 130; p. 132
36 *Ibid.*, p. 45
37 *Ibid.*, p. 76
38 Williams, *Elizabeth*, p. 277
39 Camden, *Annales*, p. 41

CHAPTER TWENTY-FOUR:
The Babington Plot
1 Morris, *Letter-books of Sir Amyas Paulet*, p. 15
2 *Ibid.*, p. 6
3 *Ibid.*, p. 6
4 Monckton, 'Beer and Ale in Shakespeare's Time'
5 Morris, *op. cit.*, p. 122
6 Labanoff, VI, p. 368
7 Morris, *op. cit.*, p. 98
8 *Ibid.*, p. 139
9 Pollen, *Babington Plot*, p. 1; Read, *Walsingham*, III, p. 9

10 Labanoff, VI, p. 281

11 Pollen, *op. cit.*, p. lvi

12 Morris, *op. cit.*, p. 152

13 C.S.P. Roman 1572–8, p. 330

14 Phillips, *Images of a Queen*, p. 108

15 Mathew, *Celtic Peoples of Europe*, p. 49

16 Paget Papers, Staffordshire County Record Office D(W) 173/3/3/280

17 Caraman, *William Weston*, p. 99

18 Hat. Cal., III, p. 140

19 Labanoff, VI, p. 345; Pollen, *op. cit.*, p. 15

20 Pollen, *op. cit.*, p. 18

21 *Ibid.*, p. 38

22 Labanoff, VI, p. 404

23 *Ibid.*, p. 294

24 Black, *Reign of Elizabeth*, p. 381

25 Pollen, *op. cit.*, p. 32; p. 45; Conyers Read, *op. cit.*, III, p. 43

26 Labanoff, VI, p. 330; p. 325; p. 309; p. 351

27 *Ibid.*, p. 362

28 Morris, *op. cit.*, p. 201

29 *Dictionnaire de Théologie Catholique* (*Tyrannicide*)

30 Pollen, *op. cit.*, p. 53; Labanoff, VI, p. 288

31 Pollen, *op. cit.*, p. 46

32 Caraman, *William Weston*, p. 81

33 Pollen, *op. cit.*, p. 49 *et seq.*

34 Chantelauze, *Bourgoing's Journal*, p. 467 *et seq.*

35 Labanoff, VII, p. 242

36 *Ibid.*, VII, p. 250

37 Morris, *op. cit.*, p. 275

38 *Ibid.*, p. 276

39 *Ibid.*, p. 267

40 Pollen, *op. cit.*, p. cxc

41 *Ibid.*, p. clxxxii

42 *Ibid.*, p. clxxxix

43 Stevenson's Introduction to Nau, *Memorials*, p. xxiv

44 Labanoff, VI, p. 438

CHAPTER TWENTY-FIVE: *Trial*

1 Chantelauze, *Bourgoing's Journal*, p. 490 *et seq.*

2 *Ibid.*, p. 490

3 Morris, *Letter-books of Sir Amyas Paulet*, p. 297

4 27 Elizabeth C.I.

5 Johnston, *Shrewsbury*, 22 October 1586

6 Stuart, *Trial of Mary Queen of Scots*, p. 86 *et seq.*; Hardwicke State Papers, I, p. 224

7 Read, *Cecil*, p. 402

8 Labanoff, VII, p. 36; Maxwell-Scott, *Tragedy of Fotheringhay*, p. 31

9 Maxwell-Scott, *op. cit.*, p. 35

10 Strickland, *Queens of Scotland*, VII, p. 428

11 Chantelauze, *op. cit.*, p. 513 *et seq.*; Maxwell-Scott, *op. cit.*, p. 51 *et seq.*

12 Chantelauze, *op. cit.*, p. 520

13 *Ibid.*, p. 522
14 Chantelauze, *op. cit.*, p. 527
15 Pollen, *Babington Plot*, p. cxcii
16 Stuart, *op. cit.*, p. 41
17 Chantelauze, *op. cit.*, p. 532
18 *Ibid.*, p. 539
19 Morris, *op. cit.*, p. 301
20 Arbuthnot, *Queen Mary's Book*, p. 127
21 Chantelauze, *op. cit.*, p. 539
22 D'Ewes, *Journals*, pp. 375 *et seq.*
23 Chantelauze, *op. cit.*, p. 544; Morris, *op. cit.*, pp. 299, 300
24 Labanoff, VI, p. 467; Morris, *op. cit.*, p. 311
25 Labanoff, VI, p. 461
26 *Ibid.*, p. 477
27 *Ibid.*, p. 456
28 *Ibid.*, p. 461

CHAPTER TWENTY-SIX: *The Dolorous Stroke*
1 Willson, *King James VI and I*, p. 73
2 Hat. Cal., XIII, p. 300
3 C.S.P. Scot., IX, p. 417
4 Rait and Cameron, *King James' Secret*, pp. 55 *et seq.*
5 *Ibid.*, Preface, p. viii; pp. 158–72; pp. 176–82
6 Willson, *op. cit.*, p. 78
7 Read, *Walsingham*, III, p. 60
8 Hat. Cal., III, p. 206
9 Chantelauze, *Bourgoing's Journal*, p. 552
10 Labanoff, VI, p. 474

11 Morris, *Letter-books of Sir Amyas Paulet*, p. 328
12 Chantelauze, *op. cit.*, p. 560; p. 579
13 *Ibid.*, p. 566
14 Teulet, *Relations Politiques*, IV, p. 163
15 Nicolas, *Life of Davison*, p. 83
16 Black, *Reign of Elizabeth*, p. 308
17 Nicolas, *op. cit.*, p. 86
18 Morris, *op. cit.*, p. 361
19 Nicolas, *op. cit.*, p. 103
20 Hat. Cal., III, p. 216
21 Maxwell-Scott, *Tragedy of Fotheringhay*, p. 168
22 Chantelauze, *op. cit.*, p. 571
23 Camden, *Annales*, p. 108
24 Chantelauze, *op. cit.*, pp. 575 *et seq.*; Jebb, *De Vita et Rebus Gestis*, II, pp. 175 *et seq.*; II, pp. 611 *et seq.*; Camden, *op. cit.*, pp. 109 *et seq.*
25 Labanoff, VI, p. 491
26 *Ibid.*, p. 484
27 *Ibid.*, p. 483
28 See Maxwell-Scott, *op. cit.*, Appendix for three contemporary accounts of execution
29 G. R. Gleig, *Family History of England*, II, iii; W. Chappell, *Popular Music of the Olden Time*, p. 519; Strickland, *Queens of Scotland*, VII, p. 487
30 Morris, *op. cit.*, p. 369
31 Camden, *Annales*, p. 115
32 Morris, *op. cit.*, p. 364

CHAPTER TWENTY-SEVEN:
Epilogue: The Theatre of the World

1 Jebb, *De Vita et Rebus Gestis*, II, p. 671, Translated Strickland, *Queens of Scotland*, VII, p. 499

2 Phillips, *Images of a Queen*, p. 163; Teulet, *Lettres de Marie Stuart*, p. 375

3 Calderwood, *History*, IV, p. 611

4 Hat. Cal., XIII, p. 334

5 Strickland, *op. cit.*, VII, p. 498

6 Hat. Cal., XIII, p. 230

7 *Ibid.*, III, p. 216

8 Pitcairn, *Collections relative to the Funereals of Mary Queen of Scots*

9 Public Record Office A.O. 1/2119/3

10 Pitcairn, *op. cit.*, p. 22

11 Public Record Office A.O. 1/2119/3

12 Teulet, *op. cit.*, p. 391; J. D. Mackie, *The Will of Mary Stuart*

13 *Ibid.*, p. 397

14 Camden, *Britannia*, II, p. 181

15 Cotton M.S.S., Titus C. VI, ff. 207–209b

16 Demster, *Historia*, II, p. 464

17 Dean Stanley, *Memorials of Westminster Abbey*, Appendix, p. 507

Bibliography

The bibliography of Mary Queen of Scots is potentially enormous: the following list contains only those works mentioned in the reference and works which have been of actual assistance in the writing of this book. The place of publication is London, unless otherwise specified, and in the case of a series, published over a number of years, only the earliest publication date is given.

Accounts of the Lord High Treasurer of Scotland. Ed. T. Dickson and J. Balfour Paul. Edinburgh. 1877.

Accounts of the Masters of Works. Vol. I. 1529–1615. Ed. H. M. Paton. H.M.S.O. Edinburgh. 1957.

Acts of the Parliament of Scotland. Ed. T. Thompson. 1814.

Acts and Proceedings of the General Assemblies of the Kirk of Scotland. Ed. T. Thompson. 1839.

C. Ainsworth Mitchell. *The Evidence of the Casket Letters.* Historical Association Pamphlets. 1927.

Inventory of Ailsa Muniments. Historical Manuscripts Commission. Vol. III. Supplement. 1431–1599.

J. W. Allen. *History of Political Thought in the 16th century.* 1941.

James Anderson, *Collections relating to the history of Mary Queen of Scotland.* 4 vols. 1727.

Mrs. P. Stewart-Mackenzie Arbuthnot, *Queen Mary's Book.* 1907.

Argyll Papers, Inveraray Castle.

M. H. Armstrong-Davison, *The Casket Letters.* 1965.

Chronicles of the families of Atholl and Tullibardine. Ed. 7th Duke of Atholl. Edinburgh. 1908.

Claude de l'Aubespine, *Histoire Particulière de la Court de Henry II.*

Archives curieuses de l'histoire de France. 1ère Serie. Vol. 3. Paris. 1834.

Bagot Papers. Folger Shakespeare Library, Washington, D.C. Microfilm in Staffordshire County Record Office.

Lady Baillie-Hamilton, 'A Historical Relic'. *Macmillan's Magazine*. Vol. LXXX.

Balcarres Paper: *Foreign correspondence with Marie de Lorraine Queen of Scotland,* from Balcarres Papers. Vol. I, 1537–48, Vol. II, 1548–57. Ed. Marguerite Wood. Scot. Hist. Soc. 3rd Series. IV. Edinburgh. 1923 and 1925.

Lacey Baldwin Smith, *The Elizabethan Epic.* 1966.

R. Bannatyne, *Memorials of Transactions in Scotland.* Ed. R. R. Bannatyne Club. Edinburgh. 1836.

Bannatyne Manuscript Ed. and introduced by W. Tod Ritchie. Vols. I to IV. Scottish Text Society. 1934.

E. Bapst. *Les mariages de Jacques v.* Paris. 1889.

A. Baschet. *La Diplomatie Venitiènne.* Paris. 1862.

E. Chisholm Batten. *Charters of the Priory of Beauly.* Grampian Club. 1877.

Jean de Beaugué, *Histoire de la Guerre en Ecosse.* Foreword by Comte de Montalembert. Maitland Club. 1862.

R. de Belleval, *Les Fils de Henri ii.* Paris. 1898.

Robert Birrel, *Diary.* 1532–1605. Included in *Fragments of Scottish History.* Ed. J. G. Dalyell (q.v.).

J. B. Black. *Andrew Lang and the Casket Letter Controversy.* Edinburgh. 1951.

J. B. Black, *The Reign of Elizabeth.* 1959.

Prosper Blanchemain. ed. *The Works of Ronsard.* Paris. 1857.

Collection Blis, *Manuscrits, Livres, Estampes et Objets d'Arts relatys a Marie Stuart.* Bibliothèque Nationale. Paris.

Anthony Blunt, *Art and Architecture in France. 1500–1700.* 1953.

James Hepburn, Earl of Bothwell, *Les Affaires du Conte de Boduel.* Ed. H. Cockburn and T. Maitland. Bannatyne Club. Edinburgh. 1829.

René de Bouillé, *Histoire des Ducs de Guise.* Paris. 1850.

Pierre Brantôme, *Oeuvres complètes.* Paris. 1823.

Pierre Brantôme, *The Lives of Gallant Ladies*. Trans. by H.M. 2 vols. 1924.

J. Bruce, *Letters of Queen Elizabeth and James VI of Scotland*. Camden Society. 1849.

W. M. Bryce, 'The voyage of Mary Queen of Scots in 1548'. *English Historical Review*. Vol. XXII. 1907.

George Buchanan, *The Tyrannous Reign of Mary Stewart*. See W. A. Gatherer.

Burke's Peerage, etc. 1963 edition.

E. Burns, *Scottish Coins*. 1887.

J. H. Burns, 'Catholicism in Defeat'. *History Today*. November 1966.

D. Calderwood, *History of the Kirk of Scotland*. Ed. T. Thompson. Edinburgh. 1842.

Calendar of State Papers, Domestic. Edward VI, Mary and Elizabeth. Ed. R. Lemor. 1856.

Calendar of State Papers, Domestic. James I. Vol. I. Ed. Mary Anne Everett Green. 1857.

Calendar of State Papers, Foreign. Edward VI. Ed. W. Turnbull. 1861.

Calendar of State Papers, Foreign. Mary. Ed. W. Turnbull. 1861.

Calendar of State Papers, Foreign. Elizabeth. Ed. J. Stevenson. 1863.

Calendar of State Papers relating to English affairs (Rome). Ed. J. M. Rigg. 1916.

Calendar of State Papers relating to Scottish affairs. Ed. J. Bain. 1898.

Calendar of State Papers, Spanish. Elizabeth. Ed. M. A. S. Hume. London. 1892.

Calendar of State Papers, Venetian. Ed. R. Brown and G. C. Bentinck. 1890.

William Camden, *Annales Rerum Anglicarum et Hibernicarum Regnante Elizabetha*. Trans. R. Norton, 1635 and T. Hearne, 1717.

William Camden, *Britannia*. Trans. Gough. 1789.

Annie Cameron, ed. *Scottish Correspondence of Mary of Lorraine*. Scot. Hist. Soc. 1927.

Annie Cameron and R. S. Rait, ed., *Warrender Papers*. Scot. Hist. Soc. 3rd series. Vol. 17. Edinburgh. 1931.

Michel de Castelnau, Seigneur de Mauvissière, *Memoirs*. Ed. Le Laboureur. Paris. 1731.

Lettres de Catherine de Médicis. Ed. H. de la Ferrière-Percy. Paris. 1880.

Philip Caraman, S. J., *John Gerard, the Autobiography of an Elizabethan*. 1951.

Philip Caraman, S. J., *William Weston, the Autobiography of an Elizabethan*. 1955.

Cecil Papers, Hatfield House.

G. Chalmers, *Life of Mary Queen of Scots*. 1818.

R. Chambers. *Life of James I*. Edinburgh. 1830.

W. Chappell, *Popular Music of the Olden Time*. 1855.

M. R. Chantelauze, *Marie Stuart, son procès et son exécution*. 1874. (Containing the Journal of Bourgoing.)

R. Chauviré, *Le Secret de Marie Stuart*. Paris. 1937.

A. Chéruel, *Marie Stuart et Catherine de Médicis*. Paris. 1858.

F. J. Child, *English and Scottish Ballads*. 1882.

Cobbett's Complete Collection of State trials. Vol. I. 1809.

Cooper, ed., *Correspondence of M. de la Mothe Fénelon*. 1838.

Cotton MSS., British Museum.

Crossby and Bruce, ed., *Accounts and papers relating to Mary Queen of Scots*. Camden Society. 1867.

C. W. and P. Cunningham, *Handbook of English Costume in the Sixteenth Century*. 1959.

Lionel Cust, *Authentic Portraits of Mary Queen of Scots*. 1903.

Sir John Dalyell, ed., *Fragments of Scottish History*. 1798.

Demster, *Historia*. Bannatyne Club. Edinburgh. 1829.

Dépenses de la Maison Royale. Register House. Edinburgh.

Sir Simonds D'Ewes, *Journals of the Parliaments during Elizabeth's Reign*. 1693.

G. Dickinson, *Two Missions of Jacques de la Brosse*. Scot. Hist. Soc. 3rd series. Vol. 36. Edinburgh. 1942.

W. Croft Dickinson, *History of Scotland*. Vol. I. 1961.

W. Croft Dickinson, *Scottish Parliament and the Trial of Treason*. Seton Memorial Lecture. University College, London. March 1956.

Dictionary of National Biography. 1909 edition.

Discours du Grand et Magnifique Triomphe Faict du Mariage de François et Marie Stuart. Ed. William Bentham. Roxburghe Club. 1818.

Diurnal of Occurrents. Ed. T. Thomson. Bannatyne Club, Edinburgh. 1833.

Gordon Donaldson, ed., *Accounts of the Collectors of the Thirds of Benefices.* Scot. Hist. Soc. 3rd Series. Vol. XIII. Edinburgh. 1949.

Gordon Donaldson, *Scotland: James v–James vi.* Edinburgh. 1965.

Gordon Donaldson, *The Scottish Reformation.* 1960.

T. Duncan, 'Mary Stuart and the House of Huntly'. *Scot. Hist. Review.* IV. 1906.

T. Duncan, 'Relations of the Earl of Murray with Mary Stuart'. *Scot. Hist. Review.* VI. 1909.

T. Duncan, 'The Queen's Maries'. *Scot. Hist. Review.* II. 1905.

Francis Edwards, S. J., *The Dangerous Queen.* 1964.

Francis Edwards, S. J., *The Marvellous Chance.* 1968.

Exchequer Rolls. Vol. 19. Ed. G. P. McNeill. Edinburgh. 1898.

Sir James Fergusson, *Lowland Lairds.* 1949.

Sir James Fergusson, *The White Hind.* 1963.

Fonds Français, Bibliothèque Nationale, Paris.

W. Forbes-Leith, ed., *Narratives of Scottish Catholics under Mary Stuart and James vi.* Edinburgh. 1885.

H. Forneron, *Les Ducs de Guise et leur Epoque.* Paris. 1877.

James Fraser of Wardlaw. *True Genealogie of the Frasers.* 1666.

Sir William Fraser, *The Book of Douglas.* 4 vols. 1885.

Sir William Fraser, *The Lennox.* 2 vols. 1874.

Sir William Fraser, *The Red Book of Menteith.* 2 vols. 1880.

J. A. Froude, *History of England from the Fall of Wolsey to the Defeat of the Spanish Armada.* 1862.

W. A. Gatherer, trans. and ed., *The Tyrannous Reign of Mary Stewart by George Buchanan.* Edinburgh. 1958.

Jules Gauthier, *Histoire de Marie Stuart.* Paris. 1875.

Frank Gent, 'The Edinburgh Castle Mystery'. *Chambers Journal.* September and October 1944.

Mark Girouard, *Robert Smythson and the Architecture of the Elizabethan Era.* 1966.

G. R. Gleig, *Family History of England.* 1836.

John Glen, *Early Scottish Melodies.* Edinburgh. 1900.

W. Goodall, *Examination of the (Casket) Letters said to be written by Mary Queen of Scots to James, Earl of Bothwell.* 1754.

W. Goodall, *Introduction to the History of the Antiquities of Scotland.* 1860.

Sir R. Gordon, *Genealogical History of the Earldom of Sutherland.* Edinburgh. 1813.

R. Gore-Browne, *Lord Bothwell.* 1935.

Albert le Grand, *Les Saints de la Bretagne Armorique.* Quimper. 1901.

L. F. Grant, *Social and economic development of Scotland before 1603.* 1930.

Papiers d'Etat du Cardinal de Granvelle. Paris. 1841.

Letters and papers of Patrick Master of Gray. Bannatyne Club. Edinburgh. 1835.

G. Guiffrey, *Lettres inédites de Dianne de Poytiers.* Paris. 1866.

P. Guillaume, 'La Mort de Français II'. *Bulletin du Société Archéologique d'Orléans.* Vol. I. No. 7. 1960.

Douglas Hamer, ed., *Marriage of the Queen of Scots to the Dauphin.* Scottish Printed Fragments. 1932.

Douglas Hamer, ed., *Works of Sir David Lyndsay of the Mount.* Scot. Text Society. 3rd series. 1931.

Hamilton Papers. Ed. J. Bain. Edinburgh. 1890.

R. K. Hannay, 'The Earl of Arran and Queen Mary'. *Scot. Hist. Review.* XVIII. 1920.

P. M. Handover, *Arbella Stuart.* 1957.

Hardwicke State Papers. Vol. I. 1778.

Calendar of the Manuscripts of the Marquess of Salisbury at Hatfield House. Historical Manuscripts Commission. 1883.

M. Dormer Harris, *Unpublished documents relating to Town Life in Coventry.* Trans. Roy. Hist. Soc. 4th series. Vol. III. 1920.

D. Hay Fleming, *Mary Queen of Scots from her birth till her flight into England.* 1897.

R. G. Heape, *Buxton under the Dukes of Devonshire.* 1948.

T. F. Henderson, *Mary Queen of Scots.* 2 vols. 1905.

T. F. Henderson, *The Casket Letters.* 1890.

John Maxwell, Baron Herries, *Historical Memoirs of the reign of Mary Queen of Scots.* Abbotsford Club. Ed. R. Pitcairn. Edinburgh. 1836.

Christian Hesketh, *Tartan.* 1963.

Leo Hicks, S. J., *An Elizabethan Problem.* 1964.

J. Hosack, *Mary Queen of Scots and her Accusers.* Edinburgh. 1969.

P. Hume Brown, *Early Travellers in Scotland.* 1891.

P. Hume Brown, *Scotland in the Time of Queen Mary.* 1904.

Letters of James v. Ed. Denys Hay, calendared by R. K. Hannay. Edinburgh. 1954.

Jamieson, *Etymological Dictionary of the Scottish Language.*

S. Jebb, *De Vita et Rebus Gestis Sereuissimma Principis Marie Scotorum Reginae, Franciase Dotoriae.* 2 vols. 1725.

Nathaniel Johnston, M. D., *Life of George Earl of Shrewsbury and Appendix to Life of Francis Earl of Shrewsbury — Matters omitted from Life of George Earl of Shrewsbury pertaining to the Execution of Mary Queen of Scots.* 1710.

M. S. Jourdain, *English Secular Embroideries.* 1910.

R. Keith, *History of the Affairs of Church and State in Scotland down to 1567.* Ed. J. P. Lawson. 3 vols. and Appendix. Spottiswoode Society. 1844.

Kervyn de Letterhoven, *Relations politiques des Pays-Bas et de l'Angleterre, 1555–1579.* Belgium. 1882.

Works of John Knox. Ed. D. Laing. Edinburgh. 1895.

John Knox, *History of the Reformation in Scotland.* Trans. and ed. by W. Croft Dickinson. 1949.

T. F. Knox, ed., *Letters and memorials of William Allen.* 1882.

Prince Labanoff (A. I. Lobanov-Rostovsky). *Lettres et Mémoires de Marie, Reine d'Ecosse.* 7 vols. 1844.

H. H. Lamb, *Trees and Climatic History in Scotland.* 1964.

Andrew Lang, *The Mystery of Mary Stuart.* 1901.

Andrew Lang, *Portraits and Jewels of Mary Queen of Scots.* 1906.

Regnier de la Planche, *Estat de France sous François II.* Ed. Henneschet. 1836.

J. D. Leader, *Mary Queen of Scots in Captivity.* 1880.

Maurice Lee, *James Stewart, Earl of Moray.* Columbia University Press. 1953.

Le Plessis, *Les Triomphes a Chenonceau.* Paris. 1557.

John Leslie, Bishop of Ross, *The Historie of Scotland.* Trans. into Scottish by Fr James Dalrymple. Scottish Text Society. 1895. Ed. Fr E. G. Gody and William Murison. Vols. I and II (to which references are given). Also Bannatyne Club edition. Vol. 39. Ed. T. Thomson. Edinburgh. 1830.

E. Levassieur, *La Population Française.* Histoire de la population française avant 1789. Paris 1889.

Mortimer Levine, *Early Elizabethan Succession Question, 1558–68.* California. 1966.

C. S. Lewis, *English Literature in the 16th century.* 1954.

D. M. Lockie, 'The Political Career of the Bishop of Ross. 1568–90'. *University of Birmingham Historical Journal.* 1953.

E. Lodge, *Illustrations of British History.* Vol. I. 1791.

S. G. E. Lythe, *Economy of Scotland. 1550–1625.* Edinburgh. 1960.

I. Macalpine and R. Hunter, *Porphyria: A Royal Malady.* B.M.A. Publication. 1968.

A. Macgeorge. ed., *Miscellaneous papers principally illustrative of events in the Reigns of Queen Mary and James VI.* Maitland Club. Glasgow. 1834.

D. Macgibbon and T. Ross, *The castellated and domestic architecture of Scotland.* 5 vols. Edinburgh. 1887.

Dan McKenzie, 'The Obstetrical History of Mary Queen of Scots'. *Caledonian Medical Journal.* Vol. XV. 1921.

J. D. Mackie, *The Earlier Tudors.* 1966 edition.

J. D. Mackie, 'The Will of Mary Stuart'. *Scot. Hist. Review.* No. 11.

J. Mackinnon, *Constitutional History of Scotland from Early Times to the Reformation*. 1924.

Sir Arthur Salusbury MacNalty, *Mary Queen of Scots: the daughter of debate*. 1960.

John MacQueen, *Alexander Scott and the Scottish Court Poetry of the Middle Sixteenth Century*. Proceedings of the British Academy. Vol. LIV. 1968.

John MacQueen and Tom Scott, ed., *Oxford Book of Scottish Verse*. 1967.

R. H. Mahon, *Indictment of Mary Queen of Scots*. 1923.

R. H. Mahon, *Mary Queen of Scots: a study of the Lennox Narrative*. 1924.

R. H. Mahon, *The Tragedy of Kirk o'Field*. 1930.

J. Maidment, ed., *Miscellany of the Abbotsford Club*. Vol. I. 1837.

Marlowe Society Collections. Vol. I. 1900.

Inventories of the jewels of Mary Queen of Scots. 1556–69. Bannatyne Club. 1863.

Libraries of Mary Queen of Scots and James VI. Maitland Club Miscellany. 1834.

Catalogue of the Tercentenary Exhibition of Mary Queen of Scots, at Peterborough. 1887.

David Mathew, *The Celtic Peoples of Europe in the Age of the Renaissance*. 1932.

David Mathew, *Scotland under Charles I*. 1955.

Hon. Mrs Maxwell-Scott, *The Tragedy of Fotheringhay, founded on the Journal of Bourgoing and unpublished MS. documents*. 1905.

Sir James Melville of Halhill, *Memoirs*. Ed. Francis Steuart. 1929 (to which references are given). Also ed. T. Thomson. Bannatyne Club. Edinburgh. 1827.

F. Michel, *Les Français en Ecosse, les Ecossiers en France*. 1862.

H. A. Monckton, 'Beer and Ale in Shakespeare's Time'. *History Today*. December, 1967.

A. Montaiglon, *Latin Themes of Mary Queen of Scots*. Wharton Club. 1855.

J. Morris, *Letter-books of Sir Amyas Paulet*. 1874.

Claude Nau, *Memorials of Mary Stewart*. Ed. J. Stevenson. Edinburgh. 1883.

J. E. Neale, *The Age of Catherine de Medici*. 1943.

J. E. Neale, *The Elizabethan House of Commons*. 1949.

J. E. Neale, *Queen Elizabeth I*. 1934. Also paperback edition, 1960, to which references are given.

J. E. Neale, *Queen Elizabeth I and her Parliaments*. 1953.

Sir Henry Nicolas, *Life of Davison*. 1823.

Sir Charles Oman, *History of the Art of War in the 16th century*. 1937.

Painted Ceilings of Scotland. M. R. Apted. H.M.S.O. Edinburgh. 1966.

Paget Papers. Staffordshire County Record Office.

Karl Pearson, 'Skull and Portraits of Lord Darnley'. *Biometriks*. XX.

Lord Eustace Percy, *John Knox*. 1937.

J. E. Phillips, *Images of a Queen: Mary Stuart in 16th century literature*. California. 1964.

M. Philippson, *Histoire du Règne de Marie Stuart*. Paris. 1891.

Le Marquis de Pimodan, *La Mère des Guises*. Paris. 1900.

R. Pitcairn. ed., *Collections relative to the Funereals of Mary Queen of Scots*. Edinburgh. 1822.

R. Pitcairn, ed., *Ancient Criminal Trials in Scotland*. Vol. I. Bannatyne Club. Edinburgh. 1833.

Robert Lindsay of Pitscottie, *History and Chronicles of Scotland*. 2 vols. Scottish Text Society. Ed. A. J. G. Mackay. 1899. 1911.

William Plot, *History of Staffordshire*. 1686.

J. H. Pollen, S.J., *Letters from Mary Queen of Scots to the Duke of Guise*. Scottish History Society. 1st Series. 1904.

J. H. Pollen, S.J., *Mary Queen of Scots and the Babington Plot*. Scottish History Society. 3rd series. 1922.

J. H. Pollen, S.J., 'Mary Stuart's Jesuit Chaplain'. *The Month*. January and February 1911.

J. H. Pollen, S.J., *Papal Negotiations with Mary Queen of Scots*. Scottish History Society. 1st series. Edinburgh. 1901.

John Pope Hennessy, *A lecture on Nicholas Hilliard*. 1949.

Dr Potiquet, *La Maladie et la Mort de François II*. Paris. 1893.

Quarterly Journal of the Royal Meteorological Society, Vol. 90.

R. S. Rait, *The Parliaments of Scotland.* 1924.

R. S. Rait and Annie Cameron, *King James' Secret: Negotiations between Elizabeth and James VI relating to the execution of Mary Queen of Scots.* 1927.

Conyers Read, *Bibliography of British History.* Tudor period. 1485–1603.

Conyers Read, *Mr Secretary Cecil and Queen Elizabeth.* 1955.

Conyers Read, *Mr Secretary Walsingham and the policy of Queen Elizabeth.* 1925.

Register of the Privy Council of Scotland. Ed. J. Hill Burton. Vols. I and II. Edinburgh. 1877.

Registrum Magni Sigilli Regum Scotorum. Ed. J. Balfour Paul and J. M. Thompson. Edinburgh. 1883.

G. Reynolds, *Nicholas Hilliard and Isaac Oliver.* Victoria and Albert Museum Exhibition Catalogue. 1947.

J. Robertson, ed., *Inventaires de la Royne d'Ecosse. Douairière de France.* Bannatyne Club. Edinburgh. 1883.

Ronsard, *Poésies choisies.* Ed. Pierre de Nolhac. Paris. 1954.

A. L. Rowse, *The England of Elizabeth.* 1950.

Alphonse de Ruble, *La première jeunesse de Marie Stuart.* 1891.

State Papers and Letters of Sir Ralph Sadler.* Ed. A. Clifford. Edinburgh. 1809.

Scots Peerage. Ed. J. Balfour Paul. 9 vols. 1904.

J. D. Scott, *Bibliography of works relating to Mary Queen of Scots.* (until 1700). Edinburgh. 1890.

G. Seton, *History of the family of Seton.* 1896.

Shrewsbury and Talbot Papers. Vol. I: Shrewsbury Papers. Calendared by C. Jamison; ed. E. G. W. Bill. Lambeth Palace Library. H.M.S.O. 1966.

Sir John Skelton, *Maitland of Lethington and the Scotland of Mary Queen of Scots.* Edinburgh. 1894.

Sir Robert Somerville, *Guide to Tutbury Castle* (published by the Chancellor of the Duchy of Lancaster).

J. Spottiswoode, *History of the Church of Scotland.* 1668.

Staffordshire Historical Collections. Quarter Session I. 1929.

Dean Stanley, *Memorials of Westminster Abbey.* 1867.

J. M. Stewart, *Scottish coinage.* 1955.

J. Stevenson, *Selections from unpublished manuscripts in the college of Arms and the British Museum illustrating the Reign of Mary Queen of Scotland.* Maitland Club. Glasgow. 1837.

Jane T. Stoddart, *The Girlhood of Mary Queen of Scots.* 1908.

Agnes Strickland, *Lives of the Queens of Scotland.* 1854.

Roy Strong, *Eworth.* Catalogue of the National Portrait Gallery Exhibition. 1966. (See also *Tudor & Jacobean Portraits,* below.)

Roy Strong, *Portraits of Queen Elizabeth I.* 1964.

John Stuart, *A lost chapter in the history of Mary Queen of Scots recovered.* Edinburgh. 1874.

Dispatches of Suriano and Barbaro. Huguenot Society Publication. Vol. IV.

G. H. Tait, 'Tudor Historiated Jewellery'. *Antiquaries Journal.* Vol. XLII. 1962.

S. and M. Tannenbaum, *Marie Stuart. Bibliography.* 3 vols. New York. 1944.

A. Teulet, *Papiers d'Etat relatifs à Histoire de l'Ecosse au 16ᵉ siècle.* Bannatyne Club. Edinburgh. 1852.

A. Teulet, *Relations politiques de la France et de l'Espagne avec l'Ecosse au 16ᵉ siècle.* Paris. 1862.

A. Teulet, *Lettres inédites de Marie Stuart.* Paris. 1859.

Marcel Thomas, *Le procès de Marie Stuart. Documents originaux présentés par Marcel Thomas.* Paris. 1956.

George Malcolm Thomson, *The Crime of Mary Stuart.* 1967

T. Thomson, ed., *Historie and Life of King James the Sext.* Bannatyne Club. Edinburgh. 1825.

Tudor & Jacobean Portraits. National Portrait Gallery Catalogue. Roy Strong. 1969.

P. F. Tytler, *History of Scotland.* Edinburgh. 1841. Vols. V, VI, and VII. Also new and enlarged edition. 1870.

Neville Williams, *Elizabeth Queen of England.* 1967.

Staffordshire Historical Collections. Quarter Session I. 1929.

Dean Stanley, *Memorials of Westminster Abbey*. 1867.

J. M. Stewart, *Scottish coinage*. 1955.

J. Stevenson, *Selections from unpublished manuscripts in the college of Arms and the British Museum illustrating the Reign of Mary Queen of Scotland*. Maitland Club. Glasgow. 1837.

Jane T. Stoddart, *The Girlhood of Mary Queen of Scots*. 1908.

Agnes Strickland, *Lives of the Queens of Scotland*. 1854.

Roy Strong, *Eworth*. Catalogue of the National Portrait Gallery Exhibition. 1966. (See also *Tudor & Jacobean Portraits*, below.)

Roy Strong, *Portraits of Queen Elizabeth I*. 1964.

John Stuart, *A lost chapter in the history of Mary Queen of Scots recovered*. Edinburgh. 1874.

Dispatches of Suriano and Barbaro. Huguenot Society Publication. Vol. IV.

G. H. Tait, 'Tudor Historiated Jewellery'. *Antiquaries Journal*. Vol. XLII. 1962.

S. and M. Tannenbaum, *Marie Stuart. Bibliography*. 3 vols. New York. 1944.

A. Teulet, *Papiers d'Etat relatifs à Histoire de l'Ecosse au 16ᵉ siècle*. Bannatyne Club. Edinburgh. 1852.

A. Teulet, *Relations politiques de la France et de l'Espagne avec l'Ecosse au 16ᵉ siècle*. Paris. 1862.

A. Teulet, *Lettres inédites de Marie Stuart*. Paris. 1859.

Marcel Thomas, *Le procès de Marie Stuart. Documents originaux présentés par Marcel Thomas*. Paris. 1956.

George Malcolm Thomson, *The Crime of Mary Stuart*. 1967

T. Thomson, ed., *Historie and Life of King James the Sext*. Bannatyne Club. Edinburgh. 1825.

Tudor & Jacobean Portraits. National Portrait Gallery Catalogue. Roy Strong. 1969.

P. F. Tytler, *History of Scotland*. Edinburgh. 1841. Vols. V, VI, and VII. Also new and enlarged edition. 1870.

Neville Williams, *Elizabeth Queen of England*. 1967.

Index